Robert Stewart

UNIONISTS DIVIDED

LIBRARY OF POLITICS AND SOCIETY

General Editor Michael Hurst

PUBLISHED

Church Embattled: Religious Controversy in Mid-Victorian England by M. A. Crowther

The Origins of Franco's Spain by Richard A. H. Robinson

The Politics of Government Growth by William C. Lubenow

The Peelites and the Party System 1846–52 by J. B. Conacher

Political Change and Continuity 1760–1885: A Buckinghamshire Study by Richard Davis

IN PREPARATION

Court and Country in Portugal 1680–1750 by John Villiers

The Countess of Huntingdon's Connexion by Alan Harding

The Pastoral Profession: the Theory and Practice of the Parish Ministry in the Mid-Victorian Church of England by Brian Heeney

ASSOCIATED VOLUMES

Quisling by Paul M. Hayes

Key Treaties of the Great Powers 1814–1914 selected and edited by Michael Hurst

UNIONISTS DIVIDED

Arthur Balfour, Joseph Chamberlain and the Unionist Free Traders

---

Richard A. Rempel

DAVID & CHARLES
ARCHON BOOKS 1972

This edition first published in 1972 in Great Britain by David & Charles (Publishers) Limited, Newton Abbot, Devon, and in the United States by Archon Books, Hamden, Connecticut

ISBN 0 7153 5702 6 (*Great Britain*)
ISBN 0 208 01308 3 (*United States*)

Set in eleven on twelve point Imprint and printed in Great Britain by Latimer Trend & Company Limited Plymouth

To Ann

Correction

In Chapter 9, THE ELECTION OF 1906, the note numbers in the text, from 9 onwards, do not correspond with those in the References section for this chapter. Numbers 9 and 10 (pages 154, 155) should be deleted; then 11 should become 9, 12 should become 10, and so on to the end of the chapter. In Chapter 11, THE FINAL PURGE, note 20 on page 201 should be deleted, and note 21 should be renumbered 20.

Contents

Preface		9
Chapter 1	The Background	11
Chapter 2	The Rise of the Unionist Free Traders	31
Chapter 3	The Conflict in the Cabinet	49
Chapter 4	The Tariff Reform Campaign Opens	64
Chapter 5	The Unionist Free Traders at Their Zenith	76
Chapter 6	The Characteristics of the Unionist Free Traders	94
Chapter 7	The Uneasy Alliance of Balfour and Chamberlain	115
Chapter 8	The Undermining of the Unionist Free Traders	134
Chapter 9	The Election of 1906	151
Chapter 10	The Eclipse of the Unionist Free Traders	171
Chapter 11	The Final Purge	187
References		204
Bibliography		219
Appendices		225
Index		231

Preface

THE ISSUES raised by Joseph Chamberlain's proclamation of Tariff Reform in 1903 have remained at the heart of many British economic controversies to the present day. This is not surprising because he initiated the first great debate on Britain's economic future after the passing of her mid-Victorian supremacy. His dream of a great imperial trading bloc with its assumed advantages of larger markets and new industrial incentives is present today in different guise. So too are the arguments of his opponents, Liberals and Unionist Free Traders, with their advocacy of cheap food and continued reliance on international free trade.

Whatever the strengths of Chamberlain's case, they were largely speculative before 1914, since free trade remained triumphant as national policy. Nevertheless, Chamberlain and his disciples managed to convert the Unionists from a primarily free trade party in 1903 largely to one of Tariff Reform by 1910. This struggle played havoc with the Unionists. Chamberlain was frustrated politically till the end of his life; Balfour was forced in 1911 to relinquish the party leadership after years of attempting to balance between fiscal factions; and one whole wing of the party, the Unionist Free Traders, was wiped out as a group by 1910. The bitter inter-party strife contributed mightily both to defeats in three consecutive elections and to many of the Unionists becoming politically intransigent in the stormy period 1906 to 1914.

The history of these Unionist divisions has never been fully told although recent historians have clarified Balfour's position in the fiscal struggle, and Julian Amery has extensively treated Chamberlain's career as a fiscal reformer. This study, it is hoped, will place the Unionist Free Traders' role more fully in perspective. The answers to many of the questions about the Unionist quarrels can be found by identifying the free traders, discovering what their political values and economic interests were, and explaining why they were so resoundingly defeated.

Sketchy accounts of the Unionist Free Traders have appeared in the biographies of the leaders. However, for many of the older members of this group the fiscal controversy represented the last, and bleakest phase of distinguished careers. Thus the treatment of this period of their political activities has been cursory. For the younger participants, such as Lord Robert Cecil and Winston Churchill, Chamberlain's campaign came at the very beginning of their careers, so that autobiographical and other accounts have stressed the later aspects of their lives. Moreover, since the Unionist Free Traders lost the battle, historians have tended to ignore them and to concentrate on the Tariff Reformers.

I am most grateful to all those who permitted me to use the private papers noted in the bibliography. Particularly I should like to thank Mrs Pamela Elliot. She and her late husband, Hubert, were kindness itself. My colleagues, Dr Brian O'Farrell and Dr Peter Becker, gave generously of their excellent judgement after reading the whole of the manuscript. The editor, Mr Michael Hurst, gave me unwavering support and encouragement and the benefit of his intellectual rigour. My most considerable debt, however, is to my former supervisor, Mr A. F. Thompson of Wadham College, Oxford.

Chapter 1 THE BACKGROUND

I

At Birmingham in May 1903 the colonial secretary, Joseph Chamberlain, called for a drastic revision in fiscal policy appealing to the country over the head of the prime minister, Arthur Balfour, and his cabinet colleagues. In October 1903 he launched his campaign for domestic protection to assist industry and to secure revenue for social reform, and preferential tariffs in favour of the colonies to promote imperial consolidation. Tariff Reform immediately became the most contentious political issue in the period between the Irish Home Rule crisis of 1885–6 and the announcement of the Lloyd George Budget of 1909.

Since 1846 Great Britain had been largely a free importing country. The establishment of free trade had coincided with her greatest economic expansion, and most Englishmen had come to consider that continued prosperity was inextricably bound up with its maintenance. Free trade was often elevated to the status of a dogma and endowed with the qualities of promoting peaceful international relations and harmony among classes within the state. Protection, by contrast, implied the denial of *laissez-faire*, trade wars, powerful and corrupt tariff lobbies in parliament, and dear food for the masses. Consequently, the battle between the Tariff Reformers and the free traders aroused deep passions. Especially in the critical months of Chamberlain's campaign late in 1903 and early in 1904, the fiscal struggle was the consuming interest of almost all politically aware Englishmen.

The controversy split the Unionists while helping to re-unite the Liberals. The Unionist Free Trade opposition was initially successful in preventing Chamberlain from rapidly committing the party to Tariff Reform. But in the long civil war from 1903 to 1910, the Chamberlainites succeeded, through superior resources and organisation, in coercing or all but wiping out their opponents, even if they failed to extirpate the doctrine of free trade itself. Among the defeated were many who had been powerful in Unionist circles.

The Unionist Free Traders can be divided into three groups. First, there were the old Whigs who had broken with Gladstone over Home Rule—the Duke of Devonshire, Lord James of Hereford, Lord Goschen, St Loe Strachey, and Arthur Elliot. These men, who had worked with the Conservatives after 1886, led the fight against their former ally of the Liberal Unionist coalition. In opposing Chamberlain the Whigs made their last bid to exercise a decisive political role only to be crushed by the Tariff Reform juggernaut. Their influence in British politics was in any case waning by 1903, but Chamberlain expedited their demise.

Secondly, the defeat of the Unionist Free Traders also marked a stage in the decline of a number of old guard Tories. The Cecils, as well as Sir Michael Hicks Beach, Lord George Hamilton, and Lord Balfour of Burleigh fought Chamberlain tenaciously —not only because of profound hostility to Tariff Reform, but also because they disliked Chamberlain and his political methods. They disapproved of what Lady Victoria Hicks Beach has tactfully described as his calculated attempts 'to draw popular applause' as well as his 'modern regard for the uses of publicity'.[1]

A third body of opposition contained some of the most promising young men in the party, such as Winston Churchill and Lord Hugh Cecil. For most of these men conversion to the Liberal Party was to prove the only alternative to political extinction. Those who remained within the party had their parliamentary careers ruined like Elliot, permanently frustrated as was the case with Hugh Cecil, or at least temporarily blighted like the latter's brother, Robert.

The fall of the Unionist Free Traders and the victory of the Tariff Reformers can only be understood by examining the relations of both factions with the large group of Unionists from 1903–6 who sheltered under the wing of Arthur Balfour. The Balfourians—Lord Lansdowne, Alexander Acland-Hood, Aretas Akers-Douglas, and others—were not completely committed to free trade. But while they were often impatient of the Cobdenite zealots who fought Chamberlain, they were extremely reluctant to allow him to impose his full policy on the party. They were justifiably sceptical of the electoral possibilities of out-and-out Tariff Reform and knew that victory for Chamberlain would inevitably mean the weakening and possibly the replacement of the present leaders.

The fiscal struggle was initiated by the most influential British political figure of the time. By 1903 no man in English public life aroused such diverse opinions and opposing passions as Chamberlain. Until his stroke in 1906, he was unsurpassed as a focus of political controversy. Many revered him as the country's leading statesman and apostle of empire, others execrated him as a shallow, ruthless opportunist, and some, such as Winston Churchill, saw him as a complex combination of both attributes.[2] Since his days as a Radical championing the 'unauthorised programme' of 1885, he had been, after Gladstone, the most elemental force in British politics.

After his breach with Gladstone over Home Rule, Chamberlain increasingly supported the Conservatives. He retained many of his Radical convictions, but at the same time, as a Radical Liberal Unionist ally of the Conservatives, he grafted a vigorous concept of empire on to his stock of reformist ideas. Chamberlain did not, however, immediately become a key figure in the Unionist alliance. For some time after 1886 he was in a weak position with only a small personal following of Radical Liberal Unionists. By mid-1889, however, Chamberlain had regained his position in the Birmingham area by, at last, routing the Gladstonians. From this citadel he rebuilt his influence on a national scale. At the Aston by-election of March 1891 his oratorical power was strikingly illustrated as the Unionist majority was quadrupled when the trend elsewhere was towards the Liberals. During this campaign he, the first of all major politicians, advocated old age pensions and thereafter coupled social reform with imperialism.[3]

As early as 1887 at Toronto, he had speculated that 'the federation of Canada may be the lamp lighting our path to the federation of the British empire'. In May 1890 he listened sympathetically to arguments for preferential tariffs in favour of the colonies urged by Colonel George Denison—long the veteran of the imperial movement in Canada. He promised to study the question and to advocate this policy if he found it in the interests of England and the empire. In 1880 when Chamberlain first became a cabinet minister, however, he had been a conventional free trader. Ironically, in view of later developments, he had delivered a masterly defence of free trade on 12 August 1881 in reply to a protectionist motion in parliament by the Conservative Charles Ritchie. Despite his defence of free trade, Chamberlain early in the 1880s had had misgivings about a policy which, in view of the rising continental and American tariffs, appeared to consist only of 'free imports'. These reservations were noticed at the time. His assistant at the Board of Trade, Sir Thomas Farrer, the 'high priest of fiscal orthodoxy', never thought Chamberlain a 'sound' free-trader.[4]

The election of 1892, at which the Unionists won thirty of the thirty-nine seats in Chamberlain's fief, caused Salisbury and Balfour to grasp more clearly his value as an ally. In the campaign of 1895 Beatrice Webb noted that Chamberlain's personality 'pervades this election'.[5] He was rewarded with the offer of any government position saving only those of Salisbury and Balfour. He chose the colonies in the hope of furthering closer union between them and the United Kingdom. After 1895, he was the leading exponent of imperialism and a firm policy towards the two Boer Republics. It was on the strength of his oratory and the issues he created out of the South African War that the Unionists won another term of office in 1900.

A supremely efficient political organiser, Chamberlain was also a superb House of Commons man and a national orator with a reputation for a slashing, compelling style. The precedents he set—his promulgation of party programmes, his establishment of the party machine, and his offer to the electorate of practical rather than moral choices—made him the 'prophet and architect of British democracy at the close of the patrician era. . . .'[6] A successful Birmingham manufacturer, he exemplified the movement of many businessmen and industrialists away from the Liberal party in the period from 1886 to 1914. Had it not been for Chamberlain and others of his outlook, the old Tory party could have sunk into reaction and irrelevance. In the climate of politics just after the South African War, Chamberlain, though approaching seventy, sought to give a fresh meaning to Unionism and to strengthen his own political position by advocating, with an imperial bias, the old creed of protection.

Despite Chamberlain's abilities and energy, the premiership was never open to him. When Salisbury resigned in July 1902, he was succeeded by his nephew, Arthur Balfour, whom Chamberlain had already accepted as the heir-apparent. The colonial secretary was fully aware of the obstacles which stood in the way of his leading the Unionists. He was a member of the minor party in an alliance. Moreover, while he was leader in the House of Commons of the Liberal Unionists numbering nearly seventy, only about a third were in his own immediate following. The rest were dominated by the Whigs and had a strong allegiance to the Duke of Devonshire, who, as the Marquis of Hartington, had been Chamberlain's onetime antagonist in the Liberal ministry of 1880–5. The tensions between the Hartingtonians and the Chamberlainites had reached a peak in 1885 when Chamberlain proclaimed his 'Unauthorised Programme' of land and social reform. These differences had been papered over in the Unionist alliance until the fiscal struggle dramatically revived the old tensions and intensified the bitterness, as free trade was one of the most profound beliefs of the Whigs.

Of greater importance in ensuring that Chamberlain would not become premier was the fact that while many Conservatives after 1895 admired the leadership of Chamberlain, some in high places still resented him as 'pushful Joe'—the exponent of disestablishment, and the Radical who in 1883 had condemned the Tory peers as those 'who toil not; neither do they spin'. Although the Conservatives were to accept the leadership of both his sons, Joseph Chamberlain could not expect similar recognition in his own lifetime.

The relations between Chamberlain and Balfour were generally cordial,[7] if each was somewhat wary of the other. Chamberlain was impulsive and emotional, warm to his friends and openly vicious to his enemies. Balfour was aloof and detached, often appearing to be above the turmoil of politics. In his speech to the House of Commons on the occasion of Balfour's death in 1930, Ramsay MacDonald was to capture the elusive nature of that baffling personality:

> He was indeed the embodiment of the leisured mind, expansive, hospitable, curious, interesting, cultured; the product of the garden rather than of the field or moorland. He saw much of life from afar.

Yet there was another aspect of Balfour's complex character, his streak of ruthlessness, which was brilliantly depicted by Churchill when he wrote that had Balfour's life 'been cast amid the labyrinthine intrigues of the Italian Renaissance he would not have been required to study the words of Machiavelli'.[8]

If Chamberlain was the more dynamic and original personality, Balfour was rightly regarded as possessing the subtlest political intelligence of his generation. He first made a conspicuous mark in political circles as chief secretary for Ireland in the late 1880s when his firmness as an administrator revealed unexpected talents causing the Irish to label him 'Bloody Balfour'. Henceforth, his career had been one of unbroken success. In 1891 Balfour became leader of the Conservatives in the House of Commons—a place gained by his debating talents, his success in Ireland, and the fact that the Conservative leaders preferred a Cecil. But if Balfour was the logical choice to succeed his uncle, he became prime minister with many enemies as well as many devoted admirers. Lord Winterton shrewdly summarised his weakness in the Unionist Party:

> Mr Balfour's enemies in the Unionist party—and they were by no means few, or unimportant—said that . . . [he] conveyed no clear message to his hearers. They protested that he had a manner *de haut en bas* with his supporters, and that he neither knew nor cared who they were. . . . They were convinced that he did not always support his colleagues and subordinates. . . . They said he was wholly out of touch with the ordinary voter . . . was in no sense a country gentleman . . . and chose his friends from among a small, exclusive, and by no means typical section of London society.[9]

When Chamberlain attempted to take the Unionist party by storm and turn it into a vehicle for imperial preference, he was able to capitalise on many of these weaknesses.

Imperial preference was of such fundamental importance in Chamberlain's last great political programme that some observations must now be made about that fiscal policy.

II

Britain faced many problems by 1900 which led to renewed agitation for tariffs. By contemporary standards the basis of taxation was too narrow to finance necessary social reforms and to pay the debts incurred in the South African War. Many manufacturers were alarmed by the competition of Germany and the USA. But the issue which both reanimated and synthesised the demands for protection was imperial preference. This issue was brought to the fore at the 1902 colonial conference when the colonies expressed a wish for closer commercial relations with Britain. Chamberlain knew when he took up imperial preference that he would be instituting a revolutionary change which would run counter to some of the deepest sentiments in the country. If preference was to be given, Britain had to put up tariffs against the world while allowing the colonies the privilege of free entry into her markets. He determined to proceed, however, for his experience as colonial secretary, where he had encountered increasing German and American aggressiveness, convinced him of the need for imperial consolidation:

> I believe in a British Empire . . . which . . . should yet, even if alone, be self-sustaining and self-sufficient, able to maintain itself against the competition of all its rivals.

In 1896 Chamberlain publicly indicated to the imperial Congress of Chambers of Commerce his hope for an imperial *Zollverein*. This ambitious proposal was viewed unenthusiastically by the colonies at the colonial conference in 1897, for they did not want to abolish their infant industries' tariffs against the motherland and thus feel the full force of British competition. Chamberlain was heartened, nevertheless, since just before the conference Canada had unilaterally cut her tariffs on British goods by 25 per cent. Chamberlain knew that without Canadian agreement his imperial aspirations would be stillborn. When Canada decided to send an infantry force to South Africa the colonial secretary, as Garvin emphasises, was delighted: 'Had not the great Dominion rallied with the rest in the Boer War he would not have been brought to stake his life upon his last crusade for Imperial unity'.[10] This preference was given, however, not for imperial, but for Canadian domestic reasons. The Canadian Liberal party was seeking to conciliate its own disgruntled supporters who were angry at the continuation of high domestic tariffs. As will be seen, Chamberlain interpreted this Canadian concession too optimistically. Nevertheless, in 1900 his hopes for progress in strengthening imperial trading links appeared justified when Canada increased the preference to 33 per cent.

At this stage a new element was introduced when Sir Michael Hicks Beach, the formidable Chancellor of the Exchequer, reimposed in April 1902 the Corn Registration Duty which had survived the fiscal revolution of 1846 but had been abolished in 1869. Its reimposition gave Canada the opportunity to raise the question of Britain's granting her reciprocal preference. The duty provided for a tax of 3d per cwt on imported grain and 5d per cwt on imported meal and flour. Hicks Beach justified this innovation on the grounds that it would help to balance his war budget and because the basis of taxation had to be broadened. He envisaged the duty as a valuable addition to the fiscal system, and when the Liberals expressed great alarm about its imposition, he disclaimed any protectionist and preferential intentions. However, Sir Wilfred Laurier in the Canadian House of Commons had already associated the duty with preference.

On 12 May Robert Borden, the leader of the Canadian opposition, demanded to know whether the prime minister, at the forthcoming colonial conference, would have anything at all to say on the possibility of a Canadian preference in British markets. Laurier replied that if preference to Canada on the corn duty were granted, then 'we are in a position to make offers to the imperial government which we could not make in 1897'. This was the famous offer seized upon by Chamberlain and his disciples as a justification for preference.

What did this 'offer', which was never specifically defined, amount to? All it meant at the colonial conference, as Chamberlain found to his chagrin, was that Canada would exempt Britain from further Canadian tariff increases. In fact, Canadian tariffs were never lowered before Chamberlain's death in 1914. Meanwhile, many Canadian Conservatives had opposed the earlier preference and advocated making their country self-sufficient industrially. These facts of Canadian political life and the development of Canadian nationalism seem to have been somewhat discounted by Chamberlain. His tendency to stress his belief in the destiny of the Anglo-Saxon race also offended many French Canadians, not least Laurier himself.

Of equal importance with imperial consolidation in motivating his advocacy of fiscal revolution was his desire to secure revenue for social reform. As early as 1895 Chamberlain had replied to a Conservative's question on how large sums for old age pensions would be raised with the startling answer 'by an import duty on wheat'.[11] His gropings in the 1890s toward a system of imperial preference buttressed by a domestic programme of reform were frustrated, however, by the attitudes within the party. While Salisbury was prime minister there would be no radical fiscal change. Moreover, some old Tories in the cabinet and the Whig wing of the Liberal Unionists were hostile to fiscal and other innovations. Their views were championed by Hicks Beach. The difference in outlook and policy between the Chancellor of the Exchequer and Chamberlain has been dealt with carefully by Julian Amery. He reveals how in 1901–2 Hicks Beach, by refusing to allot money for old age pensions, thwarted Chamberlain and then Chamberlain, by refusing to countenance economic retrenchment while the South African war continued, carried the day.[12] This protracted conflict must be borne in mind when we come to analyse the reasons for Hicks Beach's bitter attacks on Chamberlain's fiscal proposals in the spring and summer of 1903.

As the cost of the South African war came to be assessed, the clashes between Hicks Beach and Chamberlain became more acrimonious. When the war finally dragged to its close in 1902 Hicks Beach and the Treasury were forced to assess the total cost as exceeding £222 millions. Expenditure on such a scale shocked and dismayed many Unionists, and Hicks Beach and his friends in the Treasury deplored the spendthrift tendencies of their colleagues—especially of Chamberlain. It was because of this that Hicks Beach was able to stop Chamberlain's plans for an old age pension scheme, and yet felt himself forced to revive the corn duty as a means of dealing with the financial difficulties caused by the war. Soon after came Laurier's 'offer' which indicated to Chamberlain possibilities which might profitably be explored at the forthcoming colonial conference. Chamberlain was determined to seize his opportunity, and on 16 May he made his views known at a Liberal Unionist rally in Birmingham. In asserting that Britain must bind the colonies together instead of sticking to 'old shibboleths', presumably free trade, Chamberlain presaged much of what he was to say a year later. The biographer of the Duke of Devonshire maintained that 'all the policy which the colonial secretary declared more at large in May 1903 was contained in this speech . . . he had set up his standard, and his colleagues and the world had received fair warning'.[13] His immediate meaning, however, was clear enough: Laurier's suggestion must be given the most serious consideration.

During the colonial conference in July, a number of vital changes took place in the Unionist party. Salisbury's retirement on 11 July removed one obstacle from Chamberlain's path, and Hicks Beach resigned along with the prime minister because, according to the assistant secretary to the Treasury, Sir Edward Hamilton, 'he can get no support in the Cabinet'.[14] With these resignations Chamberlain's position was constantly strengthened. The departure of these two Tory stalwarts, and the lack of outstanding new talent moving into the Unionist ranks seemed to underline Chamberlain's eminence and indispensability. In addition, his son Austen received cabinet rank while a hostile colleague, Lord James of Hereford, was jettisoned. The duke continued to lead the Liberal Unionist party in the Lords. Although he had become very inactive by 1902, he was still an important political figure. Devonshire's influence with the landed classes was immense, and he had a high reputation in the country for political wisdom and integrity. The fiscal struggle was to revive his energies, and he eventually became the leader of the Unionist opposition to Tariff Reform.

One more appointment, that of Ritchie, did not appear likely to weaken Chamberlain's position. Despite the fact that prior to becoming Chancellor of the Exchequer he had been president of the Local Government Board and president of the Board of Trade, Ritchie was widely regarded as a man of modest talents.

Lord Balfour of Burleigh, Secretary of State for Scotland in 1895–1903 and later a close free trade colleague of Ritchie, spoke of his appointment as 'inconspicuous'.[15] The more damning appraisals, however, have come from Tariff Reformers who were understandably bitter at the role Ritchie played in helping to thwart Chamberlain's first attempts to institute fiscal reform. W. A. S. Hewins, a prominent economic historian, expressed a common Tariff Reform assessment when he labelled Ritchie the 'instrument of other people (Treasury officials) more important than himself'. Austen Chamberlain was even more specific, claiming that Ritchie had 'fallen entirely under the influence of Sir Francis Mowatt, the Permanent Secretary to the Treasury, a fanatical free trader'.[16] These deprecating assessments have recently been powerfully challenged by Alfred Gollin who makes Ritchie the hero of the fiscal struggle of 1903.

There is no evidence that Chamberlain, who was obviously glad to see Hicks Beach go, regretted Ritchie's advancement. It must have been of the utmost importance to him, already groping towards fiscal innovations, that the Chancellor of the Exchequer be friendly, and, after all, Ritchie had been a 'fair trader' in the 1880s. In the Treasury, where Chamberlain's schemes had already caused great anxiety, there was consternation. Sir Edward Hamilton threatened to resign, compared Ritchie unfavourably with the towering chancellors he had served in the past, and complained in his diary on 14 August 1902 'that though Ritchie has pleasant manners, his blood is not of the blue set'. In the light of the cordial relations which were to develop between the two men, and the extraordinary influence the Treasury, and especially Hamilton, was to assume over Ritchie, these remarks are ironic.

The reconstruction of the ministry gave little cause for satisfaction to most Unionists. The *National Review* lamented that 'new blood is conspicuous by its absence in this make-believe ministry'. Apart from Chamberlain and Balfour the new ministry presented to the public an uninspiring assembly. With the exception of Bonar Law, who became under secretary to the Board of Trade, able young Unionists such as Churchill and Hugh Cecil were passed over.

Along with this obvious Unionist debility, the passage of the

Education Act in December 1902 gave Chamberlain added incentive to present a new programme. This act struck directly at his political position. It superseded Forster's Education Act of 1870 by abolishing School Boards and passed control of education to the county and borough councils. In addition, it made provision for Church of England schools to be 'on the rates'. In time Forster's Act had come to appeal greatly to Nonconformists —many of whom looked to Chamberlain as their champion. Thus the new measure threatened to sunder the Unionist alliance, for education was the weakest link in the relations between Conservatives and Liberal Unionists. Among the former were many firm defenders of the Church of England and of the principle of aid to denominational schools. Among the latter were many Nonconformists hostile to subsidising denominational schools by public money.

As the clauses of the bill were worked out in the cabinet, Chamberlain took a determined stand against them and after the legislation passed, he alone of the cabinet was personally injured by the measure, both in his Birmingham fief and elsewhere where many Radical Liberal Unionists were up in arms. Chamberlain's hostility to the measure, and his bitter letters to Devonshire lamenting that 'our best friends are leaving us by the scores and hundreds never to return' were known in political circles. Since Devonshire sided with Balfour in cabinet discussions over the bill, the traditional alliance of Whigs and Nonconformists was destroyed. Balfour would not compromise on this bill and was fortified by the reports of Jack Sandars, his private secretary, who stressed that any changes in the measure 'to meet the Birmingham Liberal Unionists' would necessitate 'withdrawal of the bill and that, of course, means an election and a rout'.[17] Chamberlain eventually gave in and stayed with the administration, but his correspondence is filled with references to the deleterious effect of the Education Act on his own position and on the Unionist cause. The Secretary of State for India, Lord George Hamilton, went so far as to comment that 'the first change propagated the second. If we had no Education Bill in 1902, we should have had no Tariff Reform in 1903'.[18] This is too simple an explanation of the motives behind Chamberlain's fiscal campaign, but it is true that Tariff Reform allowed him both to regain the initiative as he set the Tory party ablaze, and to recover his position with many of the Radical Liberal Unionists despite the Education Act.

Balfour's stand on the Education Act conveys the impression that he wanted to leave no doubt in the party as to who was in command. He admitted as much to Devonshire when trying to explain Chamberlain's call for Tariff Reform in May 1903 as arising, among other things, 'from the notion that his counsels had not all the weight which his public position justified in determining the legislative policy of his colleagues'.[19] Balfour appreciated Chamberlain's abilities and valued him as a colleague. Few men in English politics, however, were as successful as Balfour in dealing with rivals—witness, for example, his intrigue against Lord Randolph Churchill from 1883 to 1886, when he consistently warned Salisbury of Churchill's ambitions and advised his uncle to give the Tory Democrat enough rope to hang himself. While the prime minister certainly did not want to lose Chamberlain, he did not want him playing the role of the over-mighty subject.

III

Chamberlain was determined to carry on with his developing aspirations for preference by trying to force his policy on the administration. On 21 October 1902 Chamberlain raised the matter of a preferential remission of the corn duty in favour of Canada. At this cabinet meeting, the discussion was apparently general and inconclusive, but a considerable amount of sympathetic interest was shown toward the proposal. Ritchie was much taken aback and lamented that Balfour, the only man who could have checked Chamberlain, was wholly absorbed in the Education Bill. An eternal pessimist, Ritchie doubted his ability to fight Chamberlain single-handed but in fact he was by no means alone. The forces which were initially to check Chamberlain—the chancellor, the Treasury, and advisors such as Lord Goschen, a former Chancellor of the Exchequer—at once began to organise.

The two men who probably did most to wreck Chamberlain's hopes for a peaceful acceptance of reciprocal preference by the government were Sir Francis Mowatt and his assistant, Sir

Edward Hamilton. Since 1894 Mowatt had been permanent secretary to the Treasury. A powerful, outspoken man, fanatically imbued with Gladstonian ideas on finance, he viewed any suggestions for preference as heretical and totally misguided. Mowatt disliked and distrusted Chamberlain and was already convinced that he would try to enhance his political fortunes by an appeal to protection when he found the time opportune. Although ill during most of 1902 and due to retire in the summer of 1903, Mowatt threw himself passionately into the fight to stop Chamberlain. Indeed, Mowatt was so incensed by Chamberlain's fiscal suggestions that when the two met by accident in the lobby of the Commons a heated argument developed.

More detached than Mowatt and probably more effective was Edward Hamilton, the Assistant Secretary. Indeed, because of Mowatt's illness, Hamilton dominated the Treasury and thereby exerted great influence upon Ritchie. In his 'Diaries', written with an eye to subsequent publication, Hamilton attempted to portray himself as a candid, straightforward civil servant. In fact, he was an accomplished intriguer with a special fondness for grand aristocrats, notably Rosebery and Devonshire, whom he considered the greatest figures in British public life. The influence Hamilton gained over Ritchie and his success in assisting him to oppose Chamberlain's plans were the most important actions of his career.

Hamilton prepared a memorandum for Ritchie giving the arguments against preference. It was circulated among the cabinet ministers on 15 November and Chamberlain's copy, with his marginal comments, is quoted lavishly by Amery. The document presents cogently the Treasury arguments: preference will lead to taxes on food and raw materials which will handicap British consumers and producers alike; it will encourage the colonies to make exorbitant demands to increase the range and rate of the duties; it will diminish British trade with foreign countries; and, in particular, will antagonise the United States. On 19 November 1902, however, a long and elaborate discussion ensued and, according to Balfour's letter to the King, 'the cabinet finally resolved that as at present advised, they would maintain the corn tax, but that a preferential remission of it should be made in favour of the British Empire'.[20]

Thus it appears that for the time being Chamberlain's views prevailed. After this decision, however, the cabinet listened to Ritchie. He made what Amery, an avowed partisan of Chamberlain, considered the reasonable demand that no official communication concerning the provisional decision should be sent to Canada which would bind them 'to continue the imposition of the tax which circumstances between now and the time of the Budget might show it would be wise to abandon'. With this suggestion the cabinet concurred. However, as Chamberlain embarked in November on a much-publicised trip to South Africa, he could feel hopeful that Balfour and his chief colleagues would stand by a policy which they appeared to have accepted in principle.

Between November 1902 and March 1903, while Chamberlain was absent, his opponents managed to spike the colonial secretary's guns—an extraordinary success in the light of his earlier victory in the cabinet and the repercussions in England of his journey through South Africa. At the height of Chamberlain's tour in February, Hamilton noted with mingled admiration and fear that his trip was 'a triumphant success' and that on his return 'he would of course be able to dictate his own terms. . . . There will be no holding him now.' The Liberal leader, Sir Henry Campbell-Bannerman, expressed similar fears to Herbert Gladstone, commenting 'for the moment Joe is the hero . . . he will come back home a very powerful political personage'.[21] Even J. A. Spender of the *Westminster Gazette*, often so critical of Chamberlain, remarked on the opening of parliament in 1903 that 'without Mr Chamberlain, parliament indeed seems like Hamlet without the Prince'. But, 'with much shuffling of feet', Ritchie was hardening against preference and slowly preparing to undercut Chamberlain's position. On 24 February he finally told the cabinet that he could not accept Chamberlain's proposals. Edward Hamilton recorded with relief:

> Ritchie has at last summoned up his courage. He has told Arthur Balfour that if preferential treatment is to be pressed he must find himself another Chancellor of the Exchequer. . . . It is very creditable of Ritchie to have put his foot down. It remains to be seen whether he is strong enough not to take it up again.

Ritchie was deluged with advice from the Treasury and from men who later became Unionist Free Traders. Unfortunately, only tantalising glimpses remain, though Hamilton on 2 March 1903 records one important incident:

> I find that Goschen had, not long ago, a talk with Ritchie and it has certainly had a great effect. Goschen regards any coquetting with preferential treatment as fatal to sound finance, and I see his advice has *taken*.

As a financial expert and former Chancellor of the Exchequer, Lord Goschen was a man of considerable influence in both financial and Unionist circles, and Ritchie was bound to give his opinion great weight. As a politician he represented the commercial and manufacturing classes in the Whig wing. In his aversion to social and electoral reform, this 'ablest of the Whig logicians' was the 'political antithesis 'of Chamberlain.[22] Goschen had worked closely with Devonshire to thwart Gladstone's first Home Rule Bill, and when Lord Randolph Churchill threatened the stability of Salisbury's administration by his precipitate resignation in 1886, Goschen stepped into his position and became a highly-acclaimed Chancellor of the Exchequer. After 1895 he had been a successful First Lord of the Admiralty until his retirement in 1900.

At Madeira on his way home, Chamberlain was informed of Ritchie's stand by his son Austen. In the meantime the Treasury prepared for the budget to be delivered on 23 April. Then on 15 March Chamberlain returned to be welcomed by cheering crowds, an ecstatic Unionist press, most of the cabinet, and a series of major receptions. However, his preference proposals had been sabotaged: in the first instance by Ritchie and his advisors, but also because Balfour accepted the claims of the Chancellor of the Exchequer.

The reason often given for Balfour's failure to support Chamberlain is that he did not want to lose another Chancellor of the Exchequer so soon after Hicks Beach's retirement. In the opinion of Tariff Reformers like Leopold Amery, however, Chamberlain made a grievous error in not demanding that the prime minister choose between Ritchie's resignation and his own. But if Chamberlain had forced a showdown in March 1903, would Balfour have supported him or made him Chancellor? If he lost and resigned Chamberlain would have found himself once more in the political wilderness unless he chose the bleak alternative of leading a revolt in the Unionist party at the head of a small rump of protectionists. So, ill and exhausted, after two cabinet councils in the last week of March he gave way sullenly to Ritchie's demands. Since preference was not to be given, he demanded, successfully, that the duty be repealed lest its retention, after Laurier's offer, give offence to the colonies.

Ritchie and the Treasury, even if they remained apprehensive about the possibilities of a counter blow, were immensely relieved at Chamberlain's retreat. The chancellor presented his conveniently free trade budget on 23 April and the preference struggle seemed ended for the moment. Ritchie in his speech went out of his way to define the position of the administration along rigid free trade lines claiming the need to repeal the duty because corn was the food of the people. It was this dogmatic approach, which could only have deepened Chamberlain's chagrin, that aroused the prime minister's full anger at Ritchie. Indeed, Balfour's latest biographer concludes that the chancellor's intransigence in the debate of 23 April made the cabinet crisis after 15 May 'inevitable'.[23] The Treasury, however, working through Ritchie had managed an internal coup of considerable dimensions.

IV

At the time that Chamberlain was defeated by Ritchie and let down by Balfour, the fortunes of the Unionist party were lower than at any time since 1895. The Education Act was in its most unpopular phase and Nonconformist agitation was reaching a peak. Within the government the hapless St John Brodrick, Secretary of State for War, desperately tried to push through an unpopular measure of army reform. The administration was being ridiculed by a group of young Unionists led by Winston Churchill, Hugh Cecil, Ernest Beckett, and Jack Seely. In the Liberal press these young men were popularly described as Hughligans because of the dominant position in the group attributed to Lord Hugh Cecil. With verve and pungency, if not always accuracy, they poured scorn on Brodrick, and execrated what they considered the lavish expenditure of government departments.

The mockery and indiscipline of the Hughligans was a severe irritant to the administration at a time when its reputation in the country was sinking badly. Although the government was producing two of the most constructive measures of the early twentieth century—the Education Act and the Irish Land Act—the Unionist administration was becoming increasingly unpopular. As early as March 1902 Sandars had painted a 'very black picture of the coming legislation' to Balfour and later in the year reported that Middleton, the Conservative agent, had pleaded that by-elections be avoided.[24] Moreover, by refusing to grant old age pensions and by alienating labour through their support of the Taff Vale judgement, the Unionists had displayed a dangerous reluctance to come to terms with some of the most urgent problems facing the nation.

Chamberlain might have met the demand for pensions if he had not been frustrated in the cabinet or if he had become prime minister. With his shrewd tactical perception as well as his own Radical past, Chamberlain knew he could not let social reform pass by default to the Liberals. What is clear is that Balfour was not the man to be prime minister when it was necessary to revivify Unionism by constructive appeals to the masses. Although he displayed great finesse and judgement in foreign policy, he appeared indifferent to large segments of British society, had little appeal for the electorate, and lacked interest in vote-getting machinery.

Unionist disorganisation and demoralisation had become more apparent while Chamberlain was in South Africa. A striking example of Unionist dissension came on 23 February 1903 when Churchill, Beckett and Seely challenged the government by proposing an amendment of Beckett's censuring Brodrick's army scheme. The activities of the Hughligans became even bolder on a further amendment against Brodrick by Ivor Guest on 12 March when twenty-six Unionists voted with the opposition. In these humiliating divisions many of those who later became ardent Unionist Free Traders consistently defied the whips. Even the Unionist press was full of accusations of timidity and delay. Castigating the government for its procrastination on the

London Education Bill, the *Pall Mall Gazette* on 27 March described Balfour and his colleagues as tending toward 'the curse of Reuben' as they sat 'shivering in philosophic doubt on the steps of a metaphysical bathing machine'. *The Times*, which had extolled the Unionist administration as recently as February, sombrely lamented by mid-March that 'the confidence of the people in the government is slipping away'.

This Unionist debility began to be reflected at the beginning of 1903 in electoral rebuffs. Defeats by decisive majorities in such traditional Tory constituencies as Newmarket, Woolwich, and Rye greatly disturbed the Unionists. The defeat at Rye on 18 March, in particular, produced a spate of reassessments. The *Standard* asked whether the issues of war and Home Rule upon which the Unionist party had relied so much since 1886 had ceased to alarm and fascinate the public. The *Daily News* proclaimed after Rye that 'one personality, namely Mr Chamberlain, can pull those political neurotics together and keep them just strong enough to go through the Session. . . . Little as he may deserve his power, it exists'. Contributing to these setbacks was the fact that the Conservative electoral apparatus had run down. So finely tuned in the heyday of Salisbury, the party machine was after 1900 increasingly neglected by the once energetic Middleton, and from mid-1903 it was clumsily and ineptly controlled by his successor, Captain Wells.

These Unionist failures, as well as his own grievances, must have determined Chamberlain to embark on Tariff Reform in May. He knew that this was the time to announce his programme before the Unionists became even more unpopular and while preference was still a live issue. Yet only a month before Chamberlain seemed incapable of any bold initiative. When he was not resting at Highbury he was brooding over the Unionist by-election losses and the decay of his party. Mary Chamberlain expressed his dissatisfaction, as well as the general view of Unionism, when she wrote to her mother in April:

> Everyone is getting very depressed over the political situation. The Government is the target for all the malcontents. It certainly has ceased to be popular and . . . one wishes that some accident might throw it out. . . . Even Mr Balfour's serenity is disturbed . . . I have never seen him as low in his mind.[25]

Other observers like Blunt, noting both the Unionist malaise and the lack of Liberal initiative, speculated that Chamberlain might make a bid with a new programme. Chamberlain recovered his energy and initiative, and determined to force the hand of his colleagues and to rout his enemies. Mrs Chamberlain wrote to her mother on 11 May that 'Joe is very preoccupied over his speech for Friday'. The speech was to throw English politics into a state of flux unequalled since 1886. Even before Chamberlain delivered his famous speech many in Britain were already profoundly disturbed about the obvious deterioration of their home and imperial markets owing to increasingly fierce foreign competition. The 'made in Germany' scare of 1896 had been followed by an even greater economic alarm in 1902 and early 1903—the so-called 'American invasion'. No cabinet minister was more concerned about these American (and German) economic dangers than Chamberlain. Although these threats were subsequently seen as less serious than they appeared at the time, Chamberlain's urgent call for fiscal change was to strike a responsive chord in the country.

Chapter 2 THE RISE OF THE UNIONIST FREE TRADERS

I

BY MAY 1903 the ministry had gained a respite. Balfour, however, had no illusions, for he later confided to the duke:

> I do not myself believe that it would have been possible . . . to have prevented the subject [of preference] coming within the sphere of practical politics in the immediate future. Joe's action has precipitated the crisis; has made it more acute and dangerous; but it would not I think in any case have been long postponed.[1]

The prime minister could deal with the clamour inside his party against the dropping of the corn duty if it came only from back-benchers, and he planned to receive a deputation on 15 May to rebuff their demands.

Balfour explained to the deputation that the tax had been withdrawn because it was unpopular and widely regarded as protectionist. He speculated, however, that if the desire for a fiscal union with the colonies ever arose from 'the great body and mass of the people' then 'a trifling duty upon food imports might be part of the general system'. Despite the doubts he had cast upon the long-term prospects of free trade, he appeared to be openly challenged by a speech Chamberlain made to his constituents the same day. The contrast 'almost stupefied' the public and politicians who knew nothing of the background of the speeches. When Balfour had first told the cabinet of his intentions, 'Chamberlain', he recalled to the duke, 'took the occasion if you remember to observe that he proposed to say at Birmingham much the same as I proposed to say to the deputation *only in a less definite manner*. The famous Birmingham speech embodies his practical endeavour to carry out this undertaking.'

In fact, however, Chamberlain reopened the whole issue publicly in an appeal to the nation to consider a change in fiscal policy. He claimed that Canada had already offered Britain substantial preferences but that 'speaking for the Government as a whole, and not in the interests of the colonies', he was 'obliged to say that it was contrary to the established fiscal policy of this country'. The colonial secretary entreated his countrymen to grasp the significance of the problem:

> I leave the matter in your hands. I desire that a discussion on the subject should be opened. The time has not yet come to settle it; but it seems to me that, for good or evil, it is an issue much greater in its consequences than any of our local disputes. Make a mistake in your Imperial policy—it is irretrievable. You have an opportunity; you will never have it again.

He closed with the threat that, although he did not believe that an election was very near, 'our opponents may perhaps find that the issues they propose to raise are not the issues on which we shall take the opinion of the country'.

The impact of Chamberlain's declaration was dramatic even though earlier pronouncements, particularly his speech of 16 May 1902 at Birmingham, had anticipated much that was included on 15 May 1903. According to the *Annual Register*, however, 'no political event in recent years has produced so startling an effect as the pronouncement on fiscal policy made by Mr Chamberlain . . . at Birmingham'. Unionists in sympathy with Chamberlain's imperial ideals looked upon the speech as a clarion call, and Leopold Amery described it as 'a challenge to Free Thought as direct and provocative as the theses which Luther nailed to the church door at Wittenberg'.[2] Liberals were exultant. The *Daily News* praised Balfour's 'free trade speech' and claimed that, speaking several hours after his chief and in full cognisance of his speech against the corn tax', Chamberlain 'opens a crusade'.

Balfour, according to Gollin, was 'scarcely ruffled' by the speech as 'it had all been said before'.[3] Chamberlain, however, soon gave him clear cause for concern. On 21 May Chamberlain made a crucial speech in the House which clearly indicated that the Birmingham speech was not an isolated outburst. In a debate on an Aged Pensioners Bill, David Lloyd George taunted the colonial secretary as an apostate over pensions. Chamberlain disdainfully dismissed the charges but insisted:

> Before any Government can consider a scheme of that kind it must know where it is going to get the funds. I do not think that old age pensions is a dead question and I think it may not be impossible to find the funds, but that no doubt will involve a review of that fiscal system which I have indicated as necessary and desirable at an early date.

The colonial secretary declared that he had entered the chamber 'accidentally', but it is clear that his statement was not simply an impulsive outburst. It has been generally accepted that Chamberlain only pronounced on pensions after being deliberately provoked by Lloyd George. But evidence indicates that he had deliberately decided to speak out, linking his imperial aspirations with social reform at home. In a memorandum written after his resignation in September 1903, Ritchie related the 'peculiar circumstances' under which this speech was delivered:

> Mr Balfour the day before told me of Chamberlain's intentions, and I had at once expressed my determination, if he did this, of rising up in my place and repudiating his authority to make such a declaration on behalf of his colleagues. This led to an interview between Mr Balfour and Mr Chamberlain which resulted in a message being sent through Mr Gerald Balfour that Mr Chamberlain had abandoned his intention and would absent himself from the House during the Debate. Notwithstanding this undertaking on Mr Chamberlain's part he was present and delivered the speech which he had promised the Prime Minister he would not make. I myself, relying on his promise, did not go to the House. I have reason to believe that Mr Balfour was much annoyed by this incident. I need hardly say that this did not improve the relations—never very cordial—which existed between Mr Chamberlain and myself![4]

This accusation, that Chamberlain had broken his word, is corroborated by Balfour. He wrote to Devonshire in August 1903 that it was difficult to defend the colonial secretary's speech in the House of 22 May. It was 'a distinct violation of an arrangement come to with me'.[5] It may be that Chamberlain would have stood by his agreement, at least to the extent of not speaking, if Lloyd George had not goaded him. But it appears more likely that his remarks were premeditated and that he was declaring war on colleagues who had presumed to reject his scheme for imperial preference.

Whatever his reactions to the speech of 15 May Balfour can have been in no doubt after 22 May that Chamberlain's fiscal opinions threatened to destroy his government. The prime minister was not disturbed by the ideas themselves, for his attitude to protection was purely empirical, and, while he considered Chamberlain somewhat alarmist in his analysis of Britain's economic and imperial position, he was prepared to inquire sympathetically into the colonial secretary's proposals. His prime aim, however, was to maintain the unity of the party and so on 27 May he informed the king that in his opinion 'there is much to be said for the scheme [of colonial preference] but . . . it is most imprudent to attempt to "rush" it either in the Cabinet or in the Country'. Nevertheless, despite his desire for caution, Balfour knew he would have to clarify his own fiscal position, for Sir Charles Dilke and Lloyd George announced that on 28 May they would initiate a fiscal discussion on the motion for adjournment of the House. Chamberlain's old comrade in arms led the assault. Dilke asserted that the colonial secretary's two speeches 'form a series' of 'momentous importance' and demanded to know the intention of the government concerning the taxation of food and raw materials and their policy for the next election. In reply Balfour stressed that there was no contradiction between Chamberlain's views and his own but he 'couldn't imagine it would be wise to put a tax on raw materials . . . nor can I say people are ready to accept and submit to a tax on food'. However, he revealed that the government would undertake a formal inquiry into the fiscal question. When pressed by Lloyd George, he added that no fiscal change would be undertaken until after an election.

Balfour had clarified his position and had gone a long way towards conciliating his most powerful colleague. Great then was his annoyance when Chamberlain rose immediately and developed further his own proposals. After stating his complete agreement 'with every word that fell from the Prime Minister', he then turned Balfour's vague point about no fiscal change being contemplated until after an election into a militant threat by proclaiming that 'undoubtedly a new mandate will have to be given the Government if the suggestions I have thrown out are to be put into practical effect'. While disclaiming, as yet, the need to tax raw materials he concluded: 'If you are to give a preference to the colonies—I do not say that you are—you must put a tax on food.'

By boldly stating his controversial views at such a moment and claiming that the prime minister was in harmony with them, the colonial secretary was forcing the pace with a vengeance. No wonder Balfour was angry at Chamberlain's presumption for, as the *Daily News* claimed, 'Chamberlain spoke more like a monarch than a Minister'.

II

Chamberlain's sudden declarations threw many free traders in his party off balance. At the Treasury, however, Mowatt acted with dispatch to bolster up Ritchie to face the new challenge. The day after the colonial secretary's speech on pensions he wrote a long, carefully composed letter to the chancellor pointing out that Chamberlain's new departure had been predictable:

> I have known for the past two years that he contemplated an appeal to the country on protection coupled with preferential treatment and old age pensions thrown in as a bait to the working class vote, and I think I may say that the Prime Minister has known it also.

Mowatt concluded on a note of flattery by presenting the crisis as a conflict of will between the chancellor and the colonial secretary:

> No one can doubt that Mr Chamberlain's recent action is largely prompted by his desire to reverse your victory in the Cabinet. If you were to resign he would have succeeded but if you remain and the Cabinet does not desert you your victory becomes more established every day. . . .[6]

Flattery, however, was not enough. According to Hamilton,

Mowatt and he were called to the chancellor's office on 26 May and told that 'he would like to go now'; but they replied, 'as civilly as we could, that he was an important man where he was but would be nobody if he resigned. . . .'

While Ritchie was being fortified, Hugh Cecil and Churchill implored the prime minister to resist Chamberlain. Lord Hugh was considered the most brilliant of Salisbury's sons and many Unionists looked upon him to lead the party after Balfour retired. This precocious, arrogant young man outlined graphically to Balfour the probable impact of protection on the party:

> Like someone in a novel I implore you to pause before it is too late. . . .
>
> From a party point of view can anything be more hazardous? . . . If the Govt. embark on Protection—under whatever specious name—our party must be split; for aught I can see Protection will do to us what Home Rule has done for the others.[7]

Churchill also entreated the prime minister to preserve the free trade character of the country. He promised that if Balfour disavowed Chamberlain, such action 'would command my absolute loyalty', but if the colonial secretary's proposals were accepted he would be obliged to 'reconsider' his 'position in politics'.[8]

These private warnings from two of the boldest young men in the party were made public in the debate on 28 May, for Churchill and Cecil spoke out vigorously against fiscal change. Their dissent centred on the belief that if the Unionists became protectionist a new type of party would arise which, in Churchill's words, would be 'rich, materialist, and secular and whose opinions would turn on tariffs'. Such an organisation would 'cause the lobbies to be crowded with the touts of protected industries'. Their protests emphasised to the world the divisions opening up in the Unionist party. What was unknown publicly was that the speeches of the young Tories had been 'prompted' by Hicks Beach, the most influential free trader in the party outside the ministry.[9]

While Chamberlain was pouring forth his ideas in May the free traders within the ministry made no public comment. However, the rudiments of a free trade wing began to evolve around Devonshire. The duke wrote to Ritchie on 29 May promising to support him. He went on to claim that although he had not

> given 5 minutes consideration to the question [of protection] since /86 [*sic*] and I do not say I am incapable of conversion . . . but I think it unlikely. What I do not intend however is to be committed by silence or acquiescence to a policy as to which I have the gravest doubts, and I shall be prepared to support as well as I can any of us who intend to keep themselves free.[10]

Ritchie replied that his views were 'practically identical' and that in the situation Chamberlain had 'wantonly created' they could not keep silent but must decide on some common action.[11] Ritchie, who had gone to Ireland on 29 May, accepted Devonshire's invitation to Lismore Castle where they were joined by George Wyndham and Lord Lansdowne, but no record of their deliberations has been found. Two days later the duke wrote to the prime minister informing him of his letter to Ritchie and warning that no more than the chancellor would he 'be committed by silence to a policy which has now [*sic*] been adopted by the Cabinet, one to which I never expect to be able to assent. . . .'[12]

Now that Chamberlain had stated his case, the free trade ministers presented the greatest threat to the administration. The prime minister therefore worked desperately in the recess from 29 May to 9 June to persuade them to accept a cabinet truce while an inquiry was undertaken into fiscal policy. The prime minister was particularly concerned to retain the support of Devonshire. The duke was the most important free trader in the cabinet, not only because he was the Liberal Unionist leader but also because of his immense prestige among the landed and indeed other classes. Balfour treated him 'with a deference he showed to no other living creature'.[13] If Devonshire could be persuaded to remain and to treat the fiscal issue as an open question for the time being, then Ritchie, George Hamilton, and Balfour of Burleigh would surely follow his lead. The prime minister was assisted in his endeavours by three leading cabinet ministers and close personal friends—Lansdowne, Lord Selborne, and Wyndham.

Lansdowne emphasised to the duke that 'so far as the immediate future is concerned—we are asked to admit only that there is a case for enquiry'.[14] Selborne stressed the danger to the party of the duke resigning: 'If Ritchie and you left the present government, then I think the Unionist party would be practically destroyed', and then 'the work of your life, the defeat of Home Rule, is jeopardised'.[15] Wyndham also implored Ritchie to save the Conservative party. 'If we break up now, we shall be wiped out and our historic party will be shattered for 30 years.'[16]

These entreaties helped to induce the duke to remain in the ministry, but the crucial factor was Balfour's decision to press for an inquiry into the condition of British commerce with a view to deciding whether or not a change in fiscal policy was advisable. Meanwhile, he assured Devonshire on 4 June that 'Chamberlain's views . . . commit no one but himself. They certainly do not commit me; although I am probably more in sympathy with him than either you or Ritchie'. As Chancellor of the Exchequer, Ritchie was to be free to state his position in the House on 9 June, but he, like the duke, agreed to the cabinet concordat proposed by Balfour. Its terms exemplify Balfour's mastery of delaying tactics:

(a) That the question is an open one; and that no one stands committed by any statement but his own.
(b) That we should be allowed officially to collect information upon the effects of the proposed policy.
(c) That, at all events for this Session, we should discourage further explicit statements of individual opinion.
(d) [That the Duke and Ritchie are not to admit their minds completely closed against a preferential arrangement.][17]

By acceptance the leading Unionist Free Traders made the first of the many compromises which were eventually to lead to their extinction. With the duke willing to suspend judgement, Balfour knew that the chances of a major free trade revolt had been greatly reduced.

By 9 June both factions in the cabinet were temporarily under control, for the colonial secretary had also agreed to the prime minister's proposals by suspending his public efforts to advance Tariff Reform. As Mrs Chamberlain told Lord Esher: 'Joe will not speak for fear of provoking more disunion'. Thus the prime minister could inform the king on 9 June that, although 'the fact of division' among the ministers 'greatly weakens our position', he hoped it would be possible to avert or at least defer a crisis which would threaten the existence of the government.

Having regained the initiative, Balfour refused to yield to the suggestions of the king that his proposed inquiry should be undertaken by a royal commission. The inquest was kept firmly in the prime minister's control, being directed by his brother Gerald, the President of the Board of Trade. Furthermore, the Treasury officials were not allowed to participate because Balfour considered them too committed to free trade. Instead of the Treasury, Balfour turned to civil servants such as Hubert Llewellyn Smith, the permanent secretary to the Board of Trade, and to young academic economists, such as Percy Ashley, who were prepared to question free trade. From their evidence the prime minister hoped to prepare a fiscal solution which would satisfy both factions in the ministry and restore his grip on policy.

Meanwhile, Unionist Free Traders outside the administration were acting with more energy and decision than their counterparts in the government. The two most active organisers were Churchill and Hicks Beach. Churchill wrote to St Loe Strachey, the editor of the *Spectator*, that 'some of us have quite taken our political future into our hands' and continued:

> it is proposed to form a League . . . to counter Chamberlain's impending campaign. Beach is taking the lead and our little group knows of at least 30 members. I will let you know more when I have seen Beach again. . . . Without organisation we are bound first to be silenced and secondly to be destroyed.[18]

A few days later Churchill reported that the League, which was to become the Free Food League on 13 July, was under way, and urged Strachey to write an editorial appealing to Hicks Beach to come forward. Churchill went further and wrote to Rosebery that 'if by the aid and under the aegis of Beach we cannot save the Tory party from Protection I shall look to you'.[19] At this early stage of the controversy Hicks Beach was the most prominent Unionist Free Trader not in office. His leadership was looked to by not only the Hughligans, but also by Whigs such as James and Goschen. Hicks Beach's talents were of such a high order that R. C. K. Ensor described him as 'a man who, though he never became prime minister, had certainly more capacity for that or any other high office than many whose luck has carried them to the summit'. He held various cabinet posts, concluding his official career as Chancellor of the Exchequer in Salisbury's government of 1895–1902. Upon his retirement in 1902 Balfour wrote that 'you have justly earned a greater financial reputation than any Chancellor since Mr G'. The essential characteristic of Hicks Beach was his intense party loyalty. Because of allegiance to his party, he was to become, by September 1903, the most powerful Unionist Free Trader supporting Balfour.

Hicks Beach's saturnine appearance and apparent fierceness helped to earn him the sobriquet of 'Black Michael'. Within the party he was 'feared rather than loved' and described by a wag as 'a bad horse to go up to in the stable'. Allied to this irascibility, however, was a nervousness which often left him ill and exhausted in the face of protracted conflict or strain of work. This weakness, which Unionist Free Traders came to know well, was explained to Lord Cromer by Hugh Cecil in 1908 when he advised the former proconsul to consult Hicks Beach:

> He is no doubt what schoolboys call a 'funk' and he has a most highly-strung temperament. But if one can get at his real mind, it is well worth doing. His judgement (where there is no risk to or strain on himself) is wonderful, and his knowledge of every intricacy of the Parliamentary game quite unrivalled. He is (where nerve is not wanted) the best of tacticians, I really believe superior, e.g. to either Mr Balfour or the Duke.[20]

At this stage of the controversy Hicks Beach was eager to combat Chamberlain's proposals. He was soon in touch with his old friend Sir William Harcourt, who wrote to H. H. Asquith on 25 May that Hicks Beach had come to see him 'full of fight and quite prepared to lead the opposition to the Chamberlain programme on the Government side of the House'.[21]

For the Liberals, Chamberlain's new programme was to heal or mute many old differences by providing in the defence of free trade a common front of action. By the end of May Campbell-

Bannerman could count on a degree of Liberal unity unequalled for nearly twenty years. 'This reckless criminal escapade of Joe's . . . is playing old Harry with all party relations', he reported happily, 'all the warhorses about me . . . are snorting with excitement.'[22]

If the Liberal leaders were spoiling for a fight, their actions did not show it, for the front bench took no part in the fiscal debates of May. As Harcourt told Campbell-Bannerman, the Unionist Free Traders were attacking Chamberlain sufficiently at present: 'I have just had a long and important conversation with Hicks Beach. . . . He is in communication with the Beckett-Winston Churchill party and their action is prompted by him'.[23] Hicks Beach also warned Harcourt that a Liberal amendment in the debate scheduled for 9 June would frighten most of the Unionist opponents of Chamberlain into supporting the administration. If they refrained from an amendment of their own, however, he was prepared to speak in opposition to Chamberlain. Liberals, therefore, contented themselves before the debate with speeches in the country denouncing Chamberlain's views.

III

When parliament reassembled on 9 June the old protectionist Henry Chaplin moved an amendment to the Finance Bill to remove import taxes from tea rather than corn. But the ensuing debate was not on the relative merits of taxing corn or tea, but on the perilous position of the Unionist party. In an explosive speech to a crowded and excited House Hicks Beach delivered a stinging attack on Chamberlain's proposals. He predicted that if they were implemented, the Unionist party would be destroyed. Ritchie's speech followed immediately. The chancellor asserted that he would be surprised if an inquiry brought to light any practical means of carrying out Chamberlain's preference proposals and therefore he felt he could not be a party to a policy which would be detrimental to both the country and the colonies. After him, other Unionists—Elliot, Sir John Gorst, Jack Seely, and Edgar Vincent—declared their free trade faith.

Despite this barrage, Balfour spoke blandly the next day and announced that, pending inquiry, he had 'no settled convictions' and denied that absolute uniformity could be expected from members of the government. He concluded by setting forth his own fiscal policy—retaliation. Asserting that imperial preference was not yet practical politics, he proposed the use of tariffs as a method of reprisal against those countries which applied them to British exports. The prime minister hoped that the threat or actual institution of such tariffs would lead other countries to reduce their tariffs on British goods. It was of small importance that the Liberals alleged that the inquiry was spurious, for the victory in the debate lay with Balfour. He had gained time to make more definite policy decisions.

Chamberlain had accepted the inquiry. Indeed, perceptive observers had noted that as Hicks Beach rose to speak in the debate, the colonial secretary slipped out of the House. This was the first public sign that some form of cabinet truce had been reached. In fact, while he remained prime minister, until December 1905, Balfour never gave his approval to another fiscal debate in the House of Commons. If the question was to be brought up, it had to be done by a free trade amendment which the government would label as a vote of censure.

While most free trade politicians and newspapers admitted to a grudging admiration for Balfour's tactics, their opinions ranged widely as to how effective it would be in muzzling Chamberlain. Hicks Beach reported to his wife that Balfour's inquiry was a 'heavy blow' to Chamberlain. At the same time Hicks Beach optimistically outlined to his wife what he thought his own future role would be:

> I dined with the 'Hughligans' last night . . . to please them. . . . I am trying to stop anything like the start of a Free Trade organisation on our side; as if Joe is quiet I don't want to make any move to disturb him, or to start what would be called a new party. My main object is to keep the government together and prevent Balfour from committing himself to Joe.[24]

Many free traders, however, disagreed with Hicks Beach and viewed the inquiry as merely a clever tactical device by the prime minister. They regarded Balfour as already committed to (or impotent to stand up against) Chamberlain despite his claim of 'no settled convictions'. John Morley cynically remarked that the inquiry 'was a pitched battle with a most accomplished bruiser on a foregone conclusion'.[25] Leo Maxse, editor of the *National Review*, openly gloated about the great service Balfour rendered Chamberlain by allowing him time for opinion to ripen in his favour. Since Balfour would probably come down on Chamberlain's side, the Unionist Free Traders would be destroyed. They would not survive like the Peelites who lost their party but won the nation, and, wrote Maxse presciently,

> compared with the Liberal Unionists after 1886, their position will be still more isolated and insignificant. They will not be able to co-operate successfully with the Nonconformist Liberals because of the Education Act, and apart from a few like Churchill who will cross the floor, the rest of the Unionist Free Traders will be opposed by Liberals and ignored by the Radical party at the next election.

Balfour sincerely saw the inquiry as a means to hold his party together. He outlined his position to Selborne complaining that he had 'exhausted every device in my power to prevent a party split. . . . As a matter of fact the difficulty is to prevent Chamberlain preaching the new doctrine *now*, in its most aggressive form. . . .'[26] Most Unionist Free Traders believed that the inquiry was a façade. Thus the duke's 'open mind' on retaliation was viewed with apprehension by Unionist Free Traders who had little faith in Balfour stopping Chamberlain and therefore regarded retaliation as the prelude to full protection. Goschen expressed these fears when he wrote to Lord Avebury, the distinguished scholar and banker, asking him to take the pulse of financial opinion in the City. Goschen then told Strachey of the pessimistic views he received:

> What I found out is not that Chamberlain will win on the food tax part of his projects, but that 'retaliation' will find much support in the City. . . . As for the Unionist party, it has suffered an almost mortal blow—all the more so as Balfour has lost much of his prestige and is regarded in many quarters as impotent to grapple with Chamberlain. . . .[27]

There were many indications that the Unionist Free Traders were being out-manoeuvred. Unionists close to the Treasury knew that its officials were being ignored by Balfour. More serious still was the obvious fact that while refraining from major speeches, Chamberlain was continuing to advance his cause. When Devonshire met Chamberlain on 20 June to discuss the future of the Liberal Unionist Association, the latter, according to James, who was present, 'burst into the room and shouted without a word of greeting: it is going gloriously, magnificently —nothing can be better. I am winning all along the line'.[28]

Strachey, meanwhile, heard rumours that Chamberlain was urging Alfred Harmsworth to start a rival to the *Spectator*—the only Unionist Free Trade press outlet apart from the *Edinburgh Review*. In fact, nothing came of this rumour, but the Tariff Reformers sought to gain control of the national and provincial press immediately after Chamberlain spoke out at Birmingham. Arthur Pearson, who controlled eleven newspapers by 1905 including the *Daily Express*, the *Standard*, and the *Evening Standard*, was the greatest capture of the Chamberlainites. The cause of Tariff Reform was also advanced by a brilliant young journalist on the *Daily Telegraph*, J. L. Garvin. By comparison, Unionist Free Trade efforts to secure assistance of any kind were not very successful. For example, early in June 1903, Hicks Beach, Churchill, and Goschen tried to win over Alderman Archibald Salvidge, the Conservative 'boss' of Liverpool. Churchill had invited him to a private dinner party, but when the free traders asked for his support Salvidge disavowed them immediately and sought an interview with Chamberlain to tell him what was 'brewing' so that the Tariff Reformer might stifle any threats to his movement in Liverpool.[29]

Chamberlain's growing power within the party was emphasised by a Tariff Reform meeting at the House of Commons on 24 June when 130 MPs met or sent letters supporting Chamberlain. The colonial secretary himself called for the meeting, but it was represented as having been spontaneously organised. From this gathering emerged the nucleus of the Tariff Reform League. Then on 26 June Chamberlain was Balfour's guest at the Constitutional Club. The prime minister and the colonial secretary exchanged lavish mutual praises and talked harmoniously about the need for extensive fiscal re-appraisal. Chamberlain reassured many of his conservative supporters by divesting himself, for the time being, of old age pensions.

The Tariff Reform rally on 24 June led the Unionist Free Traders to hold their own counter meeting from which emerged the organisation Churchill had been trying to form as early as 31 May. On 1 July fifty-three MPs and Lord Goschen held a meeting in a committee room of the House of Commons. The range of the Unionist talents and interests represented at the gathering was commented on by A. G. Gardiner of the *Daily News*. The free fooders had 'shrewd and keen men of business such as Colonel Denny'. Sir Samuel Hoare and Charles Tritton were 'powerful representatives of City opinion'. The 'young scions of the Whig Unionist houses of Cavendish, Lambton, and Peel' were for free trade. 'Rich, ambitious Tories like Robert Yerburgh and Ernest Beckett' opposed fiscal reform, as did 'the best representatives of medium Toryism' as exemplified by W. F. D. Smith. Hayes Fisher, 'deep in the inner life of official Toryism', came out against Chamberlain. The 'young hopes of neo-Toryism', Hugh Cecil and Winston Churchill, were unalterably against Tariff Reform. He concluded: 'Is there an abler Member of Parliament than Sir Michael Hicks Beach? I do not know him.'

At the meeting Hicks Beach made the last of his fire-eating speeches against Chamberlain, declaring that he would not be drummed out of his party for holding opinions which the Tory party had held for the last fifty years. In a very determined manner, Goschen, Cecil, and others proclaimed their opposition to Chamberlain. Then after a reasonably moderate resolution condemning food taxation but supporting the inquiry, a committee was set up to organise the Free Food League. Probably the Tariff Reform demonstration in the Commons on 24 June had persuaded Hicks Beach to drop the opposition, which he had expressed to his wife on 10 June, to the formation of a free trade organisation. On 13 July the League was formally inaugurated and Hicks Beach, the chairman, informed his son they had 'got rather more than 60 Unionist MPs to declare themselves against the protective taxation of food, which is the keystone of Joe's policy. . . .'[30]

On 21 July the Tariff Reform League was formed of dedicated Chamberlainite MPs, journalists, and wealthy Unionist industrialists. The Tariff Reform League was a far more powerful organisation than the Free Food League. Its financial resources were such that it could issue millions of pamphlets, could intervene actively at elections, and could establish nearly 300 constituency branches by the 1906 election. In many cases the League became synonymous with local Unionist constituency associations.

By contrast the Free Food League was only a parliamentary committee with very meagre resources. Moreover, it only sent propaganda into constituencies where the MP specifically requested their material. It had no constituency branches and did not intervene actively at elections apart from periodic pronouncements by leading free fooders, particularly the Duke of Devonshire, calling on the electors not to vote for Tariff Reformers. A list in the Elliot papers shows the peak membership to have been sixty-five MPs. From late in 1903 until the League's disappearance early in 1905 its membership dropped slowly and steadily under the impact of Tariff Reform pressure. Indeed, many Unionist Free Traders found participation in the Liberal Free Trade Union, which had been formed by Herbert Gladstone with Hugh Cecil's assistance, the most effective organisation. Nevertheless, the Free Food League did focus attention in 1903 and 1904 on both the most crucial and the weakest point in Chamberlain's programme: food taxes. Sponsored by the League, free fooders made numerous powerful speeches around the country denouncing Tariff Reform. Finally, the League was successful during 1904 in acting as a parliamentary pressure group to prevent Balfour having to commit himself wholly to Chamberlain's programme.

Liberals were relieved by the show of Unionist Free Trade strength although a number of Radicals wished to attack Balfour in parliament. Relying on Hicks Beach, Harcourt attempted to moderate such aggressiveness lest the relationship with the Unionist Free Traders be jeopardised. He maintained to Campbell-Bannerman that 'we cannot afford to dispense with their support any more than Wellington could afford to neglect the Prussians at Waterloo'. To the dismay of Harcourt, Hicks Beach then informed him that there could not be co-operation with the Liberals now that, instead of giving in to Chamberlain, Balfour had established the inquiry. This enraged Harcourt, who reported bitterly to Campbell-Bannerman of Hicks Beach that 'this cock will not fight', and that the Liberals 'had nothing to expect from their co-operation in the House of Commons'.[31] Hicks Beach's apparent initial willingness to fight, followed by his clear identification with Balfour, greatly influenced the view Liberal leaders held of the Unionist Free Traders as a timorous lot who could not be counted upon. Meanwhile, the Liberals went ahead with filling most of the constituencies where Unionist Free Traders sat with candidates of their own.

Hicks Beach and about forty of the sixty-five Unionist Free Traders believed by July that Balfour could check Chamberlain without destroying the party. Free traders with little faith in Balfour found the attitude of the Beachites most galling. Hugh Cecil, desperate to get a fiscal debate in the House, suggested to Herbert Gladstone the wording for a motion which would bring about a debate. He asserted that the least the Unionist Free Traders could do would be to walk out on a division, thus making the government look very silly. 'Whether all this is sound or not I don't know. . . . Beach knows nothing about this letter and I should guess he would disapprove.'[32] Twelve days later Cecil went even further by appealing to Devonshire to come forward. But the duke would only reply that 'as to the leadership of the Free Trade Unionists it seems to me at present that you need not look beyond Sir M. Hicks Beach'.[33]

In this uncertain atmosphere the session dragged to a close. By announcing on 7 July the dates for his autumn speaking tour, Chamberlain indicated that the cabinet concordat could not possibly last beyond September and that Balfour would soon be faced with more Tariff Reform pressure. Tariff Reformers also began to attack Unionist Free Traders in the constituencies. Exasperated by their situation, the Unionist Free Traders pressed Balfour for a day in parliament to 'discuss' fiscal proposals. When Balfour tartly refused, the free fooders were enraged. Cecil in particular was outspoken, and Balfour was moved to write to his cousin that 'I heard that you have been using rather violent language about me in the Lobby: . . . I do not mind— . . . You want a debate upon the tariff question . . . I do not want one.'[34]

In the light of these divisions the lobbies buzzed with rumours of an impending fall of the ministry and the rise of some new combination. However, Edward Hamilton on 13 August wrote in his Diary that the Balfour forces felt assured:

> According to J. Sandars there will be no serious split, and he repudiates the idea of a Hartington ministry. The Duke and others may go but Chamberlain had a large majority in the Cabinet, including as I always expected, the Prime Minister.

Chapter 3 THE CONFLICT IN THE CABINET

I

No matter what threats Tariff Reform posed to his administration, Balfour was determined to remain in power. Indeed, he nonchalantly told Wyndham's sister, Lady Elcho, that he was looking forward to the cabinet meeting, scheduled for 13 August, with much interest.[1] On the eve of this last cabinet meeting of the session, Balfour was also prepared to support Chamberlain's programme more strongly than at any time until the total commitment of the Unionists to Tariff Reform in the first election of 1910. He was ready to advocate not only retaliation, but also preferential tariffs entailing a tax on food.

On 5 August before the cabinet meeting the prime minister circulated a document composed of two separate parts. The first part was published on 16 September as *Economic Notes on Insular Free Trade.* Its general tone was vague and the main argument was that the growth of cartels and the increase of foreign tariffs rendered it necessary that the British government be armed with a weapon against any nations that imposed high protective duties. He therefore advocated giving the government power to force down foreign tariffs by means of retaliatory duties.

In addition, Balfour circulated another paper—called the Blue Paper—attached to the *Economic Notes.* The implications of this hitherto neglected paper have been dealt with extensively by Gollin and Amery. They observe that Balfour's *Economic Notes* contained no suggestions that food should be taxed or that a general tariff be imposed. Balfour in the Blue Paper advocated not only retaliation but also preference and food taxes. The latter part of this paper particularly antagonised the Unionist Free Traders in the cabinet since it accepted provisionally Chamberlain's arguments. George Hamilton later wrote bitterly that during 'the so-called truce' Balfour 'had been talked round by Chamberlain' and the 'Blue Paper was a . . . conspicuous instance of the Prime Minister's conversion'.[2]

Historians, however, have never examined the Blue Paper and have accepted only the accounts of its existence given by Ritchie and George Hamilton. By looking at the cabinet papers the controversy surrounding this document is solved. On 30 July Balfour wrote an important letter to the duke which was a rough draft of a cabinet memorandum. The main point stressed was that 'we should openly and avowedly announce that this country no longer considers itself debarred by economic theories from making the best commercial bargain it can with other countries'. Agreement on this point should be governed by the following principles:

> 1. No retaliatory duty should be threatened, or fiscal preference offered, *with a view to protecting any industry . . . against legitimate competition. . . .*
> 2. No such duty and no such preference should introduce any change into our fiscal system which would increase the average cost of living to the working-man.
> 3. . . . a retaliatory policy . . . [should not be instituted] by . . . starting with heavy protective duties against the world. . . .

Balfour concluded with the statement that he had 'shown my Memorandum (which is, of course, in a rough and provisional form) to none of my colleagues save Gerald—who agrees with it. Will you for the moment treat it as confidential'.[3]

On 1 August Balfour drew up a more polished draft and on 5 August informed the cabinet that he was circulating it along with 'the accompanying "Notes on Insular Trade" *as a Confidential Cabinet Memorandum*; what I shall do with it afterwards must depend on circumstances'.[4] The document advocated two policy maxims:

> we intend to propose no tax simply for Protective purposes. . . . [and] any readjustment of taxation, required either for the purpose of furthering freer trade with the Colonies or with foreign countries . . . should be framed so as to avoid any material increase in the budget of the working man. . . .'

Balfour noted that the scheme provided two methods of obtaining freer trade, 'namely, "preference" and . . . "retaliation" '. This memorandum was later labelled the Blue Paper.

The financial secretary to the Treasury, Arthur Elliot, recorded on 5 August that Gerald Balfour had told Ritchie, who was confused by the prime minister's treatise, that 'Arthur means to consent to a small duty on corn and meat with Colonial Preference'. The chancellor said he would resign immediately if the prime minister tried to push through such a policy.[5] The duke also prepared to take a determined stand. His answer to Balfour's letter of 30 July was a powerful memorandum of his own drawn up on 12 August and circulated to the cabinet. He was spurred to this effort because he gathered from something that was said in the cabinet on Tuesday (11 August) that 'we may be asked at once to assent or dissent from the opinions expressed in the memorandum.' The duke took particular exception to the fact that 'the Notes and the Memorandum entirely ignored the inquiry and might as well have been written twelve or six months ago'. He claimed that 'the whole policy sketched out by Mr Chamberlain could be advocated under the sanction of the principles laid down in the memorandum. . . .'[6] On 12 August Elliot commented hopefully in his 'Journal' about Devonshire's stiffening attitude:

> Hear the Duke is going to put his foot down at tomorrow's Cabinet. He will not stand any protective taxation on imported food. Victor [Cavendish] tells me he has seen a very strong memo—or paper—the Duke has prepared for the benefit of his colleagues. Will Chamberlain resign? Or what will happen? Present state of things clearly cannot last.

At the meeting on 13 August Devonshire, Ritchie, Balfour of Burleigh, and George Hamilton objected strongly and persistently to the principles of the Blue Paper. In the face of this opposition Balfour wrote to the king the next day that he did not feel hopeful about retaining the co-operation of all his colleagues 'for the scheme which he himself favours'. However, if Chamberlain 'shows a readiness to accept Mr Balfour's scheme and to modify some of the plans which he has from time to time put forward rather hastily', the prime minister was optimistic that a majority would agree to his 'moderate scheme'.[7]

Apparently at the Tuesday cabinet (11 August) there had been some disagreement as to whether a final decision on fiscal reform should be made at Thursday's cabinet (13 August). Because of the division Balfour had decreed on the Tuesday that no final verdict would be made until a cabinet meeting in September. Moreover, he was prepared to work strenuously to retain the duke:

> I am entirely in favour of postponement. I would make much greater sacrifices than that for the chance—even the off chance—of a harmonious arrangement. What do you say to 14 Sept.?[8]

In this way Balfour deliberately hinted to the duke, but to no one else, that he was considering the possible withdrawal of the Blue Paper. However, uncertainty remained. All four free trade ministers, including the duke, assumed that for the September cabinet meeting the Blue Paper would still be under review. Balfour of Burleigh gave evidence of this confusion when he wrote to the duke a week after the meeting:

> I have thought a good deal about our discussion in the Cabinet on the 13th. I am afraid that the more I reflect on this new policy, *so far as I can understand it*, the less I like it. . . . I dislike this tax on food. . . . I do not believe in us putting on any preference for the Colonies.[9]

The impasse in the cabinet was well known. Churchill informed Rosebery after the 13 August meeting that there was no agreement. Churchill would prefer the duke to form a government with Rosebery's co-operation, but, the tenacity 'of the Arthurians' hold on to office' impressed him:

> They loathe it; they despise it; they are weary and bored; but they are so absolutely convinced that England will be ruined if anyone replaces them that their patriotism and self-sacrifice lead them to swallow any quantity of dirt and humiliation to remain in Downing Street for the public interest. It is a strange point of view; and the most curious feature is its absolute sincerity.[10]

Two general conclusions emerge from the meeting of 13 August. Balfour had postponed, for the moment at least, his decision on preference, and the free trade group in the cabinet had clung together under Devonshire's leadership. Nevertheless, the duke, having achieved postponement, did not want to wreck the ministry. To Ritchie, who was all for resigning, he confessed that he did not find such a simple course satisfactory. The duke added that he had some suggestions which, if accepted by Balfour, might enable the cabinet to hold together for some time longer. Devonshire wanted the prime minister to tell his free trade ministers exactly what proposals he wanted them to accept. He wanted Balfour's agreement that no fiscal changes should be suggested until after an election, and that the present parliament should be allowed to discuss the whole matter.[11] Ritchie was perturbed at the duke's desire for compromise and exhorted him to maintain a firm stand.

Balfour's inner circle was aware of the pressure on the duke and of his own uncertainties. Sandars 'gathered' from the duke's secretary, John Dunville, that the duke was anxious to avoid a crisis involving his resignation. He disliked the pressures being put upon him to head a free trade party, but

> he feels that the demand in the interest of the country might be one he could not resist. . . .
>
> Dunville certainly left . . . the impression that if by concordat you could set some bounds and limits to the present scheme you would be in a fair way to reconcile the Duke who wants to be reconciled.[12]

This good news, Gollin maintains, held out the promise to Balfour that if he used all his blandishments, and made some compromises, the duke might be retained and the Unionist Free Trade threat to his ministry destroyed. The wavering Devonshire was the recipient of a sequence of letters from the prime minister expressing such sentiments as: 'There is no man living whose support and co-operation I think so necessary for the unity of the party, and the welfare of the country, or which I so earnestly solicit on personal grounds.' Balfour knew that if he could keep the duke he would not only hold the support of many hesitant free traders, but he would isolate the small group of active free fooders. Now that Hicks Beach was clearly not going to oppose the government, Devonshire was the only other possible focus for a strong Unionist Free Trade threat. It was therefore the prime minister's policy after 13 August to try to separate him from his free trade colleagues.

The prime minister was further encouraged by a letter from the duke on 23 August. Devonshire conceded that, while Chamberlain found in Balfour's 'paper and memorandum sufficient authority to enter upon his autumn campaign', he might detect in the 'reservations' satisfactory 'securities and safeguards'. The duke thereby indicated that he was a much less rigid free trader than his three allies. Humanitarian feelings rather than dogma prompted his fear of preference: his apprehension was that closer ties with the colonies might be purchased only at the cost of privation for the working classes.[13]

Balfour composed a very skilful reply on 27 August. The prime minister knew very well that the essential characteristics of the duke were his absolute honesty and his devotion to duty. What often appeared as dithering to his colleagues was in fact intense scrupulousness and concern about the right course. These qualities plus his unpretentiousness account for the hold he had on the loyalties and affection of many in the governing classes. Advancing age and an almost infantile grasp of economics did, however, often mean his prestige was blindly used. Balfour's first argument was that safety from Chamberlain's extremism lay in the 'steadfast co-operation' of moderate men like the duke and himself 'who are neither blind to new necessities nor too easily carried away by new enthusiasms'. Secondly, Balfour pointed out the interests which would be endangered if Devonshire failed to stand by him:

> Our business is to prevent our divisions reaching a point which may convert them into a national disaster and may deprive the greatest interests of the country of the guardianship by which since 1886 they have been protected.[14]

These powerful arguments, particularly the veiled reference to the danger of Home Rule should Devonshire depart, must have weighed heavily with the duke.

While this correspondence was being conducted, great uncertainty prevailed in the country about the future course of the government. Rumours were rife during the recess that Chamberlain was going to have to cut preference out of his programme.

By late August there were indications from the country that food taxes were not politically practicable. The Chamberlainite defeat in the Argyllshire by-election of 27 August seemed to underline the Unionist weakness at the polls if food taxes were advocated.

Despite the speculation that for the present the government would give up preference, Balfour as late as 8 September was still trying to convert the duke to the Blue Paper. On 6 September he sent the duke a set of draft resolutions advocating the principles of retaliation and preference. This and a scheme for preference which Gerald Balfour transmitted on 8 September represent the prime minister's answer to the duke's request for a policy outline before the September cabinet meeting.[15] The prime minister attempted to allay the duke's fears that preference would bring hardship to the poor by leaving corn untaxed and by off-setting the imposition of new duties on meat, fruit, and dairy produce with a reduction of the taxes on tea, coffee, cocoa, and sugar.

On 9 September, however, the duke sorrowfully replied that he did not think 'anything . . . would reconcile me to the adoption of any such compromise as is indicated in your resolutions'. He regretted that in trying to avert the disruption of the government he might have misled the prime minister as to the extent he would abandon free trade. Devonshire was resolved to resign, and while he would attend the cabinet meeting, he feared he 'should only be wasting your time'.[16]

The same day, however, Chamberlain wrote privately to Balfour offering to resign in order to speak freely in the country for Tariff Reform. The most convincing explanation for this action is given by Amery, who surmises that, realising Tariff Reform could not be forced on the administration without wrecking it, Chamberlain felt obliged to leave. Moreover, at a meeting on the occasion of Salisbury's funeral on 31 August Balfour apparently told Chamberlain of his increasing doubts about the political wisdom of committing the government to food taxes at the present time. Amery also suggests very plausibly that the prime minister told the colonial secretary that to hold the administration together Devonshire's support was important.[17] In addition, Chamberlain realised that a great propaganda campaign was required before the country would accept his programme. However, the colonial secretary must have felt confident that, as the greatest popular orator of the day, he could convert the nation and that he would have greater freedom to pursue his task outside the ministry. There was not the slightest hint that he would depart as a rebel—indeed why should he when the prime minister had already accepted his programme in principle? Thus Chamberlain believed he could promote his cause 'with absolute loyalty' to Balfour's government.

Balfour did not reply immediately and decided not to accept the resignation until he had talked with Chamberlain before the meeting and until he saw how the cabinet discussion developed. In the meantime he gave no public indication that he had received the letter. Gollin concludes that with this letter of resignation 'Chamberlain delivered himself into the prime minister's hands'.[18] This assertion may be a little melodramatic, but it is true that thereafter Balfour had greater flexibility to deal with all factions in the dispute.

II

Up to the September cabinet meeting no policy had been laid down. Neither preference nor retaliation had been accepted or rejected as only principles had been discussed. But on the eve of the crisis the prime minister was resolved that Ritchie, George Hamilton, and Balfour of Burleigh would have to leave the government. He was annoyed at their intransigence on the fiscal issue, and, according to Young, considered that they 'had shown their antagonism openly, had stirred the Party against him, had even caballed for a new administration and a new prime minister.'[19]

Ritchie was determined to resign. He was certain Balfour and Chamberlain would stick together and that preference would become the policy of the government. Ritchie and James were alarmed about the possibility of the duke yielding to the fiscal reformers, and James wrote that

> My fear is that you may not realise how much depends on you at this time. The Chamberlain people are hoping—and will do all they can to capture you—by suggestions of the *modus vivendi* feeling. If they can separate you from the Free Traders, Chamberlain's policy will become that of the Government.[20]

In fact, as we have seen, Devonshire had already decided, sorrowfully, to leave the government.

Balfour and Chamberlain, with Gerald Balfour, met for an hour before the cabinet. They decided that the colonial secretary should leave the ministry to go out as a missionary for Tariff Reform if Balfour could keep the duke in the government. The prime minister would commit his government only to retaliation while waiting on the results of the campaign. Together they may have decided on the tactics to be followed at the meeting: that Ritchie, Balfour of Burleigh, and George Hamilton would be forced to resign while every effort would be made to retain Devonshire. This is conveyed by Sandars' remark to Balfour in December 1903, when rumours were spreading of the possibility of a free trade ministry under Devonshire, that 'Joe appears to have questioned whether, as things have turned out, he was wise in counselling you to try to keep the Duke when the others went'.[21] The bargain was sealed, and Balfour's support for Chamberlain's programme apparently confirmed, by the decision that Austen Chamberlain would replace Ritchie.

At the cabinet meeting Balfour made it immediately clear to Ritchie and Balfour of Burleigh that they could not remain in the government. As Devonshire put it, 'I have never heard anything more summary or decisive than the dismissal of the two Ministers'. Then followed a general and not very clear discussion. Balfour tried to get the other ministers to agree that they were a fiscal reform cabinet without specifying the nature of the proposed reforms. This point is important for it confirms what Balfour on 22 September stated in writing to his remaining colleagues: that 'Tariff Reform' was no longer an 'open question', and support of him 'must be cordial'.[22]

When the question of preference was raised, Chamberlain implied that he could not remain if that policy was dropped. But neither he nor Balfour mentioned that they had agreed on the present impracticability of the government adopting preference. Not a word was uttered about Chamberlain's letter offering to resign, nor was it revealed that the prime minister had apparently agreed to accept it as soon as he was certain that the duke could be retained and that the intransigent Unionist Free Traders had resigned. It was to get them out of the way that he allowed the cabinet to believe he still advocated preference. Only Lord Onslow and Austen Chamberlain took Chamberlain's reference to resignation to mean that the colonial secretary was about to resign.[23] Ritchie later admitted in the Commons that he heard Chamberlain say he would resign if preference were not adopted. However, being unaware of Chamberlain's resignation letter and his pre-cabinet meeting with the prime minister, the chancellor and his allies did not grasp that Balfour had dropped preference as government policy. Whether they should have read correctly all the oblique hints in cabinet is another matter.

After this cabinet the free trade ministers met in George Hamilton's room and they met again after the cabinet of 15 September at which only foreign affairs were discussed. At this second meeting, according to Ritchie, he, George Hamilton, and Balfour of Burleigh 'resolved that all our resignations were to go in that night with a proviso on the part of the duke that before he took the final step he was to see the P.M. assuring us at the same time that there was no chance of his altering his determination to resign'.[24] On the morning of 16 September, Ritchie wrote to Elliot summarising what he and at least two of his colleagues thought to be the situation:

> All chance of a compromise is at an end. It was impossible for me to consent to either preferential treatment or retaliatory duties as proposed. . . . Chamberlain sticks to his programme. Balfour and the Cabinet support him. So I have sent in my resignation and I understand the Duke, G. Hamilton and B. of B. have done the same. . . . We could extract no scheme of any kind either from A. J. B. or Chamberlain. We were obliged to swallow the principle and leave trust to them [*sic*] the details! . . .[25]

This admirably illustrates the rigid turn of mind of the resigning free traders. As Balfour always maintained, their objections would not have been met even if food taxation had been abandoned explicitly. However, the letter reveals the prime minister and the colonial secretary playing rather dubious roles by making vague points while saying just enough to protect themselves against later charges of bad faith.

The duke, however, was in a muddle. He had no idea that Chamberlain was about to resign, but later on the same day, after the meeting of the free trade ministers, he saw the prime minister who 'hinted' that Chamberlain might resign.[26] Then, on Tuesday, 15 September, he met Balfour again, after his free trade colleagues had sent in their letters of resignation, and was informed that Chamberlain was almost certain to resign. Nevertheless, he still had doubts that the colonial secretary would in fact do so. He wrote to Balfour on Tuesday evening offering to resign but enclosing a covering note asking that Balfour correct him if he had misunderstood the situation in believing that Chamberlain remained a member of the government.

The next evening, Wednesday, the prime minister took the initiative and called on the duke at Devonshire House and read him Chamberlain's letter of 9 September or parts of it. Balfour could afford to disclose the letter, and the fact that he had accepted Chamberlain's resignation (at last), because by the evening of 16 September he had received the resignation letters of the three ministers he wanted out of the way. The duke thereupon requested that the other resigning ministers be given a chance to reconsider their position. Balfour said such a course was impossible as they were irreconcilable and that he would not be able to keep his ministry together if the three ministers were given an opportunity to reconsider their resignations. Concluding that Chamberlain's departure sufficiently altered the situation, the duke withdrew his resignation the next day.

When, on 18 September, Chamberlain's letter of the 9th and Balfour's answer of the 16th were published, Tariff Reform sympathisers were surprised at the colonial secretary's resignation. However, their surprise was outweighed by free trade dismay, for Balfour's letter, with its praise of Chamberlain, its agreement with the principles (if not the present practicability) of the whole Tariff Reform programme, and its gratification that Austen Chamberlain would become Chancellor of the Exchequer, led to only one conclusion: Balfour and Chamberlain appeared to be in reasonable agreement on the need for fiscal change and the free trade ministers had been expertly jockeyed out of the way. Moreover, the free trade ministers considered they had been deliberately deceived and this intensified their bitterness.

In the light of these confusing events, the prime minister's declaration of policy at the annual meeting of the National Union of Conservative Associations was anxiously awaited. At Sheffield on 1 October, Balfour outlined his own policy of retaliation. He asked the party to support him in urging the people to give future governments the power of imposing tariffs to be used in bargaining to lower foreign customs duties. This speech was received with prolonged cheering from the predominantly Tariff Reform audience for he was prepared to 'annul and delete altogether . . . the doctrine that you must never put on taxation except for revenue purposes'. But the speech was too strongly in favour of fiscal change to suit Devonshire and he resigned on 2 October. He had in any case felt guilty, for as he had written to the Duchess of Devonshire on 17 September he was 'not sure' he had 'behaved quite well to the other resigning Ministers who consulted me . . . and whom I told I should go too'.[27] The reproaches of free traders who felt betrayed intensified his unhappiness.

Ritchie and James had led the Unionist Free Trade assault upon the duke.[28] In a letter to the duke, Ritchie charged that Balfour and Chamberlain had concocted a plot to get rid of the three ministers. Ritchie also said that, in the light of inquiries from free traders such as Goschen and Hicks Beach, he felt obliged to make public the whole story, implying that the duke went back on his word in not resigning with the others. Devonshire replied immediately that he accepted Ritchie's account with two important qualifications: he did not think that he 'was a party to any understanding that we should all act together', and he had 'no recollection of having said to you on Tuesday that if Balfour deterred my determination you would . . . have an opportunity of reconsidering the matter'.[29] Devonshire said he would leave Newmarket to come and see Ritchie. That his integrity had been called into question distressed the duke greatly; normally politicians went to see him, not he them.

The tenacious Ritchie was not mollified and buttressed his claims by corroboration from George Hamilton that Devonshire was incorrect in both his qualifications. Hamilton telegraphed that he 'clearly understood we were acting together' and that the duke had informed them that 'if there was a change in the situation the prime minister would delay taking action'. Ritchie wrote to Elliot of his 30 September meeting with the duke, stating that Devonshire's only defence was that

> he was convinced from his conversation with A. J. B. that any proposal to let us reconsider our resignations under the altered circumstances would have broken up the cabinet: that is to say that Chamberlain would not have been a consenting party.[30]

Despite further protestations from the duke that he had been misinterpreted, Ritchie remained obdurate. Certainly he made the duke acutely unhappy and this discomfort contributed mightily to Devonshire seizing his opportunity to leave the ministry on 2 October.

Ritchie's behaviour from early in 1903 to the September crisis goes far to substantiate Gollin's high assessment of his courage as well as his contention that the chancellor has been 'the forgotten man' of the controversy. Uneasiness persists, however, that Ritchie lacked judgement: that he was often too quick to anger and too ready to resign. He was frequently uncertain of his course and behind many of his actions lay the free trade interests of the Treasury.

A number of conclusions can be drawn from these events, which mark the end of the first phase of the Tariff Reform controversy. Balfour had succeeded in keeping his administration going; he had discarded the Cobdenite cabinet ministers; and by proclaiming at Sheffield that he represented 'the Free Trade Wing' of the party, he confused many Unionist Free Traders. Chamberlain had not taken the party by storm; and he had now to take the risks of going out as a solitary missionary, leaving Balfour greater flexibility to wait on his success or failure.

The resignation crisis and the Sheffield speech weakened the position of the Unionist Free Traders in the party and in the country. Devonshire's inept handling of affairs in September and the postponement of his resignation until early in October further disorganised and confused the Unionist Free Traders. More important, Balfour's outline of retaliation at Sheffield discouraged a considerable amount of free trade agitation in the party. Many Unionist Free Traders anxious to keep their party together felt they could shelter under the mantle of retaliation without compromising their convictions. Hicks Beach's actions illustrate that turning towards Balfour which characterised many Conservative free traders. He cancelled his projected free trade speeches at Glasgow. Then writing to Harcourt he explained why he would now stick with Balfour:

> I am not at all clear as to the future of the Unionist Free Food League; and think it may not impossibly dissolve. . . . As you know, it is a very weak organisation in point of numbers and means and very many of its members are by no means prepared to oppose the principle of . . . retaliation. . . . I do not believe the policy would succeed, but it might be tried without being like Colonial Preference irrevocable.[31]

At last by early October the battle lines were drawn more clearly. If Hicks Beach and some other shied away from an active free trade stand, the free food ranks were stiffened by the additions of Devonshire, Elliot, Hamilton, Ritchie, and Balfour of Burleigh. When Chamberlain's speaking tour gathered momentum and the Tariff Reformers moved in force into the constituencies, the influence of Hicks Beach with the Unionist Free Traders declined. Churchill and Hugh Cecil continued to behave aggressively. They even refused to support the resolution in favour of Balfour at the Sheffield meeting. A difficulty which hampered the militants, however, was the lack of co-operation with the Liberals. As Churchill appealed to Rosebery:

> Beach and Goschen are old and husky. *We* are children. Joe's electric strength carries all before it. You alone can counter him and stem the tide. I hope you will make some conjunction with the Duke. . . .[32]

The Liberals regarded the resignation manoeuvres and the duke's fumblings with scorn, cynicism, and apprehension. As Campbell-Bannerman remarked to Lord Spencer, 'there is no doubt that retaliation is only Act I in the drama leading inevitably to full-blooded protection all round'; as for the duke, 'he must have lost either his nerve or his senses'.[33] Despite the Unionist discordance and two consecutive by-election victories, however, the Liberals felt no bounding confidence for the future. Chamberlain's campaign was just about to start. This protectionist drive coincided with an attempt of the Liberal Imperialists to seize control of their party and try to push Campbell-Bannerman aside. Richard Haldane informed Strachey that a 'big campaign has been initiated. The outcome of this campaign will decide who are to be in the front—the C. B. ites or our people.'[34]

Thus, at this crucial time, the free trade forces, Unionist and Liberal, were far from united. Consequently, the duke's resignation was greeted with relief by Unionist Free Traders and Liberals. Active Unionist Free Traders now felt certain that the duke would find no alternative but to assume the leadership of their group. George Hamilton wrote to him:

> I read with great satisfaction your letter to Balfour. . . . I have warned Balfour's advisors that a policy of drift . . . must ultimately leave him without a party. Chamberlain will lead the Protectionists, you the Free Traders. . . . The only hope for the future is your leadership of the Free Trade section.[35]

Chapter 4 THE TARIFF REFORM CAMPAIGN OPENS

I

CHAMBERLAIN'S TARIFF REFORM campaign, a greater crusade even than Gladstone's Midlothian tours, opened at Glasgow on 6 October. While Chamberlain's advocacy lacked the moral emphasis of Gladstone's, it was equally fervent as he attempted to elevate his appeal to the nation into messianic terms rising above his opponents' accusations of squalid protectionism. Indeed, Amery goes so far as to claim that the Glasgow speech gave Unionism, for the first time, a positive social and economic programme. With the exception of imperial preference, however, the details of his programme were taken almost word for word from the fair traders of the 1880s: a duty of two shillings a quarter would be imposed on foreign corn (with the exception of maize); a duty of the same amount on flour; a duty of 5 per cent on meat and dairy produce (with the exception of bacon); and an average duty of 10 per cent on articles of foreign manufacture. By way of compensation for so many duties on foodstuffs, there was to be a reduction of three-quarters in the duty on tea, of a half in the duty on sugar, and corresponding reductions of the duties on coffee and cocoa. In all cases colonial produce would be exempt.

Chamberlain embarked on his mission with certain advantages. He had the apparently cordial support of the prime minister and much of the Unionist party. Chamberlain could afford to devote his energies to converting the country. For this task Chamberlain had some striking assets. Except for the *Spectator* and the *Standard*, the Unionist Press quickly aligned with him, and Tariff Reformers bought up the *Standard* late in 1904. He had the unwavering support of journalists and propagandists of ability such as Garvin, Maxse, and Leopold Amery. If the economic theorists did not support him, the academic backing of his movement was provided by the indefatigable W. A. S. Hewins, the economic historians W. J. Ashley and William Cunningham, and the geographer Halford MacKinder. Powerful industrialists, particularly metal entrepreneurs of the Midlands, and Rand financiers helped amass his apparently unlimited funds and graced his various commissions and committees. In his immediate entourage, Chamberlain had an organiser of ability, Powell Williams. Until his sudden death in February 1904 he held the threads of political control for Chamberlain in the 'Duchy', was his watchdog on the Liberal Unionist Association, and took over much of the direction of the Tariff Reform League.

Chamberlain alone had the vision and energy which could link the various protectionist groups with the wider theme of imperial consolidation. In October he launched a sequence of speeches which took him through Glasgow, Greenock, Newcastle, Tynemouth, Birmingham, Liverpool, Cardiff, Newport, Leeds, and London by 19 January 1904. When he was not speaking before large and often enthusiastic audiences, he was shut up in his room at Highbury working well into the night. Only his determination enabled him to press on for he was racked by gout and the effects of high blood pressure.

This lonely eminence was one of the weaknesses of Chamberlain's position: when he was not personally campaigning—and he was sixty-seven—there was nobody of comparable force to take his place. The cabinet attempted little on behalf of Chamberlain, who, after all, had agreed to crusade as a single missionary. By contrast, Chamberlain was countered by a formidable array of speakers—Asquith, Churchill, Haldane, Rosebery, Grey, Hugh Cecil, Goschen, and Devonshire. For the first time since the retirement of Gladstone, he found his primacy in logical argument seriously challenged by Asquith, and that in sarcasm and eloquent rhetoric by Churchill. Consequently, when Chamberlain finished his tour in January he retired to Egypt for two months to recuperate. He was completely exhausted, and never regained the vigour of his 1903 campaign.[1]

Whatever the strengths and weaknesses of Chamberlain's personal crusade, informed opinion in Britain did not know whether he was winning or not. For every indication that the campaign was not succeeding, other developments gave credence to his claims that it was. Not until the by-election losses of January and February 1904 was it apparent that his first bid had failed.

Chamberlain had particularly to convert working-class voters —since 1867 a majority of the borough electorate and since 1884 a majority in the counties. To accomplish this and to rehabilitate himself as a reformer he had to link Tariff Reform with a comprehensive social programme. During the Aston by-election campaign of 1891 he had been the first influential political leader to advocate old age pensions. But hostility to this policy within the Unionist party had forced him to sacrifice it during the period 1895–1903. It has been noted how the colonial secretary on 22 May 1903 attempted to link his proposals for fiscal change with pensions, but had dropped this policy again by 26 June 1903. This continued backsliding left him open to charges of betrayal of the working classes and offset his assertions that Tariff Reform meant work for all and revenue for reform.

Moreover, the Taff Vale judgement of July 1901, which asserted the liability of trade unions for the tortious acts of their agents, also hurt Chamberlain. Organised labour soon found that the Unionists—unlike the Liberal leadership—were not prepared to reverse this harsh decision. Thus, from February to August 1903 the Labour Representative Committee and the Liberal party negotiated an electoral pact to give the former organisation a straight fight against the Unionists in thirty-five constituencies. At the time of Chamberlain's campaign the Lib-Lab alliance was unknown publicly and the extent of Labour's opposition to Tariff Reform was not fully appreciated by the protectionists. There were, however, important signs of Labour's hostility to Tariff Reform. Free traders almost to a man, Labour leaders had been incensed when Hicks Beach revived such a small duty as the corn tax.[2] At the annual meeting of the Trades Union Congress early in September all but two of the delegates condemned Chamberlain's policy as 'most mischievous and dangerous to the best interests of the people of the country'. The distrust many Labour leaders felt toward Chamberlain himself was illustrated by Ramsay MacDonald in a widely circulated little book which described the Tariff Reformer as 'all cry and no wool' and his career as 'barren of practical achievement, except in municipal work'. MacDonald spoke for the working classes in damning food taxes and expressed the attitude of most British socialists in claiming that free trade was a 'preliminary stage in the progress of Socialism'.[3]

In 1903 Chamberlain could point to the precarious condition of the economy as indicating the need for Tariff Reform. The slow-down in the rate of industrial growth from the mid-Victorian years that started after 1873 had not appreciably improved. Indeed, one economist, Wesley Mitchell, went so far as to speak of a 'deep depression' in Britain in 1903'[4] although Sir John Clapham preferred to use the term 'sluggish' when speaking of the economy generally.[5] The *Annual Register* commented that 'there have rarely been such black years as 1903 from a financial point of view. It was an almost uninterrupted twelve months of depression'.[6] In all his speeches during the campaign Chamberlain endeavoured to paint a black picture of the state of the economy but in none was this view more vividly expressed than at Greenock on 8 October:

> Agriculture, as the greatest of all trades and industries of this country, has been practically destroyed, sugar has gone, silk has gone, iron is threatened, wool is threatened, cotton will go! How long are you going to stand it.

In Chamberlain's estimation, Tariff Reform would protect vital industries against foreign competition and encourage British capitalists to invest at home. Unfortunately for Chamberlain, the economy improved greatly early in 1904, and these arguments appeared seriously compromised.

During the early stages of the campaign it became clear that Chamberlain was winning a preponderance of the Liberal Unionist politicians. At Newcastle on 20 October a conference of the Durham and North Riding Liberal Unionist Association passed a resolution declaring that the fiscal policy of the country must be reconsidered with a view to promoting imperial union and modifying hostile foreign tariffs. This resolution was carried despite the introduction of a letter from Devonshire calling on the members to avoid defining their position on fiscal policy. The resolution caused a number of free trade politicians to resign from the regional Liberal Unionist association. After this episode, Chamberlain and his lieutenant, Powell Williams, began to prod the duke and his Whig entourage to call a meeting of the full Liberal Unionist organisation to vote on the fiscal controversy. Williams took the occasion of this Tariff Reform victory to write a menacing letter to James, a dedicated follower of the duke: '*Chamberlain is going to carry all before him with the country*; and if the L. U. party does not recognise that fact then so much the worse for the L. U. party'.[7]

Tariff Reform pressure was also evident in the constituencies where several Unionist Free Traders were attacked. (When Ritchie attempted to present his version of the cabinet crisis to his constituents on 9 October, he had been almost howled down by Tariff Reform hecklers.) By 27 November four leading Unionist Free Traders—Hugh Cecil, Churchill, George Hamilton, and Elliot—had been faced with resolutions from their constituency associations in favour of Tariff Reform. Hicks Beach alone remained unmolested because he had accepted Balfour's Sheffield programme.

The Tariff Reformers had ample resources. Herbert Gladstone noted in January 1904 that the Tariff Reform League had already spent £50,000 and was seeking additional funds.[8] He ruefully estimated that Chamberlain's League was spending £5 to £10 to every pound spent by the Free Trade Union. By 3 December Haldane admitted to Almeric Fitzroy, the Clerk to the Privy Council, that he was very disquieted about Chamberlain's progress.[9] Like most free traders, he feared that Chamberlain's incessant activity and his 'raging, tearing propaganda' might rush the country into a fiscal revolution.

By early December the impact of the campaign still had not been assessed through by-elections. Before the crusade began the Unionists had been in electoral difficulties. At the seven by-elections from January to October 1903, they had lost five seats and held two by greatly reduced majorities. Consequently, the contests for Dulwich and Lewisham scheduled for 15 December, and Ludlow for 23 December, were awaited with great impatience.

II

After his resignation Devonshire received many letters imploring him to organise the Unionist Free Traders. The entreaties of his old Whig lieutenants, Goschen, James, and Elliot, plus Chamberlain's blatantly protectionist speeches, induced the duke to come forward. Goschen's conviction that 'the emergency is very serious' and that 'the fate of the Unionist Free Traders, the degree to which they may hope to have any influence on the public mind depends on your decision' convinced him he must act.[10] Still Devonshire assumed the leadership hesitantly. He was old, if still deeply involved, and he had no desire to throw out Balfour and bring in a Radical government. Moreover, the Unionist Free Traders could only be effective by working in alliance with the Liberals, and the duke's nominal responsibility for the 1902 Education Act would make any compromise difficult.

On 16 October the parliamentary committee of the Free Food League received the duke's letter accepting the presidency. The duke's acceptance was sufficient to rally the disconsolate free fooders. On 23 October sixty-five met to elect him. At the meeting, however, Hicks Beach tried unsucessfully to prevent the duke's election. He did not want to see a powerful free trade group emerge within his party outside the control of the prime minister. James commented to Balfour of Burleigh who had been unable to attend:

> Quite a scene at the F. Food Meeting yesterday.
>
> It was a good meeting, between sixty and seventy of our best Unionists present. All had come to welcome the Duke as President . . . but immediately Beach stood up and said that in his opinion the Duke ought not to be elected President until after a new constitution had been framed . . . [but his move failed]. I presume Beach worked to bring this movement to an end without bringing the Duke into a responsible position.[11]

After his election the duke's authority, especially over the Tory free traders, was still uncertain due to Hicks Beach's close identifications with Balfour. Privately by letter to Balfour on 11 October, and publicly in a speech at the Bristol Dolphin Club on 13 November with Balfour present, Hicks Beach proclaimed his final adherence to the prime minister's policy. His main aim, which he outlined to Balfour in his letter of 11 October, was to keep the prime minister within the lines of the Sheffield speech. Since Balfour promised in his reply that he would certainly not go beyond the speech, Hicks Beach felt he could legitimately work with him in an attempt to prevent Chamberlain from winning control of the party.[12]

The defection of Hicks Beach and the relative inactivity of Ritchie and Balfour of Burleigh left the burden of Unionist Free Trade leadership almost completely, save for George Hamilton, with the duke and his old Whig friends. This was not an easy task when most of the Unionist Free Traders were Conservatives, and when, according to Campbell-Bannerman, Devonshire remained 'in mortal fear of Michael'.[13] Nevertheless, the attitude of the duke and most of the active free fooders hardened against not only the Tariff Reformers, but also, on occasion, against Balfour. George Hamilton, in an indictment of Balfour, bitterly recited to his constituents at Ealing on 22 October the tale of the two pamphlets at the cabinet meeting of 13 August and made public the grievances of the free trade ministers after the cabinet meeting of 14 September.

Most audaciously of all, Winston Churchill and Hugh Cecil invaded the bastion of Birmingham itself on 11 November defying every Tariff Reform threat. Having secured the disgruntled chairman of the Central Birmingham Conservatives as a sponsor, they energetically attacked Chamberlain before three thousand roaring people at the Town Hall. They were given support by the duke who sent an open letter of best wishes to the chairman. No doubt Chamberlain's 'merry men of Birmingham' would dearly have liked to 'hustle' the two young invaders as they had Lloyd George in December 1901 when he spoke in support of the Boer cause at the Town Hall, but it could not have been done without grievous harm to the cause of fiscal reform.

Actually, despite their collaboration there were great tensions between Cecil and Churchill. Cecil wanted to preserve the Conservative party for free trade. Churchill as early as October was preparing to desert to the Liberals, and was therefore reckless in his attacks on Balfour and Chamberlain. Thus Cecil, who vowed he would 'wreck 20 Govts.' to annihilate Chamberlain nevertheless accused his friend of 'lamentable instability' by his lavish praise of the Liberal party. Churchill, on the other hand, begged Cecil to join him in a reconstituted Liberal party rather than yield to the 'melancholy satisfaction' of being a martyr to the Conservatives.[14]

In this atmosphere of increasing tension, the Unionist Free Traders held their first public rally since Devonshire became their leader at the Queen's Hall on 24 November. This gathering saw nine ex-cabinet ministers on the platform, and underlined in a forceful manner the strength of the Unionist opposition to Chamberlain. The duke made the major speech declaring that while he did not understand Balfour's policy he completely understood Chamberlain's and was determined to oppose it. The rally created a considerable stir, with the *Annual Register* describing the gathering as one of 'historic significance'. Lord Spencer's observer at the rally, Sir Ryland Adkins, spoke glowingly about the duke and assured Spencer that the Unionist Free Traders now really meant business.[15] Many reflective free trade politicians would have agreed with Elliot's comment:

> Once again the Duke has placed himself at the head of a great body of intelligent opinion to resist the prospects of reckless political ambition. . . . It is Gladstone in 1886 all over again and the Queen's Hall meeting brought to mind very forcibly the memorable gathering in the Opera House in that year when Salisbury and Hartington first stood together.[16]

III

The Unionist Free Traders proposed to adopt a more aggressive policy than mere speeches. On 10 December the executive committee of the Free Food League met and after two hours of intensive discussion determined on two lines of action. They would issue a public letter advising Unionists not to vote for Tariff Reformers at the by-elections at Dulwich and Lewisham on 15 December, and machinery would be set in motion to make common cause with the Liberals in constituencies held by Unionist Free Traders. The first decision led to the Lewisham letter published by Devonshire on 12 December advising electors not to vote for candidates who followed Chamberlain and the Tariff Reform League. On 15 December Goschen, Ritchie,

James, Balfour of Burleigh, and Hamilton—but not Hicks Beach—expressed publicly their agreement with the letter. This letter was, in fact, an open declaration of war against Chamberlain. The Lewisham declaration clearly underlined the fact that Unionist divisions were now more bitter than those of the Liberals between 1895 and 1903. (At the height of their dissensions neither the Campbell-Bannerman group nor the Liberal Imperialists had advocated withholding votes from the other or voting for the Unionists.) Lacking both the money and the organisation of the fiscal reformers, the Unionist Free Traders found such public declarations were the most effective way of retaliating against Chamberlain and Balfour. For Devonshire was furious that the prime minister was supporting the protectionist candidates.[17]

The Tariff Reform press was understandably enraged. The *Daily Telegraph* fulminated that 'with characteristic bluntness Devonshire in league with John Burns, Lloyd George, and Dr Clifford, has wiped out the armistice and declared war to the knife with all Tariff Reformers'. The *National Review* quoted Chamberlain as labelling the letter an 'encyclical of that cave of Adullam summoning all Troglodytes to abstain from voting for the Unionist candidates'. The letter also created more insecurity for Unionist Free Trade MPs. For example, the president of the Exeter Conservative Association demanded that Edgar Vincent publicly accept the Sheffield programme, as in the light of Devonshire's declaration the association now felt grave misgivings concerning his membership in the Free Food League.[18]

The letter made the by-elections, already the cynosure of all eyes, a test case between the Tariff Reformers and Unionist Free Traders. Both seats had not been contested by the Liberals since 1895, but in the light of the Unionist split they expected to win one and possibly both. In Lewisham the Unionists had a colourless and vacillating Chamberlainite, Major Coates, and in Dulwich their candidate was the 'whole hogger', Rutherford Harris, who freely admitted donating £5,000 to the Tariff Reform League. Moreover, he had been involved in the Jameson Raid, for which he had been censured by parliament, and in 1900 he had been unseated in Monmouth Burghs for illegal electoral practices. His opponent was a rising hope of the Radicals, C. F. G. Masterman.

The results of the by-elections were two resounding Unionist victories. Coates won by over 2,000 votes, only 300 less than the majority in 1895, and Harris was returned by over 1,400 votes—a drop from the majority of 3,000 in 1895 but still a substantial victory. Indeed, in a poll of nearly 80 per cent Harris won the highest vote ever recorded by a Unionist in Dulwich. Well might Chamberlain exult that the results 'exceeded my most sanguine expectations.' *The Times* quoted Maxse who gloated that 'many of us were prepared to lose one if not both of the seats and particularly with Harris anything but an ideal candidate in a great cause'. After the Lewisham letter, the results were a direct humiliation for the Duke of Devonshire, shaking estimates of his electoral influence,[19] and, as he confessed to Rosebery, showing 'a considerable amount of sympathy on the part of the working men for Chamberlain'.[20] The *Daily Telegraph* even asserted that the results 'wiped out the Unionist Free Traders as a factor in contemporary politics'.

Liberals were dismayed. On 15 December the *Daily News* had claimed that 'Free Trade is the very life's blood of London. Of all places London . . . should be the last to support protectionist candidates'. Thus it was with disappointment the next day that the same paper commented:

> Compared with the hopes aroused on the Liberal and Free Trade side the results . . . are not encouraging. . . . We do not know whether the Government will be inclined to build on the two London elections and chance an appeal to the country. . . .

Liberal apprehensions were also well expressed by Allard, the agent of the Liberal Imperialists, who wrote to Rosebery that

> allowing that expectation was pitched too high in the case of Dulwich and Lewisham, there is the melancholy fact that we were badly beaten despite certain advantages. I am forced to the conclusion that Dulwich and Lewisham have spoken for many London constituencies.[21]

Masterman later wrote of the Unionists missing a great opportunity:

> Of all the mistakes ever made by any party rendered blind by

> prosperity and ignorance time may brand as the greatest the refusal of Mr Balfour to dissolve Parliament after the Dulwich and Lewisham elections. The Chief Whip had advised it; Mr Chamberlain desired it. Fiscal Reform was in the flow of an exultant tide.[22]

Chamberlainite Arthur Griffith-Boscawen, writing in 1907, spoke of these two victories (as well as the success of Ludlow on 23 December) as temporarily arresting 'the terrible rot which over a year ago had set in at by-elections'; and he lamented that Balfour had missed the golden opportunity to dissolve while the free trade forces were still in disarray.[23] Historians, however, even Amery, have given scarcely any consideration to these contests which were regarded with such interest at the time. Elie Halévy, for example, merely comments that 'at the end of 1903 the by-elections were still so indecisive that it was possible to believe that the country was accepting the compromise between the two leaders'.[24]

Why then did Balfour not dissolve in January 1904? Since no record of his reasons for continuing in office have been found, one can only speculate. He must have considered the by-elections as insufficient evidence that the country supported Tariff Reform and so was not prepared to risk defeat—particularly since an election early in 1904, when fiscal tensions were so high, might break his party irrevocably and raise a powerful free trade coalition. Perhaps also he sought more time in the hope of eventually reuniting the party on some compromise that would reconcile both the Tariff Reformers and the free fooders. Finally, dissolution after these victories would have meant surrendering virtual control of policy to Chamberlain. For these successes appeared to be squeezing out Balfour. Little was heard of retaliation, although Mary Chamberlain complained to her mother of

> pressure having been put on members and candidates all over the country to keep to the Government Programme pure and simple, and there is no doubt that the party officials are more Balfourite than Mr Balfour himself. . . . But now an idea is getting abroad that Joe's policy is much more popular than that of the retaliationists and that the constituencies care nothing for the latter unless it means the possibilities of the former.[25]

The prime minister had no propaganda machine disseminating his policies; and the issue increasingly seemed to be a straight one of Chamberlain's full policy as outlined at Glasgow versus free trade. Even before the by-elections, on 11 December, Lady Victoria Hicks Beach quoted her father's fears that his support of the prime minister was 'all of no use—for it looks now as if Balfour would not be at all able to stand up against Chamberlain'. As Hicks Beach lamented: 'Politics have been getting worse. . . . So far as the upper and middle classes are concerned, the great bulk of the Unionist party has either gone over to Chamberlain, or is quite ready to go.'[26]

This apparent polarisation of Unionism between Tariff Reformers and free fooders threatened not only to jeopardise Balfour's bloc of supporters, but also to make the duke's group increasingly intransigent. On 23 December Sandars told Balfour that he feared Chamberlain's power 'will cause our people to press you for a declaration going further than Sheffield'. He felt that 'they will not see that nothing is more foolish than to force the pace for the good Free Fooders' who 'are certain to move towards . . . Glasgow all in good time'. Sandars further observed that he, Acland-Hood, and Akers-Douglas

> had no doubt that the stupid old Duke will be pushed over to the other side; and really he had much better go than stay as an embarrassment to our friends and an encouragement to our doubting Thomases.[27]

Chapter 5 THE UNIONIST FREE TRADERS AT THEIR ZENITH

I

UNDER THE shadow of Chamberlain's increasing power, Unionist Free Traders and some factions of the Liberal party made serious attempts from December to February 1904 to form an *entente* or even an alliance. In retrospect, the fact that an alliance did not materialise has resulted in the negotiations themselves being largely overlooked in studies of the period. But, as H. W. McCready points out, 'contemporaries were reminded of the events of 1886: history was clearly repeating itself. . . .'[1]

After the December by-elections the Liberals were apprehensive and frustrated. Much of the cautious optimism Liberal leaders felt about defeating Chamberlain's programme was badly shaken. Campbell-Bannerman might believe that the protection boom would burst, but considerable evidence went against such assessments. Many leading Liberals were gravely alarmed at the efficient organisation of the Tariff Reform machine as well as by the protectionist by-election successes. On 21 December the Liberal Imperialist, Robert Perks, reported to Rosebery that Harold Harmsworth 'says Chamberlain tells his broker . . . that he has promises of £140,000 per annum—which he hopes to bring up to £200,000'. In addition, the newspaperman claimed that 'Chamberlain's committee has 20 paid agents and speakers in the Ludlow division'. Because of the 15 December by-election successes Harmsworth also claimed that Chamberlain 'asserts now that he will win the *next* election although a few months (or weeks) ago he said he would be "badly beaten" the first and win the second'.[2]

Fear of Chamberlain's whirlwind tour sweeping the country and the Unionists exploiting an early dissolution reconciled many Liberals to a *mariage de convenance* with the Unionist Free Traders. But, as with the Unionist Free Traders, the degree of co-operation possible or desirable had scarcely begun to be considered. Campbell-Bannerman judged the Unionist Free Traders of dubious value as allies. He was perfectly aware of their antipathy to him and to the Radical wing of the Liberal party. Most Liberal leaders—even Whigs like Spencer and Liberal Imperialists such as Asquith—agreed with Campbell-Bannerman's view. In addition, other formidable difficulties stood in the way of a close arrangement: by December 1903 the Liberals already had candidates picked in all but fourteen of the constituencies held by Unionist Free Traders;[3] the latter tended to have an inflated sense of their political importance and would make excessive demands; and the Education Act of 1902 presented an almost impassable gulf between them.

By 1903 many of the Liberal leaders were of Nonconformist background. The Liberal party knew that it would be very unwise to do anything which would offend organised Dissent. Spencer, an Anglican, clearly expressed this view to Campbell-Bannerman:

> We cannot alter our attitude on Education. If we did we should greatly weaken the forces in favour of Free Trade, for we should shake the faith and confidence of the Nonconformists who think much more of Education than of fiscal policy. . . . We must get the aid and help of the Free Fooders [but] . . . if we adjusted our principles so as to sweep into our Party ranks for a time until Free Trade is vindicated the Lib. Imps., Devonshire, and the Free Trade Unionists we should trade I am afraid thousands of votes from Nonconformists.[4]

Even as staunch a Home Ruler as Spencer was quite ready to shelve Home Rule for the time being in the interests of the Unionist Free Traders, but he was not willing to retreat on education: 'To clear Home Rule for complete union with Rosebery, Devonshire & Goschen no doubt is necessary . . . but then there are other questions on which we cannot agree. Education.' The large number of Free Churchmen in the parliament of 1906 was to vindicate this view. Rev Thomas J. Law, secretary of the Free Church Council, estimated that some 200 Free Churchmen were returned to the new House of Commons as contrasted with 120 in 1900.[5] To have jeopardised the support of Nonconformity for the possibility of some thirty or forty Unionist Free Traders in the next parliament was a risk the Liberals rightly were not prepared to take.

A further difficulty the Liberals faced in negotiations with the Unionist Free Traders was the remaining division in their own party. This division weakened Campbell-Bannerman in dealing with the Unionist Free Traders as it was by no means impossible that some of the Liberal Imperialists and Whigs would come to an arrangement of their own with the free fooders. Certainly some of the Unionist Free Traders tried to exploit these divisions in the hope that Campbell-Bannerman would be deposed and there would be another leader for a free trade ministry.

Thus Haldane told Rosebery that the free fooders he was in contact with, Dickson Poynder and Beckett, stressed that 'the dangers of foreign complication in the event of even a short C. B. ministry' made their juncture with Campbell-Bannerman 'out of the question'.[6] Moreover, in October, the Liberal leader was depressed by the Liberal Imperialist hostility to him and the effects of his heart condition, and told Gladstone he was ready 'to step aside'.[7]

With Rosebery unwilling to compete for the leadership, Campbell-Bannerman apparently prepared to relinquish his position, and Spencer tired and ill, it is no wonder that Asquith seemed the only prospective head of the party. Then as contacts with the Unionist Free Traders reached a climax in early 1904, and as the by-elections turned decisively in favour of the Liberals, Campbell-Bannerman's enthusiasm for the leadership revived. Asquith played a key role at this time for his speeches restored his relations with Campbell-Bannerman and helped to re-unite the party. He agreed with Campbell-Bannerman's views on the Unionist Free Traders, and he refused to fall in with any of the vague aspirations either of the extreme Roseberyites or of the Unionist Free Traders.

Yet from November onwards, vigorous Unionist Free Trade activity induced many Liberals, including Asquith and Campbell-Bannerman, to modify their pessimistic views as to the value of working with them. For example, Elliot was sounded by a number of minor Liberals. Munro Ferguson, a confidant of Rosebery, asked him about possibilities of alliance, commenting that the fiscal issue 'is a bigger question than Ireland' and that 'the Duke is good enough for me'. It was not only Liberal Imperialists who were making advances. Masterman made a plea via Elliot for a free fooder such as Churchill to come down to Dulwich and help him against Harris. Such an action, Masterman avowed, would be 'the first step towards the compromise with the Liberal party that we both, I think, desire'.[8]

Such correspondence and the numerous social meetings did little, as the session drew near, to create a working arrangement between the two free trade groups. The first formal moves came from the Unionist Free Traders. Young free fooders urged the duke to move further against fiscal reform. With great clarity, Hugh Cecil presented the view of the Hughligans that unless organised opposition to Chamberlain was backed by an agreement with the Liberals each Unionist Free Trader would be destroyed seperately by the Tariff Reform machine.[9] It is significant that Cecil wrote the note. The duke would not have been so impressed if Churchill, who had been advocating an alliance with the Liberals all along, had written the letter. That it was Cecil, who on 29 June 1903 refused to consider co-operation with the Radical Party, claiming that 'co-operation could not be otherwise than immoral', indicates how far Chamberlain's campaign had frightened free traders who were profoundly Tory.[10] Devonshire agreed that it would be desirable to approach Spencer confidentially through Rosebery.

On the same date as the publication of the Lewisham letter, the duke asked Rosebery's advice on how fiscal debates could be initiated in the House of Commons without a division being labelled a vote of censure by the government. He also wanted to know what the Liberals would be prepared to do about safeguarding the seats of Unionist Free Trade MPs, especially if the latter voted against the government. Rosebery indicated great sympathy with the duke's predicament. Yet, while he was willing to contact Asquith on behalf of the Unionist Free Traders, he was unwilling to work with Campbell-Bannerman. Moreover, he was not very sanguine about settling the difficulties which had arisen over the Education Act. He said that though his friends were trying to arrange a compromise on education, he did not think the Nonconformists would agree to any arrangement until after an election when they would be in a stronger position.[11]

Rosebery sent the duke's letter to Asquith by whom it was conveyed to Campbell-Bannerman. These cautious interchanges did not carry matters very far, and therefore disturbed Gladstone as he had to consider the possibility of an imminent dissolution. Accordingly, on 20 December he wrote to Campbell-Bannerman outlining the need for a definite policy toward the Unionist Free Traders:

> Time is slipping away and excepting certain action which I can take here and there, nothing is being done for the serious and practical consideration of our relations with the Conservative Free Traders.
>
> The letters of G. Hamilton and Winston Churchill in today's papers seem to me to require that the Party leaders should meet at the first opportunity to determine whether any definite step can be taken to find some *modus vivendi*. . . .

Campbell-Bannerman agreed and said something must be done about constituency arrangements, public demonstrations of co-operation, and joint parliamentary action. Nevertheless, he stressed that the Liberals were in the position of power and were thus not compelled to make any compromises. The Unionist Free Traders had to come to them.[12]

James made the next approach by seeking a meeting with Asquith on 21 December. After the conversation, James summarised the position of the Unionist Free Traders and the Liberals in a memorandum circulated to leaders of both sides. The two main points were that, though at the present time grave difficulties lay in the way of a fusion between the two camps, a high level meeting should be called to see what could be done about co-operation in the constituencies. James warned the Liberals, however, that in a division on a fiscal amendment, few Unionist Free Traders could, at present, be expected to vote against the government.[13] Asquith circulated a copy of the memorandum to the major Liberal leaders. Campbell-Bannerman wryly commented that he did not 'suck much comfort out of James' statement', but it did provide a bare minimum for organised discussion.

In response to the memorandum the Liberals decided to hold a meeting of ex-cabinet ministers on 7 January 1904 to decide upon a general policy toward the Unionist Free Traders. Just before the Liberal meeting, Devonshire himself took the initiative and wrote to Spencer, raising the same two points he had brought up with Rosebery.[14] Then two days before the Liberal meeting James wrote to Asquith stressing that he hoped Spencer would reply to the duke in an optimistic manner. James attempted to put pressure on Asquith and the Liberal Imperialists: 'the Duke could not if he tried bring our Unionist F. T. members into line with you so long as Campbell-Bannerman is to lead them—our reports on this head are unanimous'.[15]

The Liberals made few concessions. Yet the duke's reply to Spencer carried things a little further as he grudgingly agreed to Spencer's insistence that the Liberal fiscal amendment would be a vote of censure. He also gave evidence of his own uneasy hold over many of his followers, particularly some of the Tory free fooders, when he implored the Liberals to keep the proposed conference secret, 'especially from Hicks Beach'.[16]

The Liberals could afford to stick to their terms as their position strengthened and the duke's position weakened. For on 11 January a sequence of earlier Chamberlain-Devonshire correspondence was published, revealing that Chamberlain had virtually captured the Liberal Unionist Association and was going to drive the duke and his supporters out. The clash gave a stimulus to rumours that the duke and his friends were about to coalesce with the Liberals. For instance, the *Annual Register* subsequently reported that the correspondence 'intensified the expectation of a Liberal and Free Food coalition'. Government circles speculated on the rise of new combinations. As early as 26 December Gerald Balfour had gloomily observed to Austen Chamberlain that he saw no explanation for the duke's Lewisham letter unless he meant

> to throw in his lot with the other side. I am inclined to think it is coming to this and that the idea of a coalition party and (if they succeed in defeating us) a coalition government formed of Liberals and Free Fooders is once more in the air.[17]

On 8 January Lloyd George made a speech at the New Reform

D

Club expressing the apprehensions of the Radical wing of the party about the rumours. He declared categorically that the Liberals would not compromise on education, and while he was prepared to welcome progressive men such as Ritchie and Churchill, he wanted nothing to do with the Duke of Devonshire. However, he concluded that he was prepared to 'see urgent reforms postponed if necessary for one Parliament in order to save the country from a change in fiscal policy'. On 13 January Campbell-Bannerman at Maidstone also emphasised that the Liberals would not compromise on their commitments. This tough line was taken to warn free fooders, but chiefly to reassure his own followers. He commented to Spencer:

> I have many indications of suspiciousness among our stalwarts that they may be sold into an alliance. So I went against any compromises last night. It is absolutely necessary that the line should be taken by some men, amidst all our colloquings! & I thought I had better do it. Winston & Co. may not like it.[18]

The Unionist *Daily Telegraph* tried to menace free fooders by announcing on 19 January that Churchill and Dickson Poynder had been 'excommunicated' and would not receive the government whip in the coming session. On 26 January Iwan Müller, the editor of the *Telegraph*, wrote a leading article claiming to have all the inside information about communications 'between Devonshire and Rosebery which have resulted in an embryonic Centre Party'. Twenty-six free fooders were supposed to have subscribed to the Devonshire-Rosebery pact which the *Daily Telegraph* labelled a 'capitulation to Clifford'—the leading Nonconformist minister. This article was obviously intended not only to intimidate the Unionist Free Traders but also to make mischief in the Liberal party by frightening the Radicals. In fact, these allegations were unfounded, for although negotiations were going on, Rosebery took no part in them. Nor was Asquith any solace to the extreme Liberal Imperialists, for he expressed complete concurrence in the cautious policies toward the Unionist Free Traders followed by Campbell-Bannerman and Spencer.[19] By late January any Liberal Imperialist hopes of capturing the party or of forming some new coalition to their advantage had vanished. Any deals the Unionist Free Traders were trying to make with the Liberals would have to be conducted through the Campbell-Bannerman–Spencer axis.

While the Liberal leader's position strengthened, the duke began to campaign vigorously against Balfour and Chamberlain. He severely criticised both Unionist statesmen in speeches at Liverpool on 8 January where he regretted that he had been deceived by the inquiry, and at the Guildhall on 8 February where he avowed that the fiscal issue was not a party question. When Balfour was at Chatsworth, the duke, according to Fitzroy, 'left no doubt in his mind that he was going over to the opposition even to the length of being ready to assume the Premiership as a means of uniting discordant forces'.[20] But Devonshire was severely handicapped by the hostility of some of the Conservative free traders to any bargain with the Liberals. A striking example of this attitude was that of George Hamilton. He refused to act with James as the Unionist Free Trade representative to discuss possible electoral arrangements with Asquith and Herbert Gladstone. Hamilton sympathised with the idea of a conference but asserted that he 'was not prepared to go further and politically associate myself with the Radicals even for temporary purposes. . . . I have fought too long and consistently against Radical doctrine to be able now to alter my attitude. . . .'[21]

In anticipation of most Unionist Free Traders being compelled to come closer into line with them, Liberal leaders began to sound out important Nonconformists as to revision of the 1902 Education Act. In response to Herbert Gladstone's suggestion about 'taking the pulse of the Free Church bosses', Campbell-Bannerman wrote to Bryce—the Liberal leader most trusted by the Nonconformists—asking him to contact Dr John Clifford, the most influential opponent of the Education Act.[22] Bryce immediately complied, asking whether Clifford could foresee any propositions on education which if accepted by Unionist Free Traders would enable Liberals to support such Unionists in the constituencies. With Nonconformist agitation against the Education Act reaching its zenith, Clifford was discouraging. In a stiff reply he said that somebody like Hugh Cecil could never be supported, and that as a minimum the Nonconformists would demand that denominational schools be excluded from government aid.[23] Such Nonconformist intransigence had earlier depressed Haldane, the one Liberal who had supported the Education Act. He commented to Perks that he was 'coming to doubt very much whether we can win the big fight without an alliance with the Duke's party'. Yet, ironically, without such an alliance, 'the yoke of his Education Act will remain on the Free Church neck for years to come'.[24]

On the eve of the session Devonshire and Spencer worked out a plan of co-operation which was the culmination of the Unionist Free Trade-Liberal negotiations. The duke promised to use all his influence to get the free fooders to vote for a Liberal amendment to the Address reaffirming faith in the free trade system and condemning food taxes.[25] On the Liberal side, the leaders would then assess the degree of help to be given on the result of the division. In return, this amendment was to be sent to the duke before the free food meeting of 2 February in case Unionist Free Traders had any suggestions which would reconcile more of them to voting for it. Despite their earlier doubts about the lack of courage of the Unionist Free Traders, the Liberals seem to have had high expectations about the number of Unionists who would come over into their lobby on the division.

The first fortnight in January was the maximum period of free trade anxiety about Chamberlain's campaign. Churchill wrote to Hugh Cecil that 'nothing could exceed the confidence of the Chamberlainites everywhere' and that 'anything may happen'. On the day that he returned from his holiday, Asquith wrote to Spencer about the plans for a free trade pact: 'the situation is so unstable that a crisis may come at any moment and there ought to be no delay in making whatever arrangements are predictable for electoral purposes'. On 13 January Campbell-Bannerman told Spencer that Gladstone was 'urgent for an arrangement with the Duke and his men'.[26]

However, even as free trade anxieties reached their climax, Chamberlain's campaign began to falter. At the mid-Devon by-election on 8 January the Liberals doubled their 700 vote majority of 1900, and Mary Chamberlain wrote unhappily to her mother that her husband was very depressed about the result. Also on 8 January the Board of Trade published the annual trade returns which showed a marked rise in exports—results confounding Chamberlain's pessimistic prophecies and contributing to the collapse of the protectionist boom. As early as 16 July 1903, Lord Esher had summarised in his *Journal* the probable connection between bad times and Tariff Reform success:

> If there are two or three bad years of trade, I think Joe will win, as everyone will be anxious to try a new scheme. If, on the other hand, the years are prosperous, the feeling will be to let well enough alone.

This view was confirmed when Tariff Reform was routed in a series of by-elections between 15 January and 13 February. At Norwich on 15 January, the Liberal candidate administered a crushing defeat to his Chamberlainite opponent. The *Daily Telegraph* attributed the result to the alliance of 'Free Fooders, Free Churchmen, and Free Fighters' but the *Standard*'s sober conclusion, that it had been 'a profound error to believe the country was being swept for Protection', was more accurate. On 20 January the Liberals increased considerably their majority at Gateshead. This victory caused the *St James Gazette*, a dedicated Tariff Reform paper, to acknowledge on 21 January that all the talk about Chamberlain 'sweeping the country' was 'prematurely sanguine'. Finally, the Liberals won two striking victories at Ayr Burghs on 30 January and in mid-Herts on 13 February. This last Unionist defeat staggered the Tariff Reformers. On 15 February the *Daily News* proclaimed that it showed 'the revolt against the Government has spread to the very heart of their Gibraltar—the Home counties', and the *Daily Telegraph* lamented that 'the Unionist party is broken beyond repair'.

Despite the satisfaction it gave them, this crash of Chamberlainism had ominous implications for the Unionist Free Traders. Whatever prospects they had had of an effective alliance with the Liberals were seriously diminished if not destroyed. The Liberals could hardly fail to agree with Devonshire when he remarked to Spencer on 31 January, 'I dare say you will be able to defeat Protection by yourselves'. If this was the case where would the Unionist Free Traders be?

II

In the light of the Tariff Reform adversity, the morale of the government was very low as the Session began. Balfour was kept away with influenza and Chamberlain went off to Egypt on 10 February to recuperate from the effects of his speaking marathon. The fortunes of the government were left to Gerald Balfour, Brodrick, Akers-Douglas, and Wyndham, of whom the first three were not noted for their oratorical prowess. Rumours circulated that the ministers left to hold the ring were bitterly divided. It was said that Balfour was going to try to retain the free fooders by disavowing full Tariff Reform. This alleged decision was supposed to have split the administration into angry squabbles between Balfourites and Chamberlainites. The confusion of the ministers over what policy to follow is clear from this letter from Wyndham to Akers-Douglas on 6 February: 'If we "hedge" too much to keep the "Free Fooders" in this debate we are more than likely to split the Party permanently. . . .'[27]

On 8 February John Morley opened the fiscal debate by proposing an amendment to the Address condemning food taxes. Gerald Balfour answered, asserting that the government was against food taxes and a 10 per cent general tariff. His speech caused wide comment, but while reassuring many anxious free fooders, he inevitably gave umbrage to the Chamberlainites. Thus on 9 February Bonar Law strongly presented the case for a preferential system based on the taxation of food and urged the adoption of tariffs to protect industry.

Government ambivalence continued on 12 February when Brodrick restricted himself to advocating retaliation, only to be answered by a full declaration of Tariff Reform dogma by Alfred Lyttelton, the new colonial secretary. On the final day, Wyndham bluntly warned the Unionist Free Traders that this was no speculative debate but one of confidence, and thus an adverse vote might mean an irrevocable severance from the party. Akers-Douglas wound up ineptly. Hoping to bring most of the free fooders into the fold, he endorsed the views of Gerald Balfour, and called for unity in the face of the grave international situation caused by the outbreak of the Russo-Japanese War on 7 February. Writing of the debate years later, Mrs Dugdale concluded, somewhat unfairly, that the former chief whip 'failed lamentably in an appeal to party loyalty. He struck the wrong note with a quavering finger. . . .'[28]

These contradictions underlined the indispensability of the absent prime minister. The administration was made to look even more foolish by the galaxy of fine speeches delivered by Liberals and Unionist Free Traders. The Liberals allowed full scope to the Unionist Free Traders, seventeen of whom made speeches. Many were of a high calibre. Hugh Cecil presented the most trenchant criticisms of Chamberlain's proposals, alleging that tariffs would promote class tensions and corrupt parliament. No personal attack on Chamberlain was more savage than Cecil's. He denied that Chamberlain was preaching a crusade and claimed instead that the Tariff Reformer had gone forth 'to stab in the back . . . those who were honestly trying to maintain their own opinions'. Often, however, Unionists scarcely listened to the speeches. Griffith-Boscawen described how, throughout the debate, Tariff Reformers and free fooders were 'far too busy enfilading each other up and down our own benches, or turning about to reply to an attack from the rear, or sniping members in front. . . .'[29]

Throughout the gyrations of the debate the Unionist Free Traders remained uncertain about what attitude to adopt on the amendment. The Liberals had manoeuvred them into a position where they had to vote for it if they were to receive help in their constituencies. On the other side the pressure was equally great to follow the party line, and some Unionist Free Traders avowed that it would be unfair to vote against the government when Balfour was absent. Francis Mildmay, a prominent backbench Unionist Free Trader, exemplified this loyalty. In *The Times* on 16 February he said he and some other free fooders voted with the government as a protest against attempts to destroy it when the prime minister was away.

Consequently, it is not surprising that the Unionist Free Trade meetings held at various times throughout the debate showed considerable diversities of opinion. Their views oscillated with each government speaker. At the first meeting on 2 February the duke read out the Morley amendment, and it was decided to wait and see before announcing any general policy. At the next meeting on 10 February, after Gerald Balfour's speech, the general consensus was in favour of supporting the government, and the next day Hicks Beach eloquently attempted to rally the party for Balfour. However, the speeches of Bonar Law and Lyttelton plus some energetic whipping by Churchill and the duke on the final day resulted in a *volte face*. On 15 February in what the *Daily Telegraph* called 'far and away the most critical division that has occurred since the memorable day on which Mr Gladstone's first Home Rule Bill was defeated', twenty-six Unionist Free Traders voted against the government, fourteen voted with the government, and twelve abstained.[30]

The overall result was a majority of fifty-one for the administration. The sixty-five MPs listed in the Elliot Papers as members of the Free Food League early in December 1903 represent its peak at any one time. Thereafter, Tariff Reform pressure in the constituencies and a reluctance of some Unionist Free Traders to oppose Balfour had resulted in the parliamentary representation of the Free Food League falling to fifty-one by February 1904. Since the Unionist majority midway through February stood at ninety-one, this membership was still sufficient to destroy the government if all had voted with the Liberals. Although Balfour survived the division, the magnitude of this Unionist Free Trade defection caused one recent historian to conclude that 'the party never really recovered from it'.[31]

Sandars and the whips were staggered at the size of the revolt. After the concessions Gerald Balfour and Akers-Douglas had made, Balfour's agent had thought almost all the free fooders would vote against the amendment. Despite the size of the defection Sandars was certain the 'concessions' had saved the day. He wrote a long account to the convalescing Balfour: 'It is perfectly clear that the only thing which has saved us from disaster has been the most rigid adherence to Sheffield. . . .' Sandars conceded that the number of recalcitrants had exceeded their worst estimates and maintained that the duke's 'advice to them last week to vote against the Government determined many of them; and the dramatic way it was given at the meeting was engineered by Winston'. The problem for the future was clear to Sandars:

> If we avoid either frightening or irritating these 25 [*sic*, 26] Unionists we shall carry on—If, on the other hand, we alarm or annoy them on the fiscal question they can turn us out at a moment's notice. . . . Beach's influence I fear counts for little.

> They are torn by Linky [Hugh Cecil] and Winston and Georgie Hamilton with the old Duke in reserve.

However, Sandars pointed out one consolation—dissension and rancour had arisen between the two free trade groups:

> Now the division was a great disappointment to the Opposition. In their estimates our numbers were to be down to the vanishing point. Accordingly, smarting from their sense of failure, they have met our malcontents with a cold smile . . . and observe that, after all, there may be greater difficulties in the way of party support in the constituencies than they had imagined.

Balfour agreed with Sandars' analysis and in his detached way minimised the possibilities of a new coalition arising. 'How', he said, 'could Tory anti-reform Free Traders work successfully for long with Cobdenite Radicals'.[32]

Nevertheless, Balfour took Sandars' estimates of the dangerous situation created by the Unionist Free Traders seriously. Right up to the 1906 election he tried to hold the administration to his policy of retaliation as outlined in his Sheffield speech of 1 October 1903. Because Tariff Reform slumped badly at the polls during 1904 and 1905, the prime minister could resist Chamberlain's requests to go beyond the Sheffield speech. By this stand, Balfour broke the free trade threat to his government from within his own party. The penalty he had to pay was the increasing antagonism of the Tariff Reformers.

The Liberals had indeed expected the government's majority to drop to the vanishing point. Accordingly, they were not willing to give support to Unionist Free Traders in their constituencies unless specific pledges were given, particularly on education. The Liberals were heartened by their increasing by-election successes. (After the February debate, references to Unionist Free Traders, save for occasional constituency settlements, almost completely drop out of the correspondence of the Liberal leaders.) The Liberals felt that the future belonged to them. Moreover, the Liberal group most in harmony with the Unionist Free Traders, the Liberal Imperialists, were now, according to Mrs Webb, at a great disadvantage:

> Within the Liberal Party, the Campbell-Bannerman, Spencer, Morley crew followed by Reid, Lloyd George, Macnamara are in

> the ascendant and are asserting their right to make the future Cabinet, and include as much or as little of the Roseberyites as they choose. . . . Little Englandism, crude democracy, economy, secularism are all again to the front in the official Liberal Party.[33]

In any case, if circumstances had been such that the duke led a ministry of free traders in early 1904, it could only have been the weaker group in a free trade combination, and a general election would probably have reduced their numbers and influence even further. It could not have been a progressive or active alliance. So long as Unionist Free Traders held a crucial place in any government, they would impede most legislation sympathetic to social reform.

The Unionist Free Traders experienced many confused reactions after the division. Sandars reported that some, such as George Goschen and Richard Cavendish, were so angry with the Liberals for refusing to support them unreservedly after the division that they were almost completely reconciled to Balfour. Not all Unionist Free Traders were downcast, however, Churchill commented to Devonshire:

> The division was satisfactory. . . . Considering the grovelling attitude of the Government and the immense concessions already made—so far as votes are concerned, this shows a great deal of determination. I hope we can begin to negotiate with the opposition for the seats of those who have voted without delay. The iron is hot now.[34]

Piecemeal constituency negotiations did go on until 1905 between Herbert Gladstone and James and about half a dozen compromises were made—with two Unionist Free Traders giving pledges to support a new education settlement.

The negotiations of December 1903 to February 1904 marked the zenith of the Liberal-Unionist Free Trade co-operation. Though the two free trade combinations still demonstrated together on platforms and at massive banquets, after February 1904 the occasional talk about new coalitions was no longer realistic. After February Devonshire, Goschen, Ritchie, Hamilton, and Hugh Cecil dissociated themselves from any Liberal aims other than the preservation of free trade. The major reason for Unionist Free Trade passivity after February 1904 was the realisation that Chamberlain would almost certainly lose the next election. Thus most of them felt little need to swallow their scruples and ask for help from the Liberals. The negotiation of the *Entente* with France in early 1904 by the ex-Whig Lansdowne convinced many Unionist Free Traders, and especially the elder statesmen, that it was better to stick to Balfour than to give the Liberals, with their pacifist wing, a chance to run foreign policy. Apprehensions concerning Liberal social legislation, such as the probable reversal of the Taff Vale decision, meant that people like Goschen had no desire to help a Radical government come to power. For there existed before 1906 that fear of Liberal social reform which, proving well justified after 1906, drove most of the Unionist Free Traders back to their party.

Most often the degree of readiness to compromise with the Liberals depended on whether the free trader was a Liberal Unionist or a Conservative. Apart from some of the Tory Hughligans the initiative for negotiations came from Liberal Unionists like Strachey, James, and Elliot. These men wanted to co-operate closely with the Liberals to get a voice in their councils when a new government was formed. This close association was advocated as the only means of permitting the Unionist Free Traders to survive and to continue to play an important role in political affairs. Consequently, they were deeply resentful of much Conservative free trade opinion which regarded any bargain with the Liberals as anathema after early 1904.

Among the Tory free traders, both a majority of the leaders and the rank and file represented men far more attached to their party than to free trade. The first leader of this section, Hicks Beach, was regarded as the prime apostate in the anti-Chamberlain movement. George Hamilton also refused to endorse a policy of vigorous co-operation with the Liberals, while Ritchie, initially so vehement, was a spent force by the autumn of 1903. Among the younger Tory free traders, a number like Hugh Cecil modified their militancy against Balfour as they realised they were separated from the Liberals by too wide a gulf. Other free traders, both Liberal Unionists and Conservatives, found it preferable after February 1904 to waive their free trade convictions and either shelter completely under the title of Balfourite or retire from politics rather than actively seek Liberal support.

Although in some cases the line between Liberal Unionist and Conservative free traders was blurred, the divergences between these two sections is fundamental to explaining Unionist Free Trade paralysis. Elliot pointed out this problem to Lord Cromer when he became President of the Unionist Free Trade Club:

> As with the Free Fooders, the difficulty has always been when it comes to action that the club is divided in opinion, not as to the merits of Free Trade, but whether Free Trade Unionists can ally themselves with the Liberals, and would be wise, as a matter of political expediency, in doing so.[35]

A small number, seventeen in all, crossed the floor to the Liberals over the fiscal question, eleven of these before 1906. Men such as Churchill, Jack Seely, Dickson Poynder, and Ivor Guest wanted to form the Unionist Free Traders into a cohesive group acting with the Liberals in a manner similar to the connection between the Liberal Unionists and Conservatives after 1886. They knew it was futile to exist as an amorphous body suspended in a political twilight between distaste of the Liberals and ineffectual resentment at both Balfour and Chamberlain. They had no sympathy with the passive policy of Hicks Beach which they considered detrimental to free trade as well as harmful to their careers. When the negotiations between the Liberals and Unionist Free Traders broke down in February 1904, the exodus to the Liberal party began.

An examination of Unionist Free Trade associations with the Liberals from May 1903 to February 1904 reveals a consistent record of failure and miscalculation on the part of the former group. By failing (or being unwilling) to act and compromise on a broad front with the Liberals, the Unionist Free Traders forfeited the chance to become an effective organisation both to safeguard free trade and to prevent their party from being taken over by Tariff Reform. Consequently, they were eliminated by Chamberlain. In so far as they did negotiate with the Liberals, they miscalculated on the extent of their own power and on the complexion of the Liberal party. Old Whigs such as James, and even the duke, never fully understood the degree to which Liberal rank and file backed Campbell-Bannerman. Also, by failing to take fully into account the nature and extent of Liberal commitments to Nonconformity and to the Labour Representative Committee, the Unionist Free Traders often acted naïvely. It was not sufficient for Hicks Beach to talk to Harcourt, or for James to meet secretly with Asquith, or even for Devonshire and Spencer to consult, to bring about successful regroupings. In a similar way, Conservative free traders like Hugh Cecil overestimated their power in the Unionist party, and they often went about trying to check Chamberlain or to influence Balfour in an overbearing manner bound to be unsuccessful.

The Unionist Free Traders had no great electoral support or party machinery. They had either to ally with the Liberals or to accept Balfour's lead. They did neither and oscillated between the two alternatives. Therefore, their actions which accentuated the split in their party were turned to the advantage of the Liberals. However, it is doubtful whether many of them could have accepted the Liberal programme after 1906; and it is certainly unlikely that in the political climate of the time the Unionist Free Traders, even if in alliance with the Liberals, could have prevented much of the legislation of the years 1906–10. So conjectures about the alternatives of close Liberal-Unionist Free Trade co-operation are really only valid for the years 1903–6. After the Liberal victory of 1906, and the subsequent move of the Liberals towards radical social reform, the Unionist Free Traders had nowhere to go but back into the Unionist party.

Since both the Liberals and Unionist Free Traders drew back from a possible alliance, the duke's group had to steer a middle course between strenuous disapproval of Tariff Reform and aloofness from the Liberals. In their different ways, both Balfour and the Liberals gave them only a minimum of attention, and Chamberlain continued to exact a very effective vengeance on them for having hobbled him at the outset of his career as a fiscal reformer.

Chapter 6 THE CHARACTERISTICS OF THE UNIONIST FREE TRADERS

I

IDEALLY THE economic and social characteristics of each Unionist MP should be analysed to understand more thoroughly the party's fiscal divisions. Such a formidable task is beyond the scope of this book. A start can be made, however, by a detailed examination of the Unionist Free Traders. In the process, some characteristics of both the Balfourites and Chamberlainites can also be discerned.

Although the Unionist Free Traders failed to develop into an effective unit to defeat Tariff Reform, they remained until 1906 a partially active and sometimes very important political group. Their significance may be seen by examining their numerical strength: of the 392 Unionist MPs in May 1903, eighty-three became Unionist Free Traders as the fiscal controversy developed.[1] These were men who publicly proclaimed their free trade beliefs and fought against Tariff Reform.

The members designated here as Unionist Free Traders are: those who signed the resolution of 1 July 1903 opposing fiscal change and, apart from four, were the original Free Food League members; other Unionists who joined the League sometime after its inauguration on 13 July; the members of the Unionist Free Trade Club; Unionists who voted against their party in fiscal divisions during 1904 and 1905; and, finally, the candidates who stood as Unionist Free Traders at the 1906 election. Inclusion under any one of these five headings is sufficient to classify an MP as a Unionist Free Trader. Most of those mentioned, however, would in any case qualify under at least two headings. The six men who do not fall under any of the categories and yet were undoubtedly free traders will be dealt with separately.[2]

Three major difficulties arise in computing Unionist Free Trade strength in the Commons. They never formed a clearly defined party but always remained simply a faction inside the Unionist alliance. Membership in their organisations tended to fluctuate. Finally, the numerous free trade sympathisers in the party who never deviated in their loyalty to Balfour are not included: men such as Edward Stanley, Sir William Anson, Sir Robert Finlay, and Victor Cavendish. On the other hand, two apparent Balfourians, Sir Francis Powell and John Rutherford, must be counted as marginally Unionist Free Traders since they came out as free traders on the eve of the 1906 election.[3]

Of the 83 Unionist Free Traders, 60 were Conservatives and 23 were Liberal Unionists. There was, therefore, a markedly higher ratio of Liberal Unionist to Conservative than the proportions in the Unionist alliance as it stood on 15 May 1903. At that time there were 328 Conservatives and 64 Liberal Unionists in the Commons. In the alliance as a whole, only 16 per cent were Liberal Unionists, whereas 28 per cent of the Unionist Free Traders were Liberal Unionists. Although about a third of the Liberal Unionists fought Chamberlain's policy, only a sixth of the Conservatives openly opposed Tariff Reform.

The Free Food League reached a peak strength of 65 members late in 1903. Elliot's list of the members shows that 49 of the 53 who favoured the resolution against protection on 1 July joined the League, followed by 16 others between 13 July and early December. Elliot referred to the 65 in a journal entry on 23 October 1903: 'held the first meeting of our Free Fooders outside of the Parliamentary Committee. . . . We have a dozen Peers and some 65 Unionist MPs with us. . . .'[4]

The Unionist Free Trade Club, which was formally inaugurated in April 1905 to replace the League, had 29 members. All of them had been members of the League except for Lord Robert Cecil, who did not enter parliament until 1906.

In addition to the 53 of 1 July and the 16 later additions to the League, 6 other Unionists (who never joined the League) showed their free trade colours by voting against the government in at least one fiscal division. In fact a total of 47 Unionist Free Traders voted with the Liberals in one or more of the six 'full dress' fiscal debates during 1904 and 1905. In addition, there were 6 men who had neither joined the Free Food League nor voted against Balfour who were re-elected in 1906 as free traders. Finally, 2 other Unionists qualify as overt free traders for the period 1903 to 1906. John Wilson (LU) crossed to the Liberals in February 1904 in protest against Tariff Reform without bothering to join the League. Henry Greene, also never a member of the League, announced in March 1905 that he would retire from politics rather than continue in a party committed to fiscal change. In parliament on 28 March 1905, the Tariff Reformer, Rowland Hunt, claimed that Hugh Cecil's recent tour through Shropshire had 'blown the Hon. Member for Shrewsbury [Greene] off the fence on the free food side'.

With the inclusion of Wilson and Greene, the total of 83 Unionist Free Traders is reached for the parliamentary period 1903 to 1906. Although this is the overall total of Unionists who revealed themselves as free traders during the three-year period, it is no indication of their concerted strength at any given time. While new opponents to Chamberlain arose periodically throughout 1904 and 1905, their numbers were more than counterbalanced by the steady capitulation to Tariff Reform pressure of already established Unionist Free Traders.

From December 1903 the Free Food League suffered a continuous decline in membership. By February 1904 the *Annual Register* noted that the membership was reputed to be 53. In fact, according to Elliot's memorandum, the membership had fallen to 51. His carefully drawn-up document appears to be authoritative. It shows, by comparison with the December 1903 list, that 12 Unionists had resigned, one had become a Liberal, and one had died. The resignation of Hoare on 31 December provoked press comment, but the other resignations were not publicly recorded. The membership dropped further during late 1904 and early 1905. On 3 August 1904 *The Times* noted that 7 free fooders were now classed as Liberals, and on 9 March 1905 claimed that Hatch had to be considered a member of the opposition. Thus there cannot have been more than 43 MPs remaining at the League's dissolution early in April 1905.

The decline in parliamentary strength of the Free Food League can be illustrated even more graphically by looking at the membership of its successor, the Unionist Free Trade Club, which was formally inaugurated on 10 April 1905. Only 29 MPs joined and 4 became Liberals between April 1905 and the 1906 election. As the strength of the Unionist Free Traders in the Commons declined from late 1903 to the end of 1905, the patrician element increased, for while the League had only 13 peers the Club contained 24. At the 1906 election 16 of the MPs were re-elected. They were joined by 5 Unionist Free Traders who entered parliament for the first time.

II

The major reason for the failure of Chamberlain's campaign was that, apart from iron and steel, the major industries in the country still prospered under free trade. Although they protested volubly, the 100,000 workers concerned with the production of iron and steel did not count heavily in the balance when compared with the much larger labour forces in industries still attached to free trade.[5] Even in the iron industry itself there was no solidarity behind Chamberlain. Mrs Wright notes that a progressive producer, such as the Cleveland iron master and Unionist Hugh Bell, 'weighed heavily on the Free Trade side'. Unlike the older, badly located producers in South Wales, such as the Ebbw Vale Coal and Iron Company, Bell felt no competition from German semi manufactured goods.[6] In South Wales itself the response to Tariff Reform varied. Lord Wimborne's family, who had managed the Dowlais Ironworks from 1787 to 1853 and retained full ownership until 1900, remained dedicated to free trade.[7] Indeed, the only groups completely supporting Chamberlain were the clearly declining industries, such as silk, hit badly by competition at home and desiring simple protection.

Cotton remained particularly strong in its commitment to free trade. This industry, which for over a century had represented the industrial supremacy of Great Britain, still accounted for nearly one-third of all exports, and furnished employment for over 600,000 workers. Ramsay MacDonald asserted melodramatically in 1903 that if Britain imposed protection 'nine tenths of the people of Lancashire would then live on American sufferance'.[8]

The coal industry, which employed 842,000 men in 1903, was particularly prosperous. The Board of Trade bluebook for 1903 noted that the proportion of manufactured to total exports had gradually fallen from 94 per cent in 1850 to 82 per cent in 1902. The main cause of the decreasing percentage was the growth of coal exports. Coal remained unshaken in its attachment to free trade.

There was also the shipping industry—with 1,000,000 men employed in shipbuilding and 200,000 as seamen—whose interests remained largely bound up with free trade. Conveying half the commerce of the world in British vessels, the profits of the carrying trade made up a considerable portion of the 'invisible income' which allowed the country to balance the excess of imports over exports.[9] Add to the men in shipping, the 1,250,000 workers in the transport industries inside the country, and Halévy's conclusion, that on the day of battle, Chamberlain would muster only a 'few scratch battalions', is easily understood.

Finally, the economic interests of the City—the society of bankers, bill and stockbrokers, and insurance agents—were dependent upon London's position as the major clearing house of world trade. The fears of German and American competition which plagued Midlands manufacturers (particularly in Birmingham and Sheffield) had little reality for those who thrived on cosmopolitan finance. Bernard Semmel sums up the free trade attachments of many of the important economic groups:

> The profits of international banking and discount operations, the premiums of and the interest on foreign loans, the dividends on foreign investments, the premiums of an international insurance network all depended on the 'cosmopolitan capitalism' based upon Free Trade. . . . These 'capitalists', the shipowners, prospering from an international common carrying trade, and the Lancashire cotton industry, still thought and acted in terms of the traditional Free Trade imperialism of the nineteenth century. . . .[10]

A major reason why the British financial world was deaf to pleas for protection from, for example, iron, steel, and tinplate industrialists, or producers of silk and linen, was that the financial interests had little connection with British industrial capitalism. The economist Joseph Schumpeter pointed out that 'everywhere except . . . in England' it transpired at the end of the nineteenth century in mature industrial states that 'monopoly capitalism' had 'virtually fused the big banks and cartels into one'. Indeed, the close alliance between high finance and the cartel magnates often went 'as far as personal identity'.[11] But in England, according to Schumpeter, and later interpreters like Semmel, 'the fundamental conflict between capitalists and entrepreneurs persisted'. Clapham obliquely supports this theory when he describes how in March 1907, during an American financial crisis caused by banks which had speculated unwisely in steel and copper, Germans became restive since 'German banking was deeply involved with industry' while the 'English remained cool'.[12]

If Schumpeter's interpretation is accurate, then many Unionist Free Traders might be expected to have had interests in financial capitalism, or in free trade industries such as cotton and coal; and Tariff Reformers could be expected to show a bias toward the world of iron and steel, or mining and investment ventures within the empire. Broadly speaking, with certain exceptions, the evidence will tend to confirm this hypothesis.

In his study of parliamentary economic interests, J. A. Thomas designates under the heading 'financial interest' the holding of directorships in banking, stock and bill broking, insurance, investment, trust, and loan companies, trading companies, and land companies.[13] The banking interests, in particular, appear to have been hostile to Tariff Reform. In the first fiscal debate of 1904, Beckett on 12 February noted about the Tariff Commission, which had been set up in December 1903, that 'wide as the right Hon. Gentleman for West Birmingham has spread his net he has not been able to capture a single banker to serve on that Committee'. Beckett was a partner in Beckett's and Co Ltd, bankers of Leeds—the last large provincial bank to remain in private hands.

Ten Unionist Free Trade MPs represented London banking interests. Fitzroy described Ritchie as 'the Chancellor of the Exchequer, who in the City is regarded as the *alter ego* of his late colleague on the Directorate of the Union Bank, Mr Schuster'. Lord Goschen had been influential in the banking world ever since he had become a director of the Bank of England in 1861 at the age of twenty-seven. His son, George, followed the family tradition for by 1903 he was a director of the Bank of Roumania, the Imperial Ottoman Bank, and the London and Country Bank.[14] After his retirement from the cabinet in 1902 Hicks Beach sat on the boards of the London Joint Stock Bank and the Bank of South Africa. Sir Edward Sassoon came from a famous banking family and was married to a Rothschild. Henry Greene's father had been governor of the Bank of England. Edgar Vincent had been governor of the Ottoman Bank at Constantinople from 1887 to 1897, and he and Alfred Rollit were particularly noted as parliamentary financial experts. Richard Cavendish was a director of four London banks. Dickenson, Tritton, and Hoare were London bankers with the last two coming from particularly distinguished banking families.

With those Unionist Free Traders who held directorships in provincial (or non-London) banks, it is more difficult to assume that they would have an interest in the maintenance of 'cosmopolitan capitalism' based on free trade. There were, in fact, only six Unionist Free Traders engaged in banking outside London. Three were located in Scotland, two (including Beckett) had their base in Yorkshire, and the last came from Dorset. The two most important in terms of number of directorships, were King of Hull and Williams of Dorset West. In addition to King's Bank Ltd, Sir Henry was chairman of four other banks (one of which was in London), while Williams was a director of two banks and a trustee of another. In Scotland, Campbell was a director of the Bank of Scotland, Baird was a director of the Clydesdale Bank Ltd, and Shaw Stewart held a directorship in the National Bank of Scotland. The last named was linked with the Baring banking family as a brother-in-law of Lord Cromer.

Thirty Unionist Traders held at least one directorship in insurance, stock or bill broking, trust and loan, investment, and land companies. Fisher, George Goschen, Hoare, Bond, Cohen, Hatch, and Guthrie were particularly important in London financial circles as was Hicks Beach who had been a director of the Economic Assurance Company since 1891. In Liverpool, McArthur and Taylor held interests in shipping insurance, as did Baird, Corbett, and Cross in Glasgow.

Among the Unionist Free Trade industrialists, a number were in shipping. This industry profited from cheap steel with which to build ships and from freights and insurance revenues gained from the carrying trade. In Belfast, Gustav Wolff was a partner in Harland and Wolff, shipbuilders, and was a director of the Union Castle Line. The other Belfast Unionist Free Trader, Sloan, was a sub-contractor to Harland and Wolff. Hain of St Ives was the chairman both of Hain's steamship line and of a steamship brokerage firm. Taylor in Liverpool was a wealthy steamship owner and head of the shipbuilding firm of Hugh Evans and Co Ltd. McArthur was closely involved in shipping insurance as a director of four maritime insurance companies. Elsewhere, Crawford Smith and Rollit each held a directorship in a steamship line.

Colonel Denny of Kilmarnock Burghs, was the most eloquent representative in parliament for the Unionist Free Traders in shipping. On 29 March 1905 he seconded a Liberal resolution stating that 'under no consideration could good accrue to shipping and its kindred industries of shipbuilding and engineering, and almost as certainly harm would result from a change in the fiscal system'. Denny defended the system of free imports claiming that Glasgow shipbuilders could buy cheap steel plates for £5 7s 6d (£5·37½) a piece, whereas their counterparts in America paid £8 15s (£8.75) a plate.

All the shipping interests in the Unionist party were by no means for free trade, however, for David McIver, MP for Liverpool Kirkdale, and a prominent shipowner trading to the River Plate, attacked Denny's arguments and queried his figures on American costs. He claimed that all but five Liverpool shipowners supported Chamberlain because foreign tariffs were steadily reducing the quantity of British manufactures in their ships. He concluded by warning that 'our carrying trade was going from us by reason of our insane persistence in this free import system'. McArthur followed and objected to McIver's views asserting that Tariff Reform would not only increase the cost of building and working ships but would also reduce the volume of trade.

Four Unionist Free Traders had interests in the cotton industry. Hornby was the chairman of a family firm of cotton spinners in

Blackburn going back over a century. Knowles of Salford was a cotton exporter, as was Rutherford in Darwen. Whitely was head of a cotton-spinning firm in Ashton-under-Lyne. Kemp, who sat for the Heywood division, was a director of the flannel manufacturing firm of Kelsall and Kemp Co Ltd. Although not a cotton industrialist himself, James had powerfully represented the interests both of his Bury constituents and of the Lancashire cotton spinners. In February 1895 he had led successfully the opposition in the Commons to the Liberal government's proposal to reimpose duties on cotton imported into India. Two other Unionist Free Traders were industrialists. Charles Seely, MP for Lincoln, and John Wilson of Falkirk Burghs, were colliery owners. Although he held no directorship, Lambton's family, the Earls of Durham, had long been colliery owners in Durham.

As the shipping industry indicated, however, no simple economic explanation will account sufficiently for the fiscal attitudes in the party. Even in the realm of finance such an interpretation will not explain completely why men remained free traders or became Tariff Reformers. In fact the percentage of financial interests among Unionists Free Traders is the same as in the party as a whole. Thomas claims there were 182 Unionist MPs in 1900 who had at least a single financial interest. That is, of the 402 MPs in 1900, 45 per cent had one financial interest whereas of the 83 Unionist Free Traders, 37 (or 45 per cent) had a financial interest.

An important distinction can, however, be drawn between the 'financial' Unionist Free Traders and the 'financial' Tariff Reformers. An examination of 75 Tariff Reformers who sat in parliament from 1903 to 1906 shows that 26 (or 34 per cent) had a financial interest.[15] This is somewhat lower than the Unionist Free Trade percentage. Significantly, 14 of the 26 also had an interest in metals, colonial investment concerns, or colonial land development companies—enterprises which stood to profit from Chamberlain's programme. For example, Alfred Baldwin and Bonar Law both held bank directorships, but the former was an iron master in Bewdley and the latter an iron merchant from Glasgow, where the industry was depressed. Similarly, Samuel Roberts held a bank directorship and Howard Vincent a directorship in an investment company. Both represented Sheffield, long the home of fair trade influence, and Roberts was a director of Cammell, Laird and Company, steel, ship, and armour plate manufacturers, while Vincent was a director of Hadfields' Steel Foundry Co Ltd. One of Sir Henry Kimber's (MP for Wandsworth) fifteen directorships was in banking, but eleven others, of which he was chairman of six, were either in Africa or in India. Though he held a directorship in the Small Dwellings Acquisition Company, and was a colliery owner, Herbert Pike Pease was also an iron master and a director of the Normanby Iron Works Co Ltd.

On the other hand, with the exception of Galloway, who was a director of Carnforth Hematite Iron Co Ltd, Hicks Beach, who was a director of the Bank of South Africa, and McArthur, who was a director of the Bank of Australia, none of the 'financial' Unionist Free Traders had any countervailing interests in metals or colonial enterprises. Moreover, Galloway and McArthur represented Lancashire constituencies. Apart from two colliery owners, four cotton industrialists and one flannel magnate, and four steamship owners—all industries largely committed to free trade—and Brotherton, who was a chemical manufacturer in Wakefield, there was almost a total absence of industrial interests among the Unionist Free Traders. W. F. D. Smith owned the chain of Smith's bookstores and Hatch was chairman of Hatch, Mansfield and Co wine merchants.

Semmel notes that the interests of 'iron and steel, building materials, glass and chemicals, all midlands products hard hit by German and American competition', constituted the heart of the Tariff Commission and the Tariff Reform League; 20 of the 75 Tariff Reformers represented midlands constituencies as opposed to only 8 of the Unionist Free Traders. In the constituencies Unionist Free Traders tended to be concentrated in free trade areas: 12 in London, 13 in Lancashire, and 4 in Glasgow—about 35 per cent of their total. At the 1906 elections over 50 per cent of the Unionist Free Trade candidates contested seats in these 3 areas.

These economic differences between the two wings of the Unionist party only serve as indicators. Both Tariff Reformers and Unionist Free Traders had significant numbers of military men, lawyers, journalists, and men of letters. If many Unionist Free Traders came from patrician backgrounds, some of the most ardent Chamberlainites also came from the aristocracy and gentry. Page Croft described the origins of the Confederacy as an attempt 'to get large numbers of young men drawn from the aristocracy and country gentlemen who would devote themselves to the cause and fight constituencies wherever and whenever they were required'.[16]

Some of the most fervent Unionist Free Traders, such as Elliot, Churchill, and Tommy Bowles, appear to have had no direct economic interest to account for their stand against Chamberlain. Yet Churchill appears to have identified his fortunes with those interests in the City, for Mrs Webb wrote of him as objecting 'to a self-contained Empire as he thinks it would destroy this cosmopolitan capitalism'. Others appear to have fought Tariff Reform for reasons ranging from intellectual conviction about the merits of free trade to the less elevated explanation of sheer personal dislike of Chamberlain.

Certain broad economic biases can be indicated. The Tariff Reformers had most of the heavy industry interests, as Semmel's examination of membership of the Tariff Reform League and Tariff Commission shows. Unionist Free Traders and Balfourites held many of the financial, and particularly banking, interests. But no clear-cut economic divisions exist between the Unionist Free Traders and Tariff Reformers. The split in the party over Chamberlain's programme cannot be explained principally on economic grounds.

III

Unionist Free Traders tended to have a high opinion of their intellectual worth and political talent. Griffith-Boscawen sarcastically commented that 'they prided themselves that they have all the clever young men and we, not being superior persons, allowed them a monopoly of this kind of boasting'.[17] Certainly, in Churchill, Elliot, Hugh Cecil, Hicks Beach, Lord Goschen, Gorst, and others it can be stated that the Unionist Free Traders showed a range of parliamentary talent unequalled by the Tariff Reformers, despite the presence of Chamberlain and later of L. Amery and F. E. Smith. In 1910 Chamberlain himself remarked to Margot Asquith that 'Winston is the cleverest of all the young men, and the mistake Arthur made was letting him go'.[18]

Most of the Unionist Free Traders were determined individualists and the prominent journalist Strachey was just as independent as his allies in the House. John Strachey commented of his father that 'had he gone into the House of Commons he would have been the despair of the Whips'.[19] Clarke writes of John Rutherford as 'swashbuckling' and a great 'challenger' staking £500 on his credentials as a free trader in 1906. When Henry Hobhouse announced he would not seek re-election, his reasons were that it was impossible for a man of independent views to make his presence felt in the House any more. He was still so nervous about Home Rule that he would not join the Liberal party, and because he objected 'so strongly to the reactionary views of the Tariff Reformers', retirement was the only alternative.

Many of the rank and file Unionist Free Traders were noted for their independence in the constituency as well as in the House. It was the popularity with their constituents of men like King and Thornton which strengthened their anti-Chamberlain attitude and enabled them to withstand Tariff Reform pressure. King had been a highly-esteemed mayor of Hull. Regard for him increased when he gave personal financial aid to the families of men killed in the Russian action at Dogger Bank in October 1904. The *Daily Chronicle* on 4 January 1906 admitted that Thornton's personal popularity posed their greatest difficulty in trying to storm the Tory citadel of Clapham in 1906. (Like many Unionist Free Traders, Thornton was one of the most old-fashioned MPs, for he always drove to the House in a coach and four.) McArthur of Liverpool and the Glasgow MPs, Corbett, Cross, Baird, and Stirling-Maxwell, all held impregnable positions because of their reputations in their constituencies.

Perhaps the most eccentric and locally entrenched Unionist Free Trader was Hornby of Blackburn. Robert Cecil wrote of him as a man from a prodigiously popular family who scarcely ever bothered to attend the House of Commons. He was always returned, however, and, like all Hornbys since 1832, at election time he used to walk the streets scattering sweets to children and calling out 'Hornby for Blackburn'.[20] Hornby, and Powell of Wigan, were perfect representatives of what Clarke describes as the 'Tory patriarchs' of Lancashire—men whose fiefs were finally destroyed by 1910. These local men were seldom the leaders in the Unionist Free Trade movement, but they held steadily to most of their Cobdenite convictions throughout the fiscal controversy.

Among the Unionist Free Trade leaders were men of great originality and courage. Elliot had long been known as one of the most independent members of the House of Commons, consistently following the dictates of his conscience rather than the whips, as his opposition to Chamberlain on the South African War had indicated. (The only other Unionists who overtly opposed the war were the great 'independents' and free traders, Leonard Courtney and Sir Edward Clarke.) M. F. E. Headlam in his account of Elliot in the *Dictionary of National Biography* calls him 'the last of the Whigs'. The Elliot family, however, was split over the fiscal issue, for his brothers, Lord Minto and Hugh Elliot, were strong Tariff Reformers.

Another family divided by the fiscal controversy was that of the Tariff Reformer Herbert Maxwell. Fitzroy remarks on Maxwell's distress when his son-in-law, the free fooder Stirling Maxwell, voted against the government in the fiscal debate of 10 March 1904. Perhaps the classic example of a family divided on the question of fiscal reform was exemplified by the clash between Edgar and Howard Vincent. The elder, Howard, after a trip around the world in 1884 developed an ardent faith in imperialism and protection. Along with Chaplin and James Lowther, Howard was one of a well-known trio of fair traders who ever since 1885 had been agitating for the Conservatives to adopt protection. Edgar, Howard's younger brother, was one of the most prominent Unionist Free Traders until he crossed to the Liberals in 1910.

A high proportion of the leading Unionist Free Traders were the younger sons of famous peers. As younger sons they had all the assurance and independence of coming from established families without, perhaps, some of the responsibilities and rewards. Elliot was the younger brother of Lord Minto. Frederick

Lambton was twin to the Earl of Durham. Richard Cavendish was a forceful free trader whereas his brother Victor, after 1908 the Duke of Devonshire, consistently supported Balfour. Both Robert and Hugh Cecil were far more militant free traders, at least in the period 1903–10, than their brother, the fourth Marquis of Salisbury. The free traders Beckett, Greville, and George Goschen all renounced their militant Cobdenism upon ascending to the peerage.

Balfour, Acland-Hood, and many Tariff Reformers often claimed that many of the aggressive Unionist Free Traders were rebellious and disloyal members of the party. Griffith-Boscawen wholeheartedly concurred with the accusation, commenting that, aside from a few respectable men like Hicks Beach, the rest of the free fooders 'were chiefly malcontents who had long been seeking every opportunity of embarrassing the government'. Balfour himself curtly answered an attack Hugh Cecil had made on him by retorting that:

> You have, in my opinion, inflicted by your methods of advocacy many injuries on the cause of free trade but none is more serious than your persistent resolve to count among the most valuable supporters of free trade persons who misuse free trade arguments, as they have misused countless other arguments, for the purpose of injuring the Government.[21]

Balfour's irritation was understandable, for a number of Unionist Free Traders were chronic malcontents. Gorst became such a difficult and cantankerous politician that he never fulfilled the great promise he had shown in reorganising the Conservative party organisation in 1872. Pemberton pursued such an independent line in the Commons that, as *The Times* wrote on 6 January 1906, he had been elected for Sunderland in 1900 without official constituency support. Sir Edward Clarke, Solicitor General in Salisbury's administration of 1886–92, had become convinced, while defending Dr Jameson in 1896, that the government was implicated in the Raid. Thereafter, he became a firm opponent of the South Africa War, and was particularly hostile to Chamberlain. After one severe attack in the Commons on the colonial secretary in October 1899, Frederick Greenwood, editor of the *Pall Mall Gazette*, wrote to J. H. Blackwood that

'Clarke's speech was smashing for Chamberlain . . . no more effective speech than Clarke's has been heard for years'.[22] Because of this and other attacks, he was forced in February 1900 to retire from his constituency, Plymouth. Robert Yerburgh had also broken with party policy in the past. In July 1898 he had attempted to raise a Unionist revolt against Salisbury's foreign policy in the Far East by holding a series of dinners for disgruntled Unionists at the Junior Carlton Club.

The activities of the Hughligans and the scrupulous independence of men like Elliot were looked upon as sheer obstructionism by Balfour and the whips. Unionist Free Traders, however, maintained that they were motivated by a desire to uphold the dignity of the private member. In 1909 Cecil attributed the 'running sore' in the party to the Tariff Reformers' disregard of 'the older doctrine of the independence of politicians' in favour of the 'enforcement of opinions by menaces' unmatched even in the 'history of religion'.[23] On 30 April 1904 Cecil claimed, looking back to Burke (in an address also at Bristol), that the member of parliament 'was a man sent by the constituency to use his own judgement'. He held this view all his life and, as president of Bournemouth East and Christchurch Conservative Association, fiercely defended, against the majority in the association, Nigel Nicolson's right to abstain from a vote supporting the government's Suez policy: 'he was sent to Parliament to be a representative of the whole Commons of the Realm . . . and not as a delegate of the particular constituency who had a right to appoint him.'[24]

Gibson Bowles reiterated Cecil's sentiments in an address to the electors of King's Lynn in 1906: 'When I first presented myself to you, I declared myself an independent man, desirous to serve, not the interests of any party, but the interests of the country.' Unionist Free Trade emphasis on the autonomy of the private member also arose from the belief that Chamberlain's methods, as Pemberton claimed, led to a debasing of politics 'by obstructing members who are not slaves to any Party Caucus'.[25]

As opposed to this individualism, the Tariff Reformers were primarily concerned to elect members who would faithfully support fiscal reform. The Chamberlainites were determined to dominate Unionist Constituency associations, principally to secure candidates who were 'sound' on tariffs. Before the 1906 election the Tariff Reformers were not strong enough to compel Balfour to proscribe the free traders in the party. In eleven instances, however, fiscal reformers contested the seats of Unionist Free Traders at the election. After 1906, Chamberlain's faction became so powerful that by January 1910 all but two Unionist Free Traders were forced to capitulate or to leave their constituencies. Unionist Free Traders observed despairingly that a former convicted criminal such as Rutherford Harris, and even a Home Ruler, were accepted by the Tariff Reformers as long as the two held 'correct' fiscal opinions.

These characteristics of the Unionist Free Traders—an economic tendency towards financial capitalism, preponderance of old-fashioned local men, and a social bias toward the patrician, as well as an aggressive independence—partly justify the familiar generalisation that the division in the party over the fiscal issue represented a division of aims between the old conservatives and the new. Robert Cecil exemplified this 'old' Conservative view in a lament to Balfour:

> It is not by any means only the Fiscal Question upon which I differ from them. It is their whole way of looking at politics. It appears to me to be utterly sordid and materialistic, not yet corrupt but on the high road to corruption.[26]

Gorst's contrast between the continuity and depth of his Tory principles and Chamberlain's political changes buttress the view that the Unionist clash was between the old and new attitudes towards politics. Certainly when the old-fashioned views of Gorst, Hornby, and Thornton are contrasted with the outlook of, say, L. S. Amery, Winterton, and Garvin, a distinct difference is obvious. Beatrice Webb's description of George Hamilton illuminates another aspect of the old style Unionist Free Trade politician. She speaks of Hamilton as 'an attractive grand seigneur' with 'exceptional personal charm and social tact'. Moreover, the insistence of Unionist Free Traders on the need to cut down government expense illustrates an outlook harking back to Peel and Gladstone rather more than any appreciation of the needs of early twentieth-century England.

Like most generalisations about the Unionist Free Traders, however, the vague description of them representing an 'older' style of Conservatism is an oversimplification. A number of younger men, both Liberal Unionists and Conservatives, who crossed to the Liberals were progressive politicians. Many of the most inveterate Tories—Chaplin, Lowther, Wyndham—were dedicated Tariff Reformers. On 31 March 1905, the *Westminster Gazette* praised Hugh Cecil's efforts to rally the 'real old Conservative party', which 'has never been reconciled to Chamberlain's demagogic methods and commercial politics'. The reason why this 'rally' never occurred was simply that many 'old Conservatives' were ardent Chamberlainites. Chamberlain's Tariff Reform Dukes and Earls—Bedford, Sutherland, Portland, and Percy—were neither parvenus nor harbingers of a 'new' Unionism.[27]

Many Tariff Reformers accused the Unionist Free Traders of being enemies of imperialism. Maxse wrote contemptuously of the 'little England free fooders' and singled out Hicks Beach as one of those 'who have always frankly hated the British Empire'. Less stridently, Leopold Amery criticised Churchill's patriotism as limited to England. 'The other, new conception, that of the Commonwealth as the object of a wider patriotism . . . has never seriously influenced his thinking. . . .'[28] Tariff Reformers dismissed the imperial aspirations of the Unionist Free Traders because they opposed Chamberlain's imperial conception. But a number of the older Unionist Free Traders could echo Hicks Beach's claim that he 'was an Imperialist when Mr Chamberlain's politics did not go beyond Birmingham'.[29] Early in the 1880s, for example, Hartington had grasped more clearly than anyone else in Gladstone's cabinet that control of Egypt was the key to safeguarding British supremacy in India and the Mediterranean.

Unionist Free Traders firmly believed that Chamberlain's scheme to achieve imperial union by tariffs was likely to produce precisely the opposite result to that intended—friction, rancour, and possible dismemberment rather than agreement.[30] Just as in parliament on 3 February 1904 Hugh Cecil lauded the imperialism which had its 'spring in duty' and derided the imperialism 'which looks only to profit', Goschen was convinced that the empire could not be knit together by

> commercial bargains with the colonies; without commercial bargains the colonies have lavished their blood in South Africa and . . . we have lavished our millions in defence of our Empire . . . asking but little in return.[31]

Some Unionists considered Chamberlain to hold a very myopic view of imperialism. Soon after Chamberlain's assertion that the free fooders were imperialists in theory but little Englanders in practice, Hicks Beach pointed out that Chamberlain left entirely out of account Britain's 'Eastern dependencies'. 'I', said Sir Michael, 'am a wider Imperialist than Mr Chamberlain, because I look upon the Empire as a whole'.

If few free traders coherently expressed their Cobdenite views, few Tariff Reformers advocated protection in a sophisticated manner. Only a minority—such as Amery, Hewins, Garvin, and Chamberlain—wholeheartedly repudiated free trade theory. Amery, in particular, was a formidable theorist. Under the pseudonym of 'Calchas', Garvin in the *Fortnightly Review* attacked the Cobdenite view that free trade tended to promote harmony in international relations. For him the fiscal struggle was 'as much a sequel of Darwinism as of Cobden'. Chamberlain's aggressive actions both in South Africa and on behalf of Tariff Reform 'taught us . . . that in foreign and commercial policy passive endurance invites aggression. . . . The only sure foundation for our amiable relations with our neighbours is the possession by us of equivalent striking power. . . .' If Chamberlain should triumph, then an age 'of feminism in British policy will close'.

For Churchill free trade represented both a 'condition' and a 'herald' of progress. As opposed to imperial emphasis, he wanted a government 'which instead of looking mainly abroad, will look mainly, if not . . . entirely, at home'. Whereas for Leopold Amery free trade led 'ineluctably to confiscatory socialism' and the 'consequent division of parties on class lines', for Hugh Cecil 'protection promoted profound social discontent'. Cecil was convinced that the 'purely conservative element in modern conservatism' found Tariff Reform anathema precisely because it was protection which would 'smooth the way for Socialism'.[32]

Thus in highly individual interpretations mixed with rhetoric both Unionist Free Traders and Tariff Reformers argued their case. As with the Chamberlainites, many Unionist Free Traders lacked the inclination and intellectual drive to correlate systematically their often rudimentary beliefs in free trade in the way Goschen, Elliot, and Strachey did. The more learned arguments of these men were often detailed and dull, though it is not correct to claim as Mrs Wright does that the Unionist Free Traders 'stood . . . heavily in the sloughs of Cobdenite argument'.[33] But at times men like Cromer sounded terribly old-fashioned and doctrinaire. The proconsul complained to Strachey late in 1903 that

> to those of my age it is rather tiresome to be under the necessity of furbishing up their old and perhaps rusty economic armour in a cause which they had every reason to believe had . . . been fought and definitely won half a century ago.[34]

It is only fair to note that the ruthless methods of the Tariff Reformers caused many Unionist Free Traders to become extremely rigid in their beliefs. For example, the driving force of the Birmingham Caucus, particularly its treatment of Hugh Cecil, caused 'the iron to enter into the soul' of Balfour of Burleigh, and made him more resolute against fiscal change than he had been in 1902.

With only a few exceptions, the Unionist Free Traders were extremely conservative about social reform. Many opposed any tinkering with the domestic market economy just as stridently as they upheld free international exchange. Their views were championed by Strachey in the *Spectator* who inveighed against Liberal reform after 1906. In 1908 he outlined to Margot Asquith his hostility to the recently passed Old Age Pensions Act:

> I did my very best . . . to get the Lords to throw out the Old Age Pensions Bill and if they had not been a set of miserable funks they would have done it. . . . My quarrel with the House of Lords is not that they pass too few Liberal measures but that they pass too many.[35]

Like Strachey, Cromer was steeped in the severe financial tradition of Peel and Gladstone so that he 'placed a sound financial system before any other consideration'. Cromer thus looked upon the Old Age Pensions Act (which merely gave each man over seventy, who did not have an income of £26 a year, 5s (25p) a week, and 10s (50p) a week to a married couple not earning over £52 a year) as largesse to the masses. In such policies he saw 'an obvious re-enactment on the stage of Imperial Britain of the prelude to the drama which had heralded the downfall of Imperial Rome'.[36]

While he never expressed his belief in sound finance quite so dramatically, Hicks Beach held the same views as Cromer. Goschen was as opposed to 'profligate finance' as Cromer and Hicks Beach. However, Elliot maintained that Goschen was always prepared, unlike Hicks Beach and Cromer, 'to spend very largely for a great purpose'. If Goschen was not ultra cautious about finance, he was extremely conservative about electoral reform. He had been the foremost opponent after 1880 of the Liberal plan for the equalising of county and borough franchise, as he believed it must 'lead to the complete monopolising of political power by a single class of the community'.[37] He was almost alone against extending the franchise and developing single member constituencies, for the Conservatives were not prepared to support him in resisting democratic reform.

A small number of Unionist Free Traders did profess their interest in and advocacy of social reform. The *Guardian* spoke highly of Austin Taylor as one of the ablest and most progressive Unionist Free Traders. Cross of Glasgow ended his election address with the slogan 'as a Unionist Free Trader and social reformer I solicit your vote'. A few Unionist Free Traders were quite advanced in their sympathies towards organised labour. For example, during the 1890s Sir Henry James had been the main ally in the House of the cotton operatives. He 'stressed the need for direct representation since he had been "much handicapped by not having the assistance of a practical man" to help him with the Factory Act of 1891'. Sir John Lubbock, later Lord Avebury, had in 1886 succeeded in carrying the first Shop Hours Act, limiting 'the hours of young persons to seventy-four a week'.[38] Thereafter, he fought tenaciously to have the act enforced. In 1909, however, Avebury entered the lists against the Budget, claiming that it was not against poverty but against the poor for it sapped energy and industry, confidence and thrift. The *Annual Register*, commenting on Unionist Free Traders standing at the 1906 election, described Gorst as a free fooder 'of somewhat socialistic tendencies'. Gorst became increasingly Radical in his old age. In 1909 he dedicated his book on Education to the Labour members in parliament and in January 1910 he stood as a Liberal candidate for Preston.

However, on such a crucial issue as old age pensions only four —Rutherford, Pemberton, Stirling-Maxwell, and Williams— advocated them, and then only through voluntary societies. (By contrast, two out of three Liberals advocated pensions by 1906.) Similarly, the few who specifically said they had an interest in the welfare of the trade unions remained vague and never favoured the reversal of the Taff Vale judgement. Unionist Free Traders' views on social reform were not very different from those of others in their party, including the Tariff Reformers, who, aside from Chamberlain and a few others, failed to stress reform.

Apart from a few younger men, most Unionist Free Traders tended to be very serious, convinced of their own rectitude and unsubtle to the point of bluntness—can there have been any 'bluffer' men in English public life in 1903 than Devonshire, Balfour of Burleigh and Cromer? Certainly no politicians can have been more certain of their values than the Cecils, Elliot, and Strachey. Although justifiably esteemed for strength of character and devotion to duty, Goschen and Hicks Beach lacked not only humour, but flexibility.

Chapter 7 THE UNEASY ALLIANCE OF BALFOUR AND CHAMBERLAIN

I

AFTER THE decisive debate of February 1904 the fiscal argument receded in the wake of international events, such as the Russo-Japanese war which had begun on 8 February and the signing of the Anglo-French agreement of 8 April. In anticipation of new challenges arising from the foreign situation, Balfour brought the Committee for Imperial Defence into existence and guided the successful collaboration of Lord Selborne and Admiral Fisher in modernising the navy. The administration also forced through such controversial legislation as the Licensing Act of 1904 and the Aliens Act of 1905.

These achievements were carried out in the midst of fierce party battles over Chamberlain's programme and determined efforts by the Liberals to exploit the fiscal divisions and destroy the government. However, the adherence of the administration to the Sheffield policy during the February fiscal debate had at least broken the free trade threat to Balfour from within his party. After this debate there were no more rumours of a Devonshire ministry. Providing the prime minister did not go beyond retaliation, Hicks Beach, often the duke, and more than half of the free fooders were prepared to support him. Nevertheless, the prime minister remained in a precarious position as he was under unremitting pressure from the Tariff Reformers to adopt the whole Glasgow programme. Balfour was only able to hold steadily to retaliation because, by February, the hopes or fears that Tariff Reform would rapidly sweep the country were dispelled. Even though Tariff Reform failed to appeal to the electorate, Chamberlain continued to add to his already considerable following within the party, and his large group could at any time have destroyed the ministry by abstaining. But as long as Chamberlain maintained his impatient loyalty, and Balfour never retreated from his Sheffield proposals, the demand of the more extreme Tariff Reformers for Chamberlain to force a dissolution was of no avail. Chamberlain had left the administration promising to support it with 'absolute loyalty'. The fact that Austen was Chancellor of the Exchequer put him under additional obligation. Finally, even if he had revolted, Chamberlain could not have, at least before 1906, won the allegiance of a majority of Conservatives in a direct showdown with Balfour.

One thing the prime minister could not prevent was the systematic attempt of the Tariff Reformers to purge the party of all free traders. Balfour was not even able to protect Hugh Cecil from being opposed by a Tariff Reformer at Greenwich. Yet Balfour was strong enough to deny Chamberlain the dissolution he desired as early as January 1904.[1] Despite the desperate pleas and threats of the Tariff Reformers, Balfour advocated the calling of two elections before any fiscal reform would be enacted. Despite protracted 'negotiations' with Chamberlain, Balfour never committed the Unionist party to a general tariff and preference until 1906.

The prime minister regarded fiscal reform as just one of his major responsibilities. His overriding concern throughout the controversy was neither the introduction of fiscal reform nor the maintenance of free trade but that of keeping his party intact. In 1929 Austen Chamberlain recalled to Mrs Dugdale Balfour's indictment of Peel: 'He smashed his party, and no man has a right to destroy the property of which he is a trustee.' Balfour accused Chamberlain of the same irresponsibility. After his resignation from the party leadership in 1911, Sandars spoke of Balfour's bitterness because 'Chamberlain had split the Party in 1903, committed it to a false step in 1909, and split it once more in 1911'.[2]

Balfour's dedication to party unity must not be construed in a narrowly partisan sense for he firmly believed that the Unionist party, dominated by members of his class, was the guardian of the nation's interests. Consequently, he felt it would be a calamity for his administration to disintegrate at a time when Britain faced so many problems. He had no confidence in the Liberals' ability to guide the country and was particularly scornful of Campbell-Bannerman's capabilities for high office. His conviction that the Unionist party alone was fit to rule was stated clearly in an election speech at Nottingham on 15 January 1906 when he claimed that it was the duty of everyone to see that 'the great Unionist Party should still control, whether in power or whether in opposition, the destinies of this great Empire'.

The prime minister was also far more interested in national security than in promoting Tariff Reform. Thus, early in January and February 1904, when the fiscal crisis was reaching a climax, Balfour was rumoured to be totally absorbed in foreign affairs. The successful negotiations of the Anglo-French *Entente* in April 1904 gave his faltering ministry a new lease of life and renewed parliamentary support. Chamberlain, on the other hand, had become fanatical about Tariff Reform, regarding it as the panacea for Britain's domestic and imperial problems. Education, licensing, 'Chinese slavery', or army reform were all either secondary or transitory issues beside the immediate, desperate need to win the country to a policy of thoroughgoing fiscal reform.

Tariff Reformers and free fooders vied for the allegiance of Balfour, members of each side often claiming him for their own. Like many free fooders, however, many of the Tariff Reformers distrusted the prime minister and felt he would play them false. Griffith-Boscawen complained that 'ever since Chamberlain's resignation the government was always taking action inimical to Tariff Reform both in the House and in the country'. Indeed, writing of the fiscal issue during 1904 and 1905, Fraser labelled his chapter on this period 'Balfourism and Betrayal'.

Only Chamberlain's restraining hand prevented Tariff Reform militants from directly attacking Balfour or trying to depose him. Until the autumn of 1905 the struggle between the two men was conducted with strained courtesies, some concessions on both sides, but no break. But the cost of this prolonged stalemate was enormous, for the increasingly overt civil war almost destroyed the party. By November 1905 Chamberlain could no longer stand Balfour's fiscal sophistries and refusal to move beyond

Sheffield. He lashed out in a series of speeches which soon destroyed the ministry. In December, Balfour was forced to resign as it had become impossible to hold his government together.

II

The Tariff Reformers had been dismayed at the concessions made to retain the free fooders in February 1904. In March, when Balfour tried to edge further away from Chamberlain, they determined to present him with an ultimatum indicating the minimum degree of fiscal change he would have to support. These developments took place over the celebrated Wharton amendment.

On 9 March a Liberal member, Pirie, in an attempt to drive a wedge between Balfour and Chamberlain, moved a resolution condemning preferential and protective tariffs. To avoid a dangerous division, the government whips placed an amendment on the order paper, under the name of a backbencher, Wharton, to the effect that the House approved of the government's policy of fiscal reform, which did not include either a general system for protection or preference based on the taxation of food. This was a clever manoeuvre designed to catch all the free fooders. It was also an attempt by the administration to unify the party on Sheffield. There was nothing new in this amendment: both Gerald Balfour and Akers-Douglas had explicitly disclaimed protection and food taxes in the debate in February. However, directly condemning by amendment what Chamberlain had been advocating for nine months was significantly different from individual ministers expressing their opinion that food taxes and protection were not practicable. The Tariff Reformers were furious because they suspected the chief whip's connivance, perhaps even Balfour's hand, behind the amendment. Wharton himself was an amiable ministerialist of 'unsettled' convictions not hitherto known 'as an organiser of private political tiger hunts'.[3]

In Chamberlain's absence his Tariff Reform lieutenants threw down the gauntlet; Griffith-Boscawen and Herbert Maxwell gathered 112 MPs together at a meeting in which the full force of outraged protectionist sentiment was expressed. The chairman, Maxwell, told Balfour that unless the amendment was cancelled the 112 would withdraw their support of the ministry. Balfour thus had the alternative of defying the Tariff Reformers or facing immediate extinction. Much to the derision of free traders, the government withdrew the amendment. The Tariff Reformers had their revenge for the February setback.

Their success, however, was temporary, for in the next fiscal debate the Unionist Free Traders counter-attacked. On 7 May another Liberal backbencher, Black, put down a motion condemning preferential tariffs. In defiance, Chamberlain himself, who had returned from Egypt on 13 April, put down an amendment which substituted for it a vote of confidence in the government. According to Austen's letter to his father, however, the position became serious for

> Beach and the Free Fooders have practically issued an ultimatum that they will not vote to omit Black's words for the purpose of substituting yours. In their numbers on this occasion are included some 20 or more men than voted against us on Pirie's motion, making from 40 to 50 in all or enough probably to put us in a minority. . . .
>
> I left Beach and Balfour together at this point—Beach saying he must have some answer to take to his Free Fooders who are holding a meeting upstairs now.
>
> Beach pretty frankly said that you were so dangerous he would not support any motion which came from you.[4]

In the end because 'the Free Fooders had worked themselves up to a great pitch of excitement . . . refusing to vote for any amendment which stood in Joe's name',[5] Balfour himself put down the amendment. This expedient partially allayed Unionist Free Trade anger for only twenty-two then voted for the Liberal motion.

While observers interpreted the withdrawal of the Wharton amendment as indicating that Balfour was not master in his own house, the crisis over Black's amendment had revealed how the prime minister could retain control by setting one side off against the other. Chamberlain was not prepared to force a showdown. He would resume his public campaign in the autumn. In the meantime, he strengthened his position within the alliance by consolidating his hold over Liberal Unionism.

On 23 March Austen Chamberlain had won a majority in the Liberal Union Club in favour of Tariff Reform. Chamberlain himself on 18 May had 'bearded the lion in his den' by confronting the duke at a meeting of the Liberal Unionist Association. His proposal, that the Council and Association be fused and reorganised on a democratic basis, was carried by a large majority. The duke and his supporters thereupon resigned. Thus ended the collaboration of Devonshire and Chamberlain, once so formidable, which had originated in 1886. Throughout June and July Chamberlain reformed Liberal Unionism, although to keep up the façade of former Whig affiliations he persuaded Lansdowne and Selborne to become vice presidents. So complete did his control become, however, that late in 1905 James lamented to Balfour that 'Liberal Unionism with all its perfect machinery, has . . . been entirely captured'.[6] Meanwhile, Chamberlain's increasing influence within the party as a whole was indicated on 8 July 1904 by the attendance at the unofficial banquet held to celebrate his sixty-eighth birthday. Maxwell and Chaplin brought together 177 MPs to acclaim him and to express their support for preference. Chamberlain's ideas and organisational abilities were thus far more successful inside the Unionist alliance than with the electorate at large. Detailed research into the characteristics of the Chamberlainite MPs is needed before this conundrum can be fully explained.

While Chamberlain gained strength during the spring and early summer of 1904, the government's decision to allow South African mine owners to import indentured Chinese workers to accelerate Rand gold production had stirred up a hornet's nest. By November 1905 there were 47,000 Chinese workers in the Transvaal. The harsh conditions of their transport and their miserable lot of underground toil and restriction to 'horde compounds' raised a wave of revulsion. To allay this opposition the government attempted, unsuccessfully, after 5 May 1904 to bar further parliamentary discussion on the matter. It became apparent that Balfour had committed a grave political blunder in sanctioning Chinese labour. He also had to face the fact that his ministry appeared increasingly decrepit and that the legislation scheduled for the session did not arouse party enthusiasm. Almost every discussion on bills dealing with licensing or army reform was characterised by near-interminable arguing and generally ended by closure. In defiance of the earnest appeals of Balfour and of the whips, large numbers of Unionists simply did not bother to attend the House regularly. Fitzroy recorded on 23 June that William Walrond, a former whip, was

> full of despondence at the position of the government. . . . The demoralisation among the ministerialists is so great that the tacit convention by which no member ever leaves the House except by the main exit is no longer observed and the calculations of the whips are liable to be upset by the discovery that the majority had dribbled away. . . .

Yet despite demoralisation, the government did pass constructive legislation in 1904, such as the Licensing Act, which was intended to reduce the number of public houses while giving compensation to those deprived of licenses by levying a toll on the trade as a whole. More important were the facts (which could not be made public) that during March the Committee of Imperial Defence was being built into the Constitution and Lansdowne and M. Cambon were entering upon the final stage of the negotiations which were to lead to the *Entente Cordiale.*

However dismal his party's condition, Esher's evaluation that the prime minister had lost control proved incorrect. No one in the cabinet contested his authority. Balfour's hold on the majority of the party was strengthened as the Unionists lost by-election after by-election, frightening the average backbencher into supporting him against Liberal demands for a general election. Since Mid-Herts on 13 February none of the nine Unionist candidates at by-elections had declared themselves for Chamberlain because of the unpopularity of food taxes. Then an ultra-Chamberlainite, W. C. Bridgeman, was selected to contest the vacant seat at Oswestry on 26 July and another 'whole hogger' was scheduled to fight North-East Lanark on 10 August. These by-elections would test the extent to which Chamberlain's growth of influence within the party would be reflected in the country.

The prospects seemed favourable to Chamberlain, particularly in North-East Lanark, where according to *The Times* two industries—the iron and steel trades and coal—were suffering from the effects of foreign tariffs. Fitzroy thought Chamberlain by 21 July held 'the key of the Citadel'; could force the government into an acceptance of his terms; and would put substance into his claims after these elections. The results, however, were two crushing defeats for Tariff Reform. In Oswestry, which had been strongly Unionist since becoming a constituency in 1885, the Liberals finally won, and in North-East Lanark the Liberal candidate retained his seat easily.

On 28 July *The Times* commented that the Oswestry election was 'very discouraging for the Unionist party and a legitimate cause for rejoicing in the Liberal camp. The result came as a great surprise to Liberals and Conservatives alike'. To those Unionists who had been asserting that only a more forward Tariff Reform policy would win elections, *The Times* retorted that 'Mr Bridgeman has not fared better than those who took the opposite line'. In the face of these defeats it is difficult to accept Amery's contention that 'July had been a month of uninterrupted success' and that Chamberlain had 'rescued Tariff Reform from the doldrums'. Sandars, who had gone on a tour to assess the condition of the party in the constituencies, reported to Balfour the depressing effects of Tariff Reform:

> Oswestry would have been won but for the 'dear loaf'. We beat them on Chinese labour, we were worsted in the villages on the cry of dear food. . . . Lanark was clearly against us on the fiscal policy. It is Joe's policy that decides these elections, as a rule, not yours . . . and so it will until we say officially that our objective is not food taxes and protection.[6]

At the end of the session the fiscal reformers began to plead with Balfour to go further towards Chamberlain. Despite all the publicity surrounding the preparations for a second autumn campaign, the Tariff Reformers knew they had to get greater support from the prime minister to achieve much success. Austen Chamberlain in a long letter to Balfour on 24 August advocated the resignation of the government and the unification of the party in opposition to lay the foundations for future victory. Austen was certain the unifying policy should be out-and-out Tariff Reform, but granted that Balfour's policy 'need not be my father's. . . . Let it be your own policy . . . but let it be one on which he and his friends can unite with you. . . .' A note of recrimination followed as he claimed that Balfour had 'encouraged my father to go out as a pioneer. . . . Are we now to tell him that we can do no more? That because some forty Free Fooders still hesitate we are unable to move?' He therefore implored Balfour to announce at the National Union meetings in October that he would summon a colonial conference and then take immediate action on the measures proposed.[7] Despite these entreaties Balfour refused to move toward Chamberlain. Sandars scathingly commented that 'you did not encourage Joe to go out as a pioneer. Joe was anxious to get out of office. Evidence of this is overwhelming'. 'Austen's letter', he continued, shows that 'Joe has failed . . . and that he wants to save what he can at some price'. Sandars concluded by advising Balfour to stand firm and wrote that

> Austen now asks you to make a bridge. For whom? Not the great mass of our party. They do not want to walk . . . on any bridge which brings them any nearer to taxation of food, and to the policy of Joe and protection.[8]

Balfour agreed with Sandars and coolly deferred replying to Austen until the latter was on the point of departing on holiday. He also took Acland-Hood's advice not to yield to Chamberlain's request that the Conservative Central Office appoint a representative to the Tariff Reform League. The chief whip maintained that such an appointment 'would be sure to be known and that the Free Fooders would at once say that Joe had finally captured the central office'.[9] Balfour then twice out manoeuvred Joseph Chamberlain to spike the guns of the autumn campaign and to prevent a repetition of May 1903. The first place Chamberlain was scheduled to speak was at Luton on 7 October. With only three days' notice Balfour accepted an engagement to speak at Edinburgh on 3 October, obviously to define his attitude before Chamberlain's speech. Indeed, he had already been advised by Salisbury: 'It is essential that Joe should publicly disapprove of your policy so in the Autumn you should go off before Chamberlain'.[10]

At Edinburgh, Balfour proclaimed his famous two-election policy. The prime minister said that if the Unionists won the next election he would summon a colonial conference to discuss preferential arrangements. If this conference agreed upon a programme, Balfour would call another election. If the Unionist won this second contest, he would enact the programme. Since all but the most optimistic Unionists expected the government to be defeated at the next election, this declaration effectively postponed the implementation of Chamberlain's programme to the distant future. As Hicks Beach cynically commented after Sandars had patiently explained the speech to him, 'both he and Joe would be under ground before anything could be done'.[11] Furthermore, the prime minister went out of his way to state explicitly that he was not and had never been a protectionist and added that if the Unionist party did become protectionist he was not the one to lead. This left no doubt in the minds of most observers that Balfour had told the Chamberlainites that he would quit the leadership of the party rather than submit to the official acceptance of Tariff Reform. The Tariff Reformers were very dissatisfied with the speech and Chamberlain himself 'was furious'.[12] At Luton four days later Chamberlain could only reluctantly agree with Balfour in repudiating the name of protectionist while protesting that he could not 'understand whatever the necessity for the second plebiscite'. In vain later on Austen Chamberlain repeatedly asked Balfour to recant on his two-election policy.

The free fooders placed varying interpretations on the speech —such was the subtlety of Balfour's declaration. Edgar Vincent admitted to Sandars that 'the Duke's mood was one of profound suspicion. He appears to think that you are merely playing . . . cards and are wheedling the party to accept Joe's scheme'. Sandars attributed this attitude to 'the hopeless torpor of the old boy's mind which has been worked upon by every malignant and mischievous seceder whose words have deprived him of any power to be fair to his former friends'. But most of the free fooders agreed with Hicks Beach's reassurances to Devonshire that there was no collusion and that Balfour intended 'to put a check on Tariff Reform agitation'.[13]

The Tariff Reformers still felt they would have another chance to influence the prime minister at the National Union meetings on 28 October at Southampton. Thirteen resolutions at the conference expressed the views of the militant Tariff Reformers. The prime minister's declaration against protection was ignored and the most important Tariff Reform resolution was pieced together from parts of Balfour's former pronouncements to make him appear a thorough fiscal reformer. As a result of this pressure it was anticipated that he would speak at length on the subject. A few nights before, however, on 24 October, ships of the Russian Baltic fleet on their way to the Far East fired on British fishing trawlers which they had mistaken for Japanese torpedo boats. This fiasco created an international incident of some gravity and Balfour used it to devote the whole of his speech to the seriousness of the foreign situation. The *Westminster Gazette* on 28 October mockingly commented that the 'Chamberlainites thought they had cornered Balfour at last but he rode away on the Russian crisis, a most excellent mount for the occasion'.

By the end of 1904 Carrauthers Gould of the *Westminster Gazette*, 'the shrewdest as well as the wittiest political caricaturist of his day', had ceased to depict Chamberlain as the 'Mayor of the Palace' and instead drew him as the 'suppliant at Canossa'.[14] Despite continuous electoral setbacks, Balfour was in a stronger position within his party by early 1905 than he had been a year earlier. On Asquith's fiscal amendment to the Address at the beginning of the 1905 session, only three Unionist Free Traders, as compared to twenty-six in 1904, voted with the Liberals. The prime minister had in no way moved closer to the Glasgow programme in his famous vague speech of 27 January 1905 when, in response to a jeer from John Morley, he summarised his fiscal views on a 'half sheet of notepaper'.

Understandably, Chamberlain was reported by Selborne to be very depressed about the prime minister's evasiveness:

> I spent Sunday with Joe at Highbury—you know how strongly I hold that there should never be a breach between you. Therefore, I report. He is in a hurt frame of mind, a rather old hurt frame of mind. He alluded bitterly to Hood & Wells & said they worked against him everywhere. . . . I told him that was Linky's [Hugh Cecil's] opinion mutatis mutandi. . . . But Arthur you ought to *see* him oftener it all comes from that; he is emotional, he is overworked & he gets down in his luck. . . . He won't ask

> to see you again—you should write him in February and ask him to come and see you.[15]

In an effort to bring more cohesion to the Unionists, Chamberlain finally had to ask for a meeting with the prime minister—so far had Balfour's 'cordiality' of September 1903 diminished.

> Since I resigned about 18 months ago I have had only one serious talk with you about the situation which has necessarily changed much in the interval. Would it not be useful that we should have a free conversation very soon? . . . where we can be alone and absolutely free from interruption.[16]

Balfour agreed and they met on 17 February. No matter how much he agreed that Joe's argument had great weight, he made no concessions about food taxes and the double election, and, as a supplement to what he had urged at the meeting, he wrote down his objections:

> The prejudice against a small tax on food is not the fad of a few imperfectly informed theorists: it is a deep-rooted prejudice affecting the large mass of voters, especially the poorer classes. . . .

The prime minister was certain Chamberlain underrated this hostility, and while Balfour felt that

> the local leaders, the squires, the middle class members of the Associations and so forth are as a rule highly sympathetic to Tariff Reform, and, indeed, often hold protectionist views which I am quite unable to share. . . . [But] the obstacle with which the candidate is confronted is not the opinion of the local leader but the absolute impossibility of inducing the mass of voters to do anything . . . [to] increase the price of bread.[17]

That Tariff Reform had no extensive hold on the electorate was Balfour's trump card in declining to adopt the Glasgow programme. Chamberlain complained, justifiably, that from the electoral point of view the present diversity of opinions in the party was 'the worst . . . that can be conceived'. He protested that he did not understand Balfour's scheme, and that he was holding back the Tariff Reform League from ejecting Hicks Beach's son and Hugh Cecil from their constituencies, but unless Chamberlain was prepared to break up the party he could get no further in making his programme 'official'.

The tension had been heightened because Churchill, who had crossed the floor (in May 1904), moved a resolution on 8 March 1905 condemning preferential tariffs based on the taxation of food. Exploiting the abilities of their new recruit, the Liberals prepared to renew the onslaught in the hope of bringing down the administration. The government only avoided a possible defeat by Lyttelton resorting to the ignominious manoeuvre of moving the previous question. (This was a device by which the government could set aside a motion by claiming that it did not raise a fair issue.) The manoeuvre exasperated many Unionists, and only the hatred many of them felt for Churchill saved the government. By the end of March, Sandars confided to Fitzroy, relations between the prime minister and Chamberlain had 'almost reached breaking point'.

Although they could not force Balfour to adopt the Glasgow programme, the Tariff Reformers could wreak vengeance on the free fooders in the constituencies. The Chamberlainites felt that if this intransigent minority could be extirpated, then the prime minister would surely be coerced into accepting their demands. By February 1905 the *Westminster Gazette* claimed that fifty Unionist Free Traders had been attacked. In fact, according to an important memorandum drawn up by Robert Cecil, only twenty-five were under assault.[18]

The most celebrated clash occurred over Hugh Cecil. Because of his prestige in the party and kinship with Balfour, he was a special target. Moreover, in the Commons on 18 May 1904 he had accused Chamberlain of physical cowardice, thereby going farther 'even' than Chamberlain's 'worst enemies'.[19] On 17 February 1905, Acland-Hood sent a letter to the Greenwich Conservative Association, which had recently asked Cecil to retire, extolling the high qualities of their MP and asking the organisation to reconsider its decision. Chamberlain interfered, however, with a letter of his own to the association members, calling on them to throw the free fooder out. In the end Chamberlain won, for Cecil contested the 1906 election without the support of his association and against a Tariff Reformer.

While Balfour and the Central Office helplessly watched the struggle in the constituencies, Austen Chamberlain on 9 March attempted to persuade the prime minister to excommunicate all the Unionist Free Traders. Using Lambton as a case in point, he noted that the free fooder

> not only voted against the Government in spite of your strong and earnest appeal for support, but he went out of his way to say that he did not accept the Government policy. . . .

Chamberlain complained that Lambton 'appears to me more dangerous than an open foe'. Would not Balfour instruct Acland-Hood to secure a candidate who at least accepts Sheffield for that would 'lay the foundations for future victory and future union'.[20]

Lambton was not 'excommunicated'. In these constituency conflicts Balfour felt a spiritual sympathy for the free fooders. But in the face of increasing Tariff Reform hostility and renewed Liberal initiative, he no longer felt able to hold his party together when free trade resolutions were moved. A Liberal backbencher, Ainsworth, informed the government on 18 March that he was going to move a resolution on Wednesday, 22 March, condemning a 10 per cent general tariff. Sandars informed Balfour that 'Hood says he cannot get a majority to defeat the motion'.[21] This information resulted in two troubled cabinet meetings on 20 and 21 March.

As a result of this predicament the cabinet decided to advise their supporters to abstain from voting on the Ainsworth motion. According to Fitzroy, Balfour asked for cabinet unanimity on the decision: 'Had there been any secessions, Mr Balfour had resolved to go.' In response to Austen's request that his father tell him what course to follow, a pencilled annotation notes that Joseph Chamberlain advised him to make up his own mind, and Austen had replied: 'This is indeed drinking to the dregs of the cup of bitterness and I have consented to drain it with my colleagues.' His father accepted his decision but he cannot have been happy for on 14 March he had written to Mrs Endicott that he thought:

> a defeat of the Government possible at any time, & I do not wish to avoid it. . . . I should like to see whether we cannot, in opposition, bring our party more into line.[22]

Ainsworth's resolution was carried by the Liberals, supported by thirty-five Unionist Free Traders, 254 to 2. Sandars, Fitzroy recorded, was 'jubilant over the success of the Prime Minister's action and the progress it marked in the gradual isolation of Chamberlain'.

In the face of these rebuffs Chamberlain came to London to restrain his more extreme followers from open attack on Balfour. On 10 April he began holding a series of parliamentary meetings. To impress Balfour with the strength of his following, Chamberlain on 14 April led a deputation of 142 MPs to present a memorandum to the prime minister requesting him to clarify his ambiguities. Balfour promised a reply after Easter. His answer led to intense negotiations between Balfour and Chamberlain during the last fortnight in May.

Drawing mainly from a memorandum by Maxwell, who was present at the discussions, one account presents a lucid summary of the talks illustrating Balfour's ambivalent and devious treatment of the Tariff Reformers. On 16 May Chamberlain, accompanied by Maxwell, met with Balfour and Lansdowne. Chamberlain apparently was not optimistic, for just before they gathered he told Maxwell that he expected 'precious little' as things were 'going very badly'. To their surprise the prime minister said that 'whatever happened, Tariff Reform, including Colonial Preference must be *the* foremost article in the Unionist programme', and 'he accepted . . . an all-round tariff on imports'. In response to Maxwell's request, that if there was no dissolution until after the colonial conference scheduled for 1906 Balfour would go to the country on the resolutions passed at the conference, the prime minister seemed agreeable. In the evening of 17 May they met again, and Balfour appeared just as conciliatory.

The prime minister's unexpected compliance was of brief duration. Apparently, he soon 'caved in' under pressure from a free food delegation protesting to him against his concession of agreeing to telescope the Edinburgh policy into a single election programme. Their objections were reinforced by Lansdowne, who on 18 May, had written a long letter to Balfour deprecating any 'treaty for announcement to the party' since it would be 'regarded as a capitulation rather than a compromise'.[23]

Convinced by these arguments (or given the excuse) to retreat,

Balfour on 26 May informed Chamberlain that he could not allow a colonial conference to assemble before an election. Nevertheless, the prime minister still was prepared to stress the primary importance of Tariff Reform, especially in its colonial aspect, to the House the next day and at his impending Albert Hall speech. Balfour really felt, however, he had given little away. He wrote to Hugh Cecil in the eve of the 29 May debate:

> If the debate takes an anti-Joe turn please do not improve the occasion by attacking him. This may be excusable when things are going his way . . . but it is both un-Christian and foolish when they are not.[24]

In fact, Balfour did not speak in parliament on 29 May for, according to Acland-Hood, he was 'suffering from a severe chill'. The prime minister was still expected to announce the terms of the 'Eirenicon' on 5 June to a meeting of the National Union at the Albert Hall. However, to the chagrin of the already disappointed Tariff Reformers, the prime minister merely announced that Tariff Reform was the first point in the Unionist programme. Chamberlain remained patient and claimed publicly that he understood Balfour as saying that 'Tariff Reform would be the most important part of Unionist policy and that colonial preference would be the first item in a future Unionist programme'.

Unionist Free Traders were astonished at the interpretation Chamberlain put on Balfour's words. The prime minister told Wyndham's sister, Lady Elcho, that Chamberlain's interpretation of the Albert Hall speech 'has driven the Free Fooders wild'.[25] In the Commons on 7 June, Hugh Cecil replied to Chamberlain's allusion, that those who would not accept Tariff Reform should leave the party, with the insult that Unionist Free Traders would not depart 'at the bidding of one, who . . . was, after all, in his origin, only an alien immigrant'. Cecil was violently angry at Chamberlain's 'annexation' of the prime minister:

> he affirms that you have made Colonial Preference the first article in the party programme!!!! and winds up by hoping that every 'bigoted' Cobdenite who does not agree with him (like me) will leave the country. Insolent scamp. I who remember him preaching disestablishment and the doctrine of ransom.

With characteristic insouciance Balfour replied to his cousin's somewhat hysterical letter five weeks later:

> As regards Joe, I have not read his speech yet but I gather from reports that it does not conduce to peace. I really do not know which is worst—the right or the left wing of the party.[26]

Balfour was determined to play down the fiscal issue as he was immersed in foreign affairs. The *Entente* appeared increasingly essential when the Germans brought about the first Moroccan Crisis in May and June 1905. On 1 June, Britain's ally, Japan, annihilated the Russian Baltic fleet in the Tsushima Straits. But the 1902 Alliance was maintained without seriously endangering the *Entente* for in August the English and French fleets exchanged visits which were highly popular. Moreover, Balfour's need for time, to see the artillery equipped with new quick-firing guns, also encouraged him to perpetuate his fiscal subtleties.

There was also important domestic legislation to be enacted. An attempt to cope with growing unemployment in London was made by the Unemployed Workmen Bill. The principle was to assist 'respectable workmen' temporarily out of work to get new jobs by setting up a local organisation in each metropolitan borough and a central organisation for the whole of London. More controversial was the Aliens Act which prohibited as immigrants all lunatics, idiots, financial insolvents, and criminals (apart from political offenders). Both measures were calculated to win the sympathy of many in the working classes who felt threatened by trade fluctuations and by the competition of foreign immigrants. Balfour also planned to ask parliament in 1906 to effect a redistribution by which Ireland would lose thirty seats.

In the spring of 1905, observers were startled to read an article in the June issue of *Nineteenth Century* by Wilfred Ward, the prominent Catholic apologist and biographer of Cardinal Newman, called 'A Political Fabius Maximus'. The article eulogised the prime minister and asserted that he had seen the impracticability of Chamberlain's plans from the beginning and had used Fabian tactics to defeat the Tariff Reformer. Ward included some harsh criticism of Chamberlain's impulsiveness, of his 'overwrought nerves', and of his attempts to saddle the party with a rigid programme. Finally, he traced the relationship between the two men from the Wharton amendment to the 'walking out' tactics of March 1905 and concluded that Balfour had won his victory over Chamberlain.

This article was greeted with much cynicism by many free fooders, who neither believed Chamberlain had been defeated by the prime minister nor that Balfour disagreed with the Tariff Reformer's ultimate aims. In fact, the article was a clever piece of Balfourian propaganda, for in September 1905 Elliot was astonished when Ward called on him and 'said Arthur Balfour urged him to write the article and Sandars went through the proofs carefully before the article was sent to *Nineteenth Century*. . . .'[27]

III

While Balfour dallied with the Tariff Reformers and the free fooders and prepared to lead the government for yet another session, Chamberlain was getting ready to launch open war. He was sixty-nine and could not afford to wait much longer. Moreover, Balfour's decision in May against holding a colonial conference before an election had been irritating enough, but when the prime minister informed him that there would not be a dissolution before the spring Chamberlain's patience gave way. His frustration was increased as he had been unable to penetrate the central organisation of the Conservative party. Acland-Hood told Sandars, he was

> a bit sick of Joe's complaints. He has been trying all along to break into the central office. He tried first to seduce the cook (me), then he tried the kitchen maid (Wells), and now he is trying it on with the lady of the House (AJB). . . . Well, he won't get in.[28]

Even before the direct attacks on Balfour, Sandars was writing anxiously to his chief about Chamberlain's men preparing to make trouble at the forthcoming National Union meeting. It was a speech by the unfortunate Londonderry which finally caused Chamberlain to speak out against the prime minister. On 1 November at Sunderland, Londonderry spoke of the dangerous split in the party and blamed it on Chamberlain's policy. On

3 November, Chamberlain lashed out savagely in reply, ostensibly at Londonderry but really at Balfour. In his speech he described as 'humiliating' the prime minister's tactic of allowing the Liberals to pass fiscal resolutions by advising Unionists to disregard them. After this outburst the two Unionist leaders became openly hostile. On 11 November, Balfour, who was staying with Londonderry, gave a speech in which he devoted much praise to the latter.

The battle continued at the National Union meetings at Newcastle on 14 November. Chaplin's amendment for preference and a general tariff was carried by 698 votes to 2. Ward Humphries' amendment to it, that the conference should simply declare the 'half sheet of notepaper' sufficient, was overwhelmingly defeated, securing only eight votes. In addition, a resolution criticising the party organisation and clearly aimed at the leadership of Balfour and Acland-Hood was carried. Balfour attempted to conciliate neither the Tariff Reformers nor the free fooders. Rather whimsically, he merely commented that he was not afraid of the opposition but was 'afraid of his friends'.

Chamberlain put the seal on his capture of the National Union when he spoke at a Liberal Unionist rally at Bristol on 21 November. Maintaining he was loyal to the prime minister, he nevertheless scathingly commented that 'no army was ever led successfully to battle on the principle that the lamest man should govern the march of the army'. This last attack made it impossible for Balfour to continue. On 4 December Balfour resigned to make way for the Liberals thinking that the feuds within the Liberal party were so profound that Campbell-Bannerman would be unable to form a government.

Chapter 8 THE UNDERMINING OF THE UNIONIST FREE TRADERS

I

THE UNIONIST FREE TRADERS in the years 1904–5 represented a divided group strategically outmanoeuvred by Balfour and mercilessly hounded by Chamberlain. During the long Unionist twilight after February 1904 Balfour's skill in restraining Chamberlain largely accounted for the relative passivity and confusion of the Unionist Free Traders. The prime minister's refusal to adopt the whole Chamberlain programme enabled most of them to keep at least a tenuous connection with the party. Their loyalties were illustrated by the fact that immediately after the fiscal debate on 17 February 1904 only nine voted against the government on the first Chinese Labour debate. Indeed, Sandars reported with relief to Balfour after this division that the free fooders were only revolting in force on the fiscal question.[1]

The allegiance of most Unionist Free Traders, however, was severely tested by the crisis over the Wharton amendment. When the government whips announced the amendment, leading free fooders such as Ritchie and George Hamilton advised abstention on the original Liberal motion. Great was the Unionist Free Trade consternation when the Tariff Reformers' ultimatum forced Balfour to withdraw the government amendment. Consequently, the administration was once more shaken by a revolt in the division on the motion of the Liberal Pirie. Twenty-five Unionist Free Traders voted with the Liberals, nineteen abstained, and only seven followed Hicks Beach in supporting the government.

Two general conclusions about the free fooders can be drawn from their crisis. First, it appeared unlikely that even under great provocation more than twenty-five to thirty free fooders would be prepared to vote against the government. Secondly, the decisive show of Chamberlainite strength finally determined a number of young militants to leave their party and join the Liberals. Giving as reasons the withdrawal of the Wharton amendment and his hatred of Chinese 'slavery', Jack Seely on 17 March announced he would resign his seat in protest and stand again as a Unionist Free Trader. Since James had arranged with Herbert Gladstone that the Liberal candidate would retire, Seely was re-elected unopposed. On his reintroduction into the House by his brother and Elliot there was tremendous cheering from the Liberals and Unionist Free Traders.[2] When, however, on 30 March he dramatically announced his resignation from the Conservative party, such an uproar ensued that Seely could not be heard. Churchill, who tried to appeal to the Speaker to restore order, only managed to get a few sentences out.

This noisy incident demonstrated Unionist anger at those free fooders who changed sides. The venom of Tariff Reformers was especially directed against Churchill whose provocations, such as 'thank God we have a Liberal party', had justifiably stirred their wrath. This indignation led to a disorderly scene in the Commons on 7 April. As Churchill started to speak, Balfour left the chamber, probably as a calculated snub. When Churchill protested to the Speaker, all the Unionists except the free fooders followed the prime minister. Some stopped at the doors to jeer at Churchill. Only Gorst spoke on his behalf, execrating his fellow Tories for behaviour they should have desisted from at least out of respect for the late Lord Randolph.

Thereafter, the only logical step for Churchill was to join the Liberals. During the Easter recess of 1904 he accepted an invitation to stand as a Liberal for North-West Manchester at the next election, having previously rejected invitations from half a dozen other constituencies to run as an independent free trader. The prospect of identifying his fortunes with the citadel of free trade had 'fired his imagination'.[3] He had in fact been preceded in his change of party by his cousin Ivor Guest who had announced in *The Times* on 7 April that he would contest Cardiff as a Liberal at the next election.

Of the seventeen Unionist Free Traders who became Liberals only four went on to play a major political role. As Lord D'Abernon, Edgar Vincent in 1920 was the first British ambassador to the Weimar Republic. Dickson Poynder became Governor of New Zealand in 1910 and during the war was first Under Secretary of State for the Colonies from 1914 to 1915 and then Under Secretary of State for India. Seely became Secretary for War in 1910 and held the position until forced to resign at the time of the Curragh 'mutiny'. In 1906, Churchill was amply rewarded, not only for his defence of free trade but also for his election campaign, with the position of Under Secretary of State for the Colonies. With the Colonial Secretary, Elgin, in the Lords this meant that Churchill, Asquith at the Exchequer, and Lloyd George at the Board of Trade held the key positions in the Liberal government against Tariff Reform attacks in the Commons.

These defections weakened the Unionist Free Traders in a number of significant ways. The Hughligans ceased to exist as five of them became Liberals. After Beckett succeeded his uncle as Lord Grimthorpe only Hugh Cecil remained active of that energetic band that had been labelled a new fourth party early in 1903. Robert Cecil expressed the anger of Tory free traders at Churchill's change of party and at the actions of Dickson Poynder who tried to get the Unionist Free Trade Club to pass resolutions on rigid free trade lines, thereby making a deeper breach with the ministerialists. He accused Dickson Poynder of using

> the Club as a recruiting agency for the other side. He means to join them and naturally wishes to take over as many of his friends as he can. Such men do the Unionist Free Traders great harm. Winston's career blacked our face very much and if the Club is to be run by his imitators it will be the most powerful asset to Chamberlain that has yet been discovered.[4]

Finally, the fact that those who crossed the floor were mainly young men meant that the Unionist Free Traders were increasingly a group of old politicians. (For example, Hicks Beach was the 'father' of the House—a position which Kennaway inherited after 1906, while Powell was seventy-seven in 1904—the oldest man in the House.)

As Balfour perceptibly withstood much of Chamberlain's pressure, it became more difficult for the Unionist Free Traders to agree on voting against the government. On the other hand, when Chamberlain aggressively demonstrated his power—as over his final capture of the Liberal Unionists on 18 May—large numbers of free fooders were prepared to vote against Balfour. The same day as this Tariff Reform success the House divided on John Black's fiscal resolution condemning taxation of food and welcoming 'the declarations of Ministers that the Government is opposed to such taxation'. Up to the day of the debate it was generally understood that the government meant to allow its supporters to vote as they pleased and the Unionist Free Traders intended to support Black. But under Tariff Reform pressure, Balfour at the last moment informed them that he considered the motion one of lack of confidence, and Acland-Hood put a three-line whip on the Unionists. This government decision threw the Unionist Free Traders into confusion and at a meeting of the Free Food League to consider the new situation no unanimous decision could be agreed upon. Despite the duke's advice to support the amendment, only twenty-two voted against the government.

The duke was always most aggressive when Chamberlain took direct steps to annex the Liberal Unionists—hence his advice to all free fooders to vote for Black's motion. When Chamberlain on 10 June 1904 displayed his new Liberal Unionist Council, adorned by Lansdowne and Selborne, the duke made another of his spasmodic major efforts. He published an open letter on 2 July calling on all voters to support the Liberal candidate at the forthcoming Chertsey by-election. This manifesto differed from the earlier Lewisham letter in advising electors to vote for the Liberal and not just to withhold votes from the Tariff Reformer. Much to the duke's humiliation, the Tariff Reformers—as in the case of Lewisham—held the seat.

Unionist Free Trade belligerency oscillated with the barometer of Chamberlain's fortunes. Since from July 1904 to June 1905 he made no progress in the country and appeared checked by Balfour, the Unionist Free Traders were relatively passive. Indeed, *The Times* on 12 August 1904 remarked that 'at the close of the Session it is impossible to indicate the exact numerical strength of the Unionist free fooders in the House of Commons'. Although *The Times* noted that forty-one Unionist Free Traders had so far voted against the government at least once on fiscal divisions, many others had consistently abstained, thus giving no clear indication of whether or not they were out-and-out free traders.

At the nadir of Chamberlain's fortunes during February and March 1905, the Unionist Free Traders showed scarcely any activity at all. On the Liberal amendment to the Address at the beginning of the 1905 session only three free fooders—Elliot, Dickson Poynder, and Richard Cavendish—voted with the opposition, and five (including Hugh Cecil) walked out. Asquith had moved the amendment which asked for a dissolution, and Hugh Cecil made a most eloquent speech, criticising Chamberlain but supporting Balfour. As Edward Hamilton recorded in his Diary, the free fooders were guided in their decision to support the government by the fear that 'they would be playing Chamberlain's game if they put the government out.'[5] In the *Spectator* Strachey advanced another reason for the reluctance of the free fooders to vote with the Liberals since they insisted on 'attacking the seats of the Unionist Free-traders'. It was just before this fiscal debate that Devonshire had addressed a frank letter to Elliot forbidding a Unionist Free Trade fiscal amendment:

> You suggested the possibility of our moving an amendment of our own on the Address. . . . I can see nothing to be gained by such a move, which I think will only tend further to break up the F. T. Unionists and alienate a section of them. . . . I am not sure that we did not go too far last Session in constantly voting against the Govt., wh. may be a filip [*sic*] for our feelings, but tends to alienate Unionist F. T. opinion, and does not conciliate the Opposition.

The duke elaborated on what he thought the future role of the Unionist Free Traders would be:

> I have pointed out over and over again that the circumstances are altogether different from those of /86 when L. Unionists were prepared to enter into a virtual alliance with Conservatives . . . . [and] our business seems to me to keep together a sound centre of the Free Trade Opinion in the party to wh. it may gravitate back after the experience of the election.[6]

However, when Balfour in March 1905 refused to take the opportunity of dissociating himself further from Chamberlain, many Unionist Free Traders once more became aggressive. Their belligerence resulted from Balfour's policies regarding Churchill's motion of 8 March, condemning food taxes, and Ainsworth's motion of 22 March, condemning a general tariff. Their first protest came on Balfour's attempt to outflank Churchill's motion by moving the previous question. The free fooders were outraged by this 'unprecedented proceeding against a private member's resolution on a private member's night'. However, although Hicks Beach thought the prime minister had behaved 'very badly', he and the Cecil-dominated group refused to vote against the government.

Since the Unionist Free Traders had drawn away from the Liberals, Hicks Beach by 1905 had reasserted some of his influence over the less aggressive members. On 18 March 1905 Fitzroy wrote of Hicks Beach's tacit understanding with Balfour by which he would support the government and try to hold the free fooders in line provided that the prime minister did not go beyond Sheffield. More militant free traders continued to distrust Hicks Beach. Many felt as Elliot that his only strong feeling was dislike of Chamberlain and, holding this limited attitude on the fiscal question, Hicks Beach 'rendered all strong action by the League impossible'.

Balfour survived the division on 9 March by forty-two when few expected the majority to exceed twenty. The fact that only fifteen Unionist Free Traders voted against the government is surprising since many of them were antagonised by a tactic Balfour had employed just before the division. He sent a confidential letter to the free fooders and authorised Hayes Fisher, his spy in the free food ranks, to read it. After much arguing the Unionist Free Traders declined to hear the letter for the reason that it could not then be kept confidential. This was supposed to be a private decision. The free fooders were therefore astonished on 17 March to read the leading article in the *Daily Telegraph* accusing them of insulting the prime minister by refusing to hear his letter. Elliot expressed their resentment:

> Whoever sent the story untrue and unfair as it was betrayed the confidence of all of us and was evidently motivated by

> malicious feelings against James, Goschen and G. Hamilton who were singled out for abuse. . . . These Free Food meetings are worse than useless if confidences cannot be kept.[7]

Consequently, when Ainsworth's motion against a general tariff came up ten days later, the free fooders were in a very obstreperous mood. In the face of this hostility and because of the disintegration in his own ranks, Balfour adopted the expedient of leading the bulk of his party out of the House of Commons.

The Unionist Free Traders did not maintain this aggressive behaviour for they knew, as did everybody, that Balfour's walking-out manoeuvre was a rebuff to Chamberlain. Indeed, from March until July 1905, the Unionist Free Traders were clearly dominated by the views of those who wanted to collaborate closely with Balfour, notably the Cecils and Hicks Beach. The most striking result of this attitude was Hugh Cecil's memorandum early in April 1905 which suggested the publication of a manifesto signed by leading Unionist Free Traders subscribing to Balfour's views as expressed at Sheffield and Edinburgh. He advocated driving a deeper wedge between Balfour and Chamberlain. The idea was dropped because the duke and Goschen strenuously objected not only to proclaiming publicly such fiscal views, but also because they had no faith in such a declaration separating Balfour and Chamberlain. As Goschen said to Devonshire, he was 'dead against publication. I think it will weaken the Unionist Free Traders. . . . It will not stiffen Balfour and I don't believe it will have the slightest effect on him'.[8] Even after Chamberlain claimed at St Helen's on 3 June that he welcomed the prime minister's lead on Tariff Reform, the Cecil-Hicks Beach connection took no action although Hugh Cecil protested vigorously in private to Balfour. During the summer of 1905 an open division of the Unionist Free Traders seemed likely. In July Elliot wrote:

> It will hardly be possible to keep the Cecil party long, which is strongly Balfourian, in harmony with the majority of the Club which long ago despaired of Balfour as any check upon Chamberlain. I told the Duke that there was a good deal of dissatisfaction in the Club with the Cecil policy.[9]

II

The reason the Unionist Free Traders did not break up in 1905 is that the warfare Chamberlain waged against them in the constituencies kept them together in self-defence. As early as 13 January 1904, Ratcliffe Cousins, a prominent member of the Tariff Reform League, claimed in *The Times* that the League 'is by resolution determined to oppose the return of all Free Traders whether Unionist or Radical, and we shall use the whole of our organisation for this object'. Early in 1905 Robert Cecil complained to Sandars that he did not think Balfour had 'a glimmering of what has been going on in the constituencies'. He 'demanded' that the prime minister make some public reprobation of the attempts of the Tariff Reform League to proscribe Unionist Free Traders.

In the memorandum Robert Cecil circulated to Balfour and to leading Unionist Free Traders, it was pointed out that Tariff Reform attacks had been made on the seats of twenty-five free fooders and, as Cecil elaborated, this was by no means an exhaustive list. In addition, seven Unionist Free Traders, of whom the most important was Hicks Beach, only escaped attack by announcing they would withdraw from the House before the next election. Cecil granted that some of the attacks were made on 'bad party men' but maintained they were not attacked for their 'party delinquencies' but only after they had declared themselves free traders. Cecil claimed that Chamberlain had taken a personal part in 'stirring up opposition' to Unionist Free Traders:

> (1) He avowed in the House of Commons that he had tried to persuade [Henry Page] Croft to stand as a Tariff Reformer against Abel Smith in Hertford. . . .
>
> (2) He wrote to [Jack] Hills endorsing his candidature against Elliot though at that time the local organisation had neither rejected Elliot nor adopted Hills.

In a memorandum composed soon after the 1906 election, Acland-Hood replied to Cecil's accusations. He noted that six of the twenty-five had become Liberals. Of the five that retired, he claimed, rather ingenuously, that fiscal opinion in their constituencies rather than Tariff Reform League pressure had determined their departure. He observed that in another five cases the Tariff Reform League had withdrawn. Indeed, he believed that 'in nearly every case' where the candidate asked the Tariff Reformers to withdraw they complied. He could not say the same for the free fooders, for they

> addressed meetings in constituencies where they were not wanted by the Party; many of these meetings were organised by and almost entirely attended by Radicals. I think a careful analysis would show that the F. F. Kettle was considerably blacker than the T. R. L. pot.[10]

Chamberlain claimed that he had justification for his attacks since, with the Lewisham letter, the Unionist Free Traders had been first to declare open warfare. This was only an excuse, however; letter or no letter, Chamberlain was determined to purge the party of free traders. He defiantly acknowledged Hugh Cecil's accusation in the House of Commons that he had tried to persuade Page Croft to stand as a Tariff Reformer against Abel Smith in Hertford. In direct contravention of Acland-Hood's letter asking the Greenwich association to support Cecil, Chamberlain wrote a letter to endorse the Tariff Reform candidate, Hamilton Bridges Benn. He was so angry at the Chief Whip's intervention, according to Amery, that he ordered the Tariff Reform League 'to do everything in our power to help Benn'.

The form of the Tariff Reform purge is illustrated by Elliot's case at Durham City. On 19 September 1903, he resigned his position as financial secretary to the Treasury. Two days later he pessimistically reflected in his journal that he would probably lose his seat because of the militant protectionist feelings of members of his association. On 23 October after his association expressed itself dissatisfied with his letter explaining his resignation, he went to Durham to defend himself. Then in January 1904 a branch of the Tariff Reform League was formed in the constituency to organise opposition against him. In December 1904 two Unionist MPs, Seton Karr and Sir George Doughty, held a Tariff Reform meeting against Elliot. In January 1905, Jack Hills, a Tariff Reformer completely unknown to the area, was adopted by the association, and Elliot was thereby disowned.

The final outcome of this struggle was that at the 1906 election Elliot stood as a Unionist Free Trader supported by the Liberals. Hills had telegrams of support from both Chamberlain and Balfour at the election.

The pattern of Elliot's ejection and defeat was repeated in an essentially similar way with many of the free fooders. There were a few exceptions. For example, George Goschen complained that because he had told his constituents he was opposed to food taxes a Tariff Reformer was accepted two days later by his association. His indignation was increased since both Gerald Balfour and Akers-Douglas had spoken against taxation of food in the February fiscal debate. No doubt because of Lord Goschen's past services, Acland-Hood and the central office found the son another seat at Bolton.

The Unionist Free Traders had three courses open to them in their attempts to counter Chamberlain's attacks. They could appeal to Balfour for help, as the Cecils did; they could look to the Liberals for constituency support; or they could launch a counter-offensive against Tariff Reform candidates. The first course was ineffectual. By 1906, Balfour could do little to help Unionist Free Traders even though Acland-Hood had pleaded to Sandars that 'under no circumstances ought Hugh Cecil to be opposed', for he was 'our best card amongst the young men against Winston Churchill'.[11]

Balfour indicated both his helplessness and his anger at the internecine struggle when he replied to one of Hugh Cecil's numerous requests that he assist harassed Unionist Free Traders:

> Just as I think Chamberlain has done much injury to what I believe to be his fundamental object—Imperial Unity—by his attempts to harness all sorts of particular and selfish interests to his Imperial car; so I think the free fooders have also done great injury to free trade by their appeals to ignorance and prejudice and by the exaggerated importance they have given to any objections that may be made to a re-arrangement of our duties on food.

The prime minister claimed that not only had Unionist Free Traders 'aided our opponents', but also averred that 'some of them have been as much animated by distrust and even hatred of Joe as by a scientific ardour for truth'.[12]

running candidates against us. Lord James is evidently on the same tack. I think they are throwing away the position for the sake of keeping with us the timid and half-hearted men. The Duke ought to be the head and soul of the Free Traders on the Unionist side.[15]

III

The unwillingness to wage all-out war against Chamberlain showed the great weakness of the Unionist Free Trade organisation. The Free Food League, launched with such initial enthusiasm, soon became ineffective through the inactivity of many members and the attempts of Hicks Beach to render it politically innocuous. Indeed, by March 1904, he was trying to resign from the organisation he had founded, and was only prevailed upon to remain by the entreaties of the other vice presidents. However, although he agreed to stay on as a vice president, Hicks Beach said he was so disillusioned with politics he would 'simply stand aside'. Subsequently, in January 1905, Hicks Beach suggested to Devonshire that 'the only thing to be done is to let it [the League] drop quietly out of existence'. By early 1905 the duke himself was disconsolate, remarking to Elliot that he had been 'practically maintaining the Free Food League' and that he 'must continue to do so as long as the organisation exists'.[16] The scale of the duke's expenditure on the League does not appear to have been very high. On 11 August 1904 the secretary of the Free Food League, Manners Sutton, gratefully acknowledged the duke's cheque of £500 which was part payment of the latter's subscription to the League.

Many free fooders besides Hicks Beach were not sorry to see it absorbed into the Unionist Free Trade Club which had formally been brought into existence on 1 December 1904. Until it was dissolved in mid-1910 the Club was the centre of their activities. After 1905 it was the only Unionist organisation or social club not to be linked to Tariff Reform. Since the fortunes and weaknesses of the Unionist Free Traders are so closely bound up with this Club, its origins must be traced in some detail.

It was started by the Liberal Unionists Elliot and Strachey, and its inception directly related to Chamberlain's final capture of the Liberal Union Club. After Chamberlain called the meeting of the Liberal Unionist Council in February 1904 to discuss fiscal reform, the duke and his Whig friends boycotted the meetings but did not resign from any Liberal Unionist organisations. The Tariff Reformers continued their efforts to force all the free traders out of the Liberal Unionist Association. On 23 March 1904, Austen Chamberlain, Selborne, and Arnold Forster carried a fiscal resolution at the annual meeting of the Liberal Union Club. They defeated Elliot's amendment declaring the neutrality of the Club on the tariff question by seventy-two votes to forty.

Immediately after this encounter Elliot and Strachey sent out circulars to all Liberal Unionist Free Traders inquiring whether they would consider setting up an organisation. Nothing, however, was done until the duke formally retired from the old Liberal Unionist Association at the meeting of 18 May 1904. The real issue had been whether the association should be transformed from an aristocratic into a democratic body. Chamberlain claimed that party policy on the fiscal issue should be determined by the choice of the local associations while the duke protested that such an important question could not be solved merely by a majority vote among the rank and file.[17] Then on 12 June the 'new' Liberal Unionist Council, with Chamberlain as president, was announced. When the Liberal Union Club met on 29 June 1904 to pass a verdict on Chamberlain's reconstruction, Elliot moved an amendment against approval which was rejected by 108 votes to sixty-four. After this result, in the words of Sir Henry Lucy, Elliot 'sprang to his feet' and led the dissenting members into another committee room to found a Unionist Free Trade Club open to both Liberal Unionists and Conservatives.[18]

At the beginning the Club was a Liberal Unionist organisation in which Conservatives only slowly, and reluctantly, took part. For example, Hugh Cecil only joined on 10 July 1905, and another Conservative, Abel Smith, became a member in 1909 after the Tariff Reformers had ejected him from his seat. The duke himself also held aloof from the Club at first. He was influenced by James who had been left sitting when Elliot led his troop out and was furious at what he thought was a premature action. However, after Chamberlain announced the membership in his new association on 14 July both James and the duke became enthusiastic about the Club and the duke agreed to become president.

On 1 December 1904 the Club was brought into formal existence and the first general meeting was held on 10 April 1905. Devonshire became president and George Hamilton, Balfour of Burleigh, Ritchie, and James were named vice presidents. The real work, however, was done by Elliot who was Chairman of the Executive Committee. At the height of its influence in 1905 the Club had over 320 members including a distinguished galaxy of peers.[19] As a rallying point for free traders in the Unionist party, the Club remained a continual vexation to Chamberlain. However, like the Free Food League, the later organisation never approached the power and influence of the Tariff Reform League.

With only twenty-nine MPs joining, the new institution was markedly less well represented in parliament than the old Free Food League had been. The Club never had resources comparable to those possessed by the Tariff Reform League. Elliot noted on 1 March 1905 that subscriptions amounted to £3,000 with £2,000 promised annually.[20] Although many Unionist Free Traders were very wealthy—Devonshire was the richest man in England—they never seriously attempted to harness their own and other financial resources for free trade. Because they did not form a definite party they were never able or willing to tap the funds of the great free trade interests in England.

Some of their financial stringency arose from the attitudes of men like Sir Henry King, a wealthy Hull banker, who refused to contribute to a fund-raising campaign in January 1909. King replied cantankerously to Robert Cecil's inquiry about help:

> I do not understand the object of your appeal. I was under the impression that the Unionist Free Trade M.P.'s were all pretty well off & well able to take care, each of his own cabbage patch. . . . I am not prepared to contribute to a plan of aggression against Tariff Reformers. . . . I seek peace within the party, not a sword . . . [and so] I have deliberately stood aloof from the Unionist Free Trade League [*sic*].[21]

Another cause of the financial weakness of the Club was the dilemma Cromer described to Hugh Cecil:

> On the one hand we cannot fight unless we have money, on the other hand we cannot get any money unless we show a disposition to fight. Hence, we are rather moving in a vicious circle.[22]

The inhibiting financial circumstances of the Unionist Free Traders were illustrated in their problems concerning the press. Many Conservative Free Traders were dissatisfied that the *Spectator* was their only press outlet apart from the *Edinburgh Review*, edited by Elliot. The *Standard*, while not specifically representing the Unionist Free Trade point of view, was the only Unionist daily hostile to Chamberlain. However, late in 1904, much to the chagrin of the free fooders, Arthur Pearson purchased the *Standard* and annexed it to the Tariff Reform machine. Pearson was a powerful newspaper magnate who owned the *Daily Express*. He also was the Chairman of the Executive Committee of the Tariff Reform League. Sandars reported to Balfour the Unionist Free Trade alarm about the transaction: 'Beach came in to see me yesterday evening in full cry about the "Standard".' Sandars also reported that William Galloway, Unionist Free Trade MP for South-West Manchester, had 'offered to find £60,000' and take over the Manchester *Courier*. Harmsworth outbid him, however, and Galloway feared thereafter that the *Courier* would exert enormous Tariff Reform influence in Manchester.[23]

The Cecils then tried to float a new newspaper which would accept Balfour's Sheffield policy. Elliot said that they were working through Samuel Jeyes, formerly the editor of the *Standard*, and were promised £200,000 from the wealthy London financier Albert Speyer. Hugh Cecil wanted it to be 'purely Balfourian'. The motive was

> to have a newspaper so that when the Government was turned out it could run Balfour against Chamberlain. It is evidently *encouraged*, if not actually supported by several members of the Cabinet, and I cannot doubt that the whole thing is known to Balfour himself.

Cecil claimed that such a paper

> was never intended to trim a balance as A. J. B. does. It was to be unmistakably . . . anti-Chamberlain, but at the same time Beachian (as Beach was twelve months ago . . .). But now the

> best prospect is . . . 'Goschenian' or 'Devonshiresque' let us say, I don't care so long as it is against J. C.![24]

Nothing came of the project, partly because funds were not forthcoming, but also because Devonshire would not support the venture as 'it would be years before it would acquire any influence' and it would probably be 'too Tory-oriented'.[25]

This abortive scheme appears to have been connected with another press development. On 25 January Moberly Bell, the owner of *The Times*, offered Elliot a column and a half three days a week to be devoted exclusively to Unionist Free Trade affairs. At first they were utterly baffled by this offer from a newspaperman who had been unalterably on Chamberlain's side from the beginning. Although Devonshire thought they 'could get nothing better', Goschen, Strachey, and Hugh Cecil were completely opposed to acceptance. Elliot was certain that Bell and Buckle, aware of the rumours of a projected Unionist Free Trade paper, were eager 'to get our sanction for an authorised . . . column or two before the new Unionist Free Trade journal appears'. Whatever the reason for the offer, it was declined.

Other attempts by the Cecils to get control of a paper in 1905, particularly the *Observer* or the *Morning Post*, were thwarted first by the greater resources of Northcliffe, who bought the *Observer* and in the second case by the Tariff Reformer Fabian Ware becoming editor of the daily.

Thus, when the tension between Balfour and Chamberlain broke out into open war in November 1905, the Unionist Free Traders were in a weak position. They had little power with the press. Their numbers and influence had fallen considerably since early 1904. Balfour's devices for controlling Chamberlain had neutralised much of the Unionist Free Trade activity while leaving the Tariff Reformers almost a completely free hand to attack free fooders in the constituencies. Finally, the Unionist Free Traders had failed, partly through insufficient activity, to acquire the organisation and resources necessary to allow them to remain for long an effective unit for the defence of free trade.

Chapter 9 THE ELECTION OF 1906

I

THE RESULTS of the 1906 election represented an overwhelming victory for the Liberal party. After Balfour's resignation on 4 December 1905, Campbell-Bannerman had moved swiftly to bring the Liberal Imperialists into line and to establish an administration which obviously contained more ability than its predecessor. The dispatch and assurance with which Campbell-Bannerman formed his ministry and then dissolved to go to the country indicated the confidence most Liberals felt about the outcome of the election. Churchill reassured Morley, one of the few Liberals pessimistic about the election, that 'it will be a great majority—one of the greatest ever known'. However, although most Liberals were optimistic, none expected a landslide of the dimensions of 1832. The final results showed that the government had won 513 seats—Liberals, 377; Labour, 53; Nationalists, 83. The opposition won 157 seats of which 132 were Conservatives and 25 Liberal Unionists. The Liberals had returned to office with a majority of 84 over all other parties combined. In the light of this Liberal success and Unionist discomfiture, the Unionist Free Trade remnant was almost totally neglected after the election.

During the election many Unionist Free Traders embarked upon a period of ambitious activity comparable only to their negotiations with the Liberals in 1903 and early 1904. By this time, however, the Unionist Free Traders were almost completely isolated. Since the breakdown of negotiations with the Liberals in February 1904, the Unionist Free Traders had gained no concessions of any importance from them, save for an assurance that Home Rule would not be considered in the next parliament. In fact, only seven Unionist Free Trade candidates were free of a Liberal opponent, and three of these candidates ran for University seats. Chamberlain meanwhile had revealed the extent of his hostility for he vowed that he 'would rather have a Liberal Free Trader in the House than X who fawns on me and stabs me in the back'.[1] The behaviour of Balfour towards the Unionist Free Traders was not directly hostile but was just as harmful as that of Chamberlain. They were never sure of Balfour's position at any time and this uncertainty often paralysed the Unionist Free Traders.

When Chamberlain destroyed the ministry in November 1905, many Unionist Free Traders hoped that the prime minister would finally disavow the Tariff Reformers. Hugh Cecil informed Balfour that the duke was going to extend 'a sort of olive branch' and implored his cousin not to disregard the overture.[2] The duke himself was not very hopeful. As he wrote to Balfour, he was 'afraid that the last two years have rather increased than diminished the difference of the views which we take on the only question which divides us'. However, the duke offered to support Balfour if he would make a firm anti-protection declaration in his Manchester speech scheduled for 9 December. Balfour's reply, that he would 'keep steady to the course . . . hitherto steered', as well as his refusal to single out the Tariff Reformers for criticism, ended the chances of a last-minute rally of the Unionist Free Traders to him.[3] On 9 December, James ruefully noted in his journal that 'there is no tendency in Balfour to incline towards free trade, and so now, with the general election immediately in front of us, we Unionist Free Traders have to go our own way'.[4]

Balfour's rebuff set the election course for the Unionist Free Traders. Elliot in his 'Journal' noted on 15 December that 'Hugh Cecil has finally reached the despairing point with Balfour' and that the duke said 'he can never really have any confidence in him'. Even Hicks Beach, as early as 3 December, had become so angry over Balfour's refusal to attack Chamberlain openly that he lamented to James that 'you old Liberals can easily enough go back—but I cannot leave the Unionist Party—my father would turn in his grave if I were to do so'.[5]

Unionist Free Trade policy took shape after 20 December with an assertion of independence both from Chamberlain and indirectly from Balfour. The Executive Committee of the Unionist Free Trade Club passed a resolution urging all Unionist Free Traders 'to use their utmost exertions to prevent the adoption of a fiscal policy involving a general tariff and preference'. The duke welcomed this declaration and went beyond it. He published an open letter to Elliot on 1 January urging Unionist Free Trade electors to vote for free trade candidates. The duke remained certain that feeling in the government and the country made it 'in the highest degree improbable' that the Liberals would incur the risks of another Home Rule Bill. Therefore, Unionist Free Traders must exert all efforts both to prevent Tariff Reformers being elected and to secure the presence of a large number of Unionist Free Traders in the next parliament.

By emphasising the need for a large Unionist Free Trade contingent in the new parliament, the duke disregarded the Balfourite candidates and implicitly invited the electors to vote Liberal in constituencies where there were no Unionist Free Traders. The duke could not, of course, directly disavow Balfour. In much publicised letters, however, James in *The Times* on 3 January and Strachey in the *Spectator* on 6 January explicitly called upon the electors to vote for the Liberals in the absence of a Unionist Free Trade candidate.

By January 1906, however, Unionist Free Traders had overestimated their political influence. The Unionist Free Trade Club was so feeble that it played no role in constituency affairs. By contrast, the Tariff Reform League had established nearly 300 constituency branches by January 1906.[6] Most of the Unionist Free Trade candidates managed to retain the support of their local associations only by mixing retaliation in with their free trade principles. Even this was not always sufficient protection from attack, as the case of Hugh Cecil showed. If candidates expressed their free trade views vigorously—as with the case with Elliot, Gorst, Bowles, and Pemberton—they ran without any official backing. The Unionist Free Traders were also severely handicapped before and during the election by a lack of financial resources. All the Unionist Free Trade Club did was to circulate 250,000 selected leaflets of the old Free Food League and sell 12,000 penny copies of a pamphlet on free trade written by Ernest Hatch.[7]

The third and most damaging of their disabilities was their

limited electoral appeal. Since 1903 Chamberlain and the Liberals had succeeded in impressing upon the mass of the electorate that there were only two fiscal alternatives: Liberal free trade or some variant of Unionist Tariff Reform. For those Unionists who believed in free trade, but were loathe to vote Liberal, abstention was often a more attractive alternative than backing a schismatic Unionist Free Trade group.[8] Thus, although the correspondence of Unionist Free Traders is filled with references to supporters in the constituencies, such sympathisers were seldom organised properly and were intimidated by the Tariff Reform juntas which soon dominated most Unionist local associations.

II

Even with so many disabilities, 48 of the original 83 Unionist Free Traders sought re-election in 1906. The depletion of their ranks was modified by the appearance of 8 new candidates. By the time of the election, however, 12 Unionist Free Traders had become Liberals, 22 had retired, and one had died.[9] The retirement of 22 Unionist Free Traders, 27 per cent of their total, is only little higher than the total retirement percentage, 23 per cent within Unionist ranks in the period from May 1903 to January 1906.

It is evident, therefore, that Chamberlainite pressure on Unionist Free Traders did not drive them from the field in large numbers. Of course, those twelve who crossed to the Liberals by 1906 in a sense 'retired' from the party and if they are considered in the Unionist Free Trade retirement group, the percentage goes up to 41 per cent. One last problem which arises in computing these percentages is that it is difficult to ascertain how many of the twenty-two Unionist Free Traders retired solely because of Tariff Reform. For example, Hicks Beach had first been elected to parliament in 1864 and would no doubt have retired from the Commons to accept a peerage in any case. The fact that fifty-six candidates stood for election, who had professed themselves as against Tariff Reform, shows the limits of Chamberlain's power before 1906. When Tariff Reform came to dominate the party after 1906, there was no alternative for Unionist Free Traders but to capitulate to Chamberlainism.

A larger percentage of Unionist Free Traders by 1906 had made their peace with the party organisation and their constituencies by accepting Balfour's policies. By January 1906, in fact, only sixteen MPs and four new candidates can be regarded as absolutely 'hard core' Unionist Free Traders.[10] These were the men who put their free trade views and opposition to Chamberlain in the front line of their speeches and electoral addresses. Except for Hugh Cecil and Goschen, none of them gave even a passing or grudging acceptance to any part of Balfour's fiscal policy. The sixteen represented the activists of the Unionist Free Trade group and consequently were those whom the Chamberlainites most wanted to keep out of parliament. Thus Tariff Reformers ran against eleven of the intransigents. In particular, Chamberlain and the Tariff Reform League wanted to drive from parliament Hugh Cecil, Elliot, and Gibson Bowles—their most articulate critics within the party.

Hugh Cecil had even carried his crusade against protection into Birmingham itself, vehemently attacking Chamberlain's values as materialistic and leading to extravagance and corruption. Chamberlain, infuriated by these attacks, retaliated in word and deed. Thus, in October 1905, Cecil fulminated to Balfour that the Tariff Reformers 'were spending £50 a day' to try to throw him out of Greenwich.[11] Balfour regretted the course taken by Chamberlain, and told Robert Cecil that he had 'set in motion the only machinery I have at my command' to induce Lord Hugh's Tariff Reform opponent to withdraw.[12] Balfour himself would not intervene directly, despite pleas from Salisbury and many other Unionists. Hugh Cecil's constituency chairman, one of the few members of the association supporting the Unionist Free Trader, claimed that 'a word' from Balfour 'would be of infinite value' in strengthening Cecil's position. The only 'machinery', however, that Balfour would 'set in motion' was a letter from Acland-Hood on 10 January to the members of the Greenwich Conservative Association urging them to support Cecil. This belated concession prompted the constituency chairman to telegram Balfour in Manchester on 12 January asking 'may we not say the Chief Whip's action has your approval?'[13] Balfour did not reply, and one last, fruitless telegram was dispatched to him on 13 January, just before the polling in Greenwich.

Cecil made whirlwind tours, speaking in Bristol and London, as well as in Greenwich and adjoining constituencies. The *Morning Post* on 28 December quoted him as attacking Chamberlain, who, he said, 'had engaged in a system of Renaissance style assassination of opponents by parliamentary bravos'. The Liberal press made great capital out of this inter-Unionist fight; the *Daily Chronicle* and *Manchester Guardian* carried detailed day-by-day accounts of the situation in Greenwich. So effective were the Liberals in exploiting this split that on the eve of the election the *Daily Chronicle* had to warn voters not to let their sympathy run away with them by voting for Cecil who was, after all, a 'Tory of Tories' and, if he lost, would be given a safe seat after the election. The *Guardian* reported on 4 January that Cecil was so unwilling to compromise that even those Liberals who would 'gladly have thrown in their lot with him' were rebuffed.

In the struggle to capture the Liberal Unionist party, Chamberlain had found Elliot a most determined foe. To destroy Elliot, Chamberlain sent one of the most gifted Tariff Reformers, Jack Hills, to contest the Elliot seat at Durham. In the *National Review* of January 1906 Maxse described 'the direct confrontation of Tariff Reform and free trade' at Durham as a key fight in which fiscal reformer must defeat 'one of the ablest and most respected members of the House of Commons'. When Hills succeeded in ousting Elliot, Liberal papers echoed the *Guardian*'s comment of 17 January that his defeat 'deprives the Unionist party in parliament of one of its best brains and characters'.

While he lacked the influence of Cecil and Elliot, Gibson 'Tommy' Bowles was a most colourful critic of Tariff Reform. Of all the bitter words exchanged during the election, none equalled in vehemence those passed between Bowles and Chamberlain. In his letter to Alan Burgoyne, the Tariff Reform candidate at King's Lynn, Chamberlain spoke of Bowles as a 'pathetic nondescript' who never lost an opportunity of stabbing his party in the back. In the *Morning Post* of 8 January the Unionist Free Trader replied that Chamberlain had 'singled him out for attack with a malignancy only equalled by the vehemence of his onslaught on Lord Hugh Cecil'. Bowles ended his indictment by describing Chamberlain's career as having descended to 'a depth of infamy not hitherto sounded' comparing him unfavourably to the Thugs of India and to Judas Iscariot.

The rest of the Unionist Free Traders, thirty-five candidates of the fifty-six, acquiesced to some degree in Balfour's programme. (One Unionist Free Trader, G. Wolfe of Belfast is in a category all his own as he never even mentioned the fiscal question in his election address, campaigning solely on support of Protestantism.) The thirty-five accepted the policy of negotiation and retaliation against hostile tariffs and agreed to the calling of a 'free and unfettered' colonial conference to discuss imperial problems. It is misleading to assume, however, that because many Unionist Free Traders accepted this programme that they had jettisoned their free trade principles. The thirty-five Unionist Free Traders who supported negotiation and retaliation to reduce high foreign tariffs phrased their pronouncements so as to make a travesty of the view that they went part of the way with Chamberlain. They argued in their election addresses like R. E. Dickinson, of Wells in Somerset, that retaliation would lower foreign tariffs so that England could experience the benefits of 'real free trade'. Eleven of them explicitly stated that they were free traders and King of Hull Central and Mildmay of Totnes proclaimed that 'like my leader, Mr Balfour, I belong to the free trade wing of the Unionist party'. This was not an interpretation of Balfour that Chamberlain would have accepted.

Expediency, and not faith in Balfour's proposals, appears to have motivated many of the Unionist Free Traders who accepted retaliation. By accepting this policy they retained the support of the Central Office and hoped to prevent Tariff Reformers from attacking them. However, in the case of Abel Smith in East Herts and Bentinck in Nottingham South, who proclaimed that they consistently supported Balfour's policy, this loyalty was not sufficient to prevent the Tariff Reformers from trying to persuade their associations to disown them.

The Unionist Free Traders who conceded the need for retaliation looked upon Balfour's policy only as an interim measure to lower foreign tariffs. For example, Thornton was prepared to support retaliation in outrageous cases. However, he would wan 'each proposal submitted to Parliament before a final decision'. Holding these views, Unionist Free Traders differed widely from fervent supporters of Balfour such as the mercurial Wyndham, who preached 'the "official" programme' but 'served it up so "piping hot"—hot with anger against the foreigners; hot with enthusiasm for our colonies—that the delirium grows'.[14] Akers-Douglas held a view of fiscal change very different from that of the Unionist Free Traders even though they all supported the Sheffield and Edinburgh proposals. According to *The Times* of 1 December 1905 he saw 'no difference in the Conservative party with regard to the necessity of tariff reform but only a slight difference as to the methods of carrying it out'.

Of the 574 Unionist candidates in 1906, 55 per cent or 308 supported Balfour's proposals without endorsing Chamberlain's Glasgow programme.[15] Thirty-five of the Unionist Free Traders are included in this percentage but none of them were zealous for fiscal reform. The wide variety of attitudes represented under the general title of 'Balfourite' can also be illustrated by reference to preference. While often expressing some vague agreement on the desirability of calling a colonial conference to discuss imperial problems, 25 of the 35 Unionist Free Traders, or 73 per cent, explicitly stated in their election addresses that they could not agree to the taxation of food. Of the 12 who made no specific mention of opposition to food taxes in their addresses, all but 6 had been members of the Free Food League and so had been hostile to preference in the past. On the other hand, of the total number of Balfourite candidates, only 29 per cent or 89 of the 308 expressed specific opposition to food taxes.[16]

Austen Chamberlain was chagrined that Balfour allowed many free traders to remain in the party who gave lip service to the cause of fiscal reform 'whilst hedging round their adhesion by conditions which in practice would make any reform impossible'.[17] Joseph Chamberlain was equally bitter in his open letter to Lord Ridley of the Tariff Reform League on 8 February 1906 when he demanded that the Unionist Free Traders be purged from the party. He indicted them as Unionists who 'while nominally supporting Balfour are clearly opposed to his policy'.

III

Sixty per cent of the Unionist Free Trade candidates were concentrated in four areas. There were 10 seats contested in London, 11 in Lancashire, 5 in Glasgow, and 3 in the Universities.

The London Unionist Free Traders had normally safe seats: where seats had been contested in 1900, their majorities ranged from 4,000 to 1,000. Most of the constituencies were in well-to-do areas. For example, only in Thornton's constituency in Clapham, in George Bowles' constituency in Norwood, and in Cecil's constituency at Greenwich did the *Guardian* by 1 January think that there had been sufficiently large inflows of working class voters since 1900 to give the Liberals any chance of winning in a straight fight against the Unionist Free Traders.

Robert Cecil and Burdett contested the aristocratic and plutocratic quarters of East Marylebone and South Paddington. In East Marylebone the *Guardian* reported that there was 'a Chamberlainite intrigue very similar to that in Greenwich'. The local Tariff Reformers were unhappy with Robert Cecil's selection and unsuccessfully attempted to persuade the retiring Unionist, Edgar Boulnois, to come forward as a protectionist candidate. Then they tried to get Sir Samuel Scott, the Unionist candidate in West Marylebone, to put pressure on Cecil to retire. Out of admiration for Cecil, Scott refused and, although he was a Chamberlainite, he said that he would resign from the Tariff Reform League if Cecil were opposed. On 7 January, Balfour intervened with a letter in favour of his cousin to which Cecil replied that he thought it would 'extinguish the last embers of Tariff Reform opposition'.[18] However, the opposition did not cease, and Cecil informed Balfour on 10 January that the only reason he was not opposed by a protectionist was that the Tariff Reformers had 'too short notice to get a decent one'.

In Norwood the local Tariff Reformers were outmanoeuvred by George Bowles. After he had been selected, his association demanded that he support their resolution in favour of preference. He publicly refused, maintaining that preference was not included in the official programme. Thereupon the Tariff Reformers backed down. Despite Bowles' popularity many

Liberals felt that the Unionists would lose the seat because, as the *Guardian* stated on 3 January, of the 'feeling that their former M.P., Sir Charles Tritton, a man of high character, has been hustled out of the way by the Tariff Reformers'.

In the other London constituencies, Fisher fought for the 'well-to-do residential neighbourhood of Fulham', while W. F. D. Smith, the bookseller, and Cohen contested the 'flourishing shopping centres of Strand and East Islington'. Rollit fought for South Islington and Clarke stood for one of the two City seats. Thornton, the grandnephew of Henry Thornton of the Clapham sect, stood for Clapham where he had secured a 4,420 vote majority in 1900. This elderly gentleman was immensely popular, and his standing with the electorate was enhanced by the fact that he lived in Wilberforce's house and rode to Westminster on horseback. All ten London candidates were Conservatives, and, with the exception of Burdett, who was very progressive, mirrored the cautious views of their well-to-do constituents, being opposed to social reform and concerned to cut down on national expenditure.

Lancashire represented the area where Unionist Free Traders thought they would have the best chance of retaining their seats. As early as 2 December 1903, Hugh Cecil had written to Devonshire on the gloomy electoral prospects of the Unionist Free Traders, predicting that outside of Lancashire none would be returned. In August 1903 a special subcommittee of the Free Food League, under the direction of James, had been set up to study means of strengthening Unionist Free Trade influence in that county. Many Unionists participated in the powerful non-party Free Trade League in Manchester under the chairmanship of a local cotton manufacturer, Tootal Broadhurst.

To enhance their electoral prospects, Goschen and Lucas left their Sussex constituencies of East Grinstead and Portsmouth to stand in the cotton towns of Bolton and Bury. In the Liverpool Exchange and East Toxteth divisions, McArthur and Taylor added defence of the Protestant interest to their advocacy of free trade. Taylor was unopposed as the Liberals were in substantial agreement with him. All the other Unionist Free Traders in Lancashire faced Liberal rivals. Although McArthur had been a strong free trader in 1903 and 1904, the *Guardian* claimed on

4 January that by the election he was 'a sub-species of Balfourian all by himself'.

In Blackburn Hornby, according to the *Pall Mall Gazette* of 17 January, was expected to have an easy run, for his cotton mills employed hundreds of hands in Blackburn. Hornby also called upon Blackburn to support its new Unionist candidate, Drage. Knowles asked his constituents 'to support a Salford man for Salford'. Like Knowles, Galloway stressed his local connections in South-West Manchester, maintaining that his family had links with the constituency going back over 100 years. Both he and Knowles were exposed to constant heckling at their meetings because, the *Guardian* on 10 January stated, they had expressed themselves as not unsympathetic to retaliation. In Ashton-under-Lyne, the *Guardian* maintained that Whitely would probably lose because 'although he claims to be a free trader, he has not acted with the Unionist Free Traders in the House'. Powell at Wigan and Rutherford at Darwen made no issue of their free trade views but both were generally recognised as Unionist Free Traders.

One Unionist Free Trader, William Peel, left his constituency of South Manchester to stand for Harrow. Contests in South Manchester were generally decided by the populous district of Moss Side which was largely composed of people 'intimately engaged in the Manchester export trade', and they of all people saw nothing alluring in even mild fiscal reform. Since Peel had accepted retaliation, the *Guardian* concluded on 1 January that no one was surprised that he 'was loath to come before the electors again'. Elsewhere in Lancashire fights between local Tariff Reformers and Unionist Free Traders delayed the selection of some candidates. In Accrington and Burnley the delay was so long that no Unionist candidates were ever chosen for the election. Five of the Unionist Free Traders who represented Lancashire constituencies had become Liberals before 1906.

In the Glasgow divisions, Cross at Camlachie, Corbett at Tradeston, Stirling-Maxwell in the College division, and Baird at Central were all strong free traders. All but Baird became Liberals between 1906 and 1910. All were local men: Baird came from a family of great Scottish iron masters; Stirling-Maxwell was a Glasgow shipping magnate; Corbett was a wealthy merchant noted for his philanthropy; and Cross was a Glasgow lawyer. All four had been ambivalent publicly on their fiscal views; however, by 10 January, *The Times* noted with alarm that the Glasgow MPs were turning indisputably to free trade. In particular, Cross, formerly considered a Chamberlainite, had 'recently undergone a considerable change' and was now a strong free trader. Because of this trend the Tariff Reformers succeeded in bringing forward a protectionist from London, one A. L. Rosenthal, to contest the seat against Corbett. Elsewhere in Scotland, Shaw Stewart, Lord Cromer's brother-in-law, contested East Renfrew, and George Younger, later to be a famous Conservative backbencher, fought for Ayr Burghs.

In the Universities, Gorst tried to retain his Cambridge seat against a Tariff Reformer, and Strachey opposed the sitting member for Edinburgh and St Andrews, as did W. S. Smith at Glasgow and Aberdeen. The most exciting confrontation was at Cambridge. Gorst had been elected unopposed in 1895 and 1900. However, in November 1904, a committee of University Tariff Reformers met to criticise his political conduct. Gorst 'was not allowed to be present but was informed that he could no longer be supported'. Only on 28 December 1905 was he told that he was charged with being an unfriendly critic of the late government. Two Tariff Reformers, Rawlinson and Butcher, were selected to run for the two seats. The *Guardian*, in a leader, maintained that it was 'the duty of every Free-trader and every Liberal to defeat this intrigue'.

Apart from the above four areas the Unionist Free Traders were scattered about England in no particular pattern. Gray fought to hold on to West Ham North, while Sassoon stood for Hythe. Bentinck and Bond contested South and East Nottingham respectively. In the former case, Bentinck's uncle, the Duke of Portland, used his great influence in Nottingham on behalf of his nephew. In another instance, aristocratic influence was withdrawn as the Grosvenor family, led by the Duke of Westminster, ceased to support the duke's nephew, Yerburgh, at Chester. Westminster, while remaining nominally a Liberal, had become an enthusiastic advocate of Tariff Reform.

In Hull Central, the personal popularity of King, long a distributor of largesse to the poor in his constituency, ensured that he would hold his seat. In Sunderland, the *Guardian* thought that Pemberton would defeat his protectionist opponent as the Liberals, 'out of personal admiration for Mr Pemberton and the pluck of his free trade stand', were at first disposed to vote for him and the one Liberal candidate. However, a Labour candidate was selected early in January and, by the middle of the month, Liberal supporters appeared to have discarded Pemberton 'to try to outdo Newcastle' where a Labour candidate had already won. In Durham City a decisive majority was predicted for Elliot over the Tariff Reformer Hills, as the Liberal Association had formally resolved to support him. 'Tommy' Bowles of King's Lynn faced both a Tariff Reformer and a Liberal as did Charles Seely at Lincoln. Seely's Tariff Reform opponent, Page Croft, gave a graphic account of the Unionist struggle at Lincoln. Amid scenes of great heat and excitement, his supporters captured the Constitutional Club from the 'Seelyites', and Liberals tried to throw Page Croft in the river. At first Balfour would not support him, and it was only five days before the poll, 'on the very strong representation of Joe Chamberlain, that Mr Balfour gave way and sent me the usual letter'.[19]

In the West Country only Mildmay, Edgar Vincent, and Kennaway, of Totnes, Exeter, and Honiton, were Unionist Free Traders. Although Mildmay and Vincent had both voted for Pirie's fiscal resolution of 9 March 1904 they were opposed by Liberals as they had supported the Sheffield programme. Occasionally Unionist Free Traders who had retired exerted their influence on the side of Liberal candidates. Thus H. D. Greene, who had retired from Shrewsbury, advised his former constituents on 16 January to vote for the Liberal as Tariff Reform 'would bring disaster, impoverishment, and suffering upon all classes of the community'.

IV

It is difficult to assess accurately the effect of the Unionist Free Traders on the election and particularly their part in contributing to the Liberal landslide. The 56 free trade candidates secured a little over 240,000 votes or 4·5 per cent of the total 5,458,000 cast. Of the total Unionist vote of 2,346,000 they polled about

10 per cent. If only the 'hard core' Unionist Free Traders are considered, their percentages are very low indeed: a little over $1\frac{1}{2}$ per cent of the total and nearly $3\frac{1}{2}$ per cent of the Unionist vote.

These figures, however, fail to reflect the importance of the Unionist Free Traders in the election. The fact that eleven constituencies were contested by both Tariff Reformers and Unionist Free Traders allowed three Liberals to slip in at Greenwich, King's Lynn, and Sunderland, where Unionist Free Traders would have won if they had not faced Tariff Reformers. Durham and Cambridge University, however, were lost to Tariff Reformers in straight fights, while in the two Scottish Universities' seats Chamberlainites threw back Unionist Free Trade challenges. The competition between the two Unionist factions likewise made no difference in Lincoln and South Islington where Liberals polled more than the combined votes of Unionist Free Trade and Tariff Reform candidates. Of the Unionist Free Traders who faced Tariff Reformers only Sloan and Corbett, who also faced a Liberal opponent, managed to hold on to their seats.

Of greater importance was the fact that the existence of an articulate Unionist Free Trade minority served to emphasise the deep division within the party, thereby inducing thousands of electors who were normally Unionist in sympathy to abstain or vote for the Liberals. Russell concludes that by proclaiming the divisions in the party, the Unionist Free Traders tended 'to create a climate of opinion making it easier for the floating voters to support the Liberals'.[20] The Liberal press publicised and exploited Unionist divisions. Spender claimed that the attempt of Balfour and Chamberlain 'to create an Irish scare . . . was largely countered by the Duke of Devonshire, who declared that if there was a danger [to the Union] . . . [it] lay in the possibility of Unionists becoming identified with Protection'.[21] The old Gladstonian Radical, Francis Allston Channing, recognised the Unionist Free Trade contribution. Speaking of how much his majority at Kettering had increased over 1900, he attributed this and many other gains to the support of dissident Unionists: 'It was plain to me that my forecast was sound, that there would be a landslide of Free Trade Tories who would make no other sign than that silent vote [for Liberal candidates].'[22] In North-West Manchester, Churchill freely acknowledged that Unionist Free Trade votes had helped him, just as their withdrawal contributed to his defeat in 1908.

Liberals were thus not unaware of the help given them by Unionist Free Trade votes, but they would have derided the assertion of the *Spectator* that the Unionist Free Traders 'turned the scale in the last election'. Whatever the degree of support Unionist Free Traders had brought to the Liberals little was given in return save for support to Lambton and Taylor and promises of support to Elliot. In the latter's constituency, Lord Durham complained that not only had Liberals been sluggish in voting but that many of them sympathised with Tariff Reform and therefore abstained.[23]

Other Unionists observed the effects of the Unionist Free Traders on the election. In his Diary on 14 January, the day after Balfour's defeat at East Manchester, Lord Newton recorded that he had never seen the former prime minister so low. Among the causes of Balfour's dudgeon was the fact that 'the Duke of Devonshire and Lord Hugh Cecil had done him a lot of harm'.[24] On 8 February 1906, Acland-Hood commented on the confusion Unionist Free Traders sowed in voters' minds by their participation in Liberal free trade organisations. Iwan Müller, in a memorandum to Balfour on the disaster, declared that a 'special cause' of the débâcle

> was the defection of the Duke of Devonshire . . . The Duke's influence was always . . . enormous with a class which is mainly Conservative—viz. the well to do middle and upper middle classes. They are politically timorous and suspicious; their ideal leader is a 'safe' man preferably belonging to the 'aristocracy' with a 'stake in the country'. . . . In their suspicious way they thought there must have been something 'shady' when the Duke felt obliged to retire. . . . [The Duke's effect on the election] was much strengthened by the aloofness of another safe man . . . Sir Michael Hicks Beach. And coupled with their sapping influences were the attacks by our own free lancers . . . which surpassed anything that happened in Gladstone's day.[25]

The Tariff Reformers were equally angry at the 'treachery' of the Unionist Free Traders. On 22 January the *Morning Post* called for a purge of all Unionist Free Traders so that 'only men who are prepared to fight to the bitter end can have a place in the reconstructed party'. This led to such immediate post-election actions as expelling Balfour of Burleigh from the Constitutional Club, the Chamberlainites charging that his advice to the electors of Chelsea to vote Liberal had cost Tariff Reform the seat.

Of all the groups in the Unionist alliance, the free traders were the hardest hit by the election. The figures usually given for the 157 Unionists returned are: 109 Chamberlainites, 32 Balfourites, and 16 Unionist Free Traders. (In fact, Balfour probably had more and Chamberlain fewer supporters.)[26] On 6 March 1906, the duke spoke publicly of the 16 (and of 3 members of uncertain allegiance) and confessed sadly that 'this number was small even if we were to include—which I am afraid we cannot—the followers of Mr Balfour'. Unfortunately for the Unionist Free Traders, most of their ablest people—Hugh Cecil, Elliot, Bowles, and Goschen—were defeated and could only watch from the sidelines. Proportionally, the supporters of Balfour hardly did any better for they were outnumbered by the Tariff Reformers three to one. Thus, in February 1906, Chamberlain was able to demand successfully that Balfour commit the party more fully to fiscal reform.

V

After the shock of their defeat wore off, some of the Unionist Free Traders became very disturbed at the size of the Liberal majority. They feared that a torrent of Radical legislation would result. At the same time, the belief that the election results would destroy Tariff Reform somewhat compensated for this otherwise hopeless situation. It was with great dismay that they heard of intense Tariff Reform displeasure with Balfour and open threats to replace him with Chamberlain. This move caused Lord Goschen to appeal to all Unionists on 20 January to forget their differences 'in view of the national necessity of offering as united a front as possible to the tremendous forces now opposed to every form of Unionism'. This entreaty had no effect on the struggle for control of the policy and party machinery, and the crisis reached grave proportions at the beginning of February.

Even Chamberlain's letter to *The Times* of 2 February, saying he was not in the running for the leadership, failed to allay the fears of anti-Chamberlainites for long, since on 8 February, in an open letter to Lord Ridley, the Tariff Reform leader disclosed his demands. He called upon Balfour to convene a party meeting to discuss the future position of Tariff Reform. His followers could not accept Balfour's 'half sheet of notepaper' but would advocate preference and also a general tariff. If Tariff Reform were dropped, there would be no alternative but to form a wholly separate group of fiscal reformers in the House. He did not contest Balfour's position, for the 'leader of a party seven-tenths of which are Conservatives should be a Conservative'. But he was very angry that Balfour had 'accepted without protest the statement of the Free Fooders that under no circumstances . . . will they assent to any duty on corn'. Chamberlain also demanded a reform of the party organisation which the election had shown to be inefficient. Change would involve the decision as to whether the central organisation was to remain an autocratic and non-representative body, or whether, with a democratic electorate, it ought to be strictly representative and 'responsible to the party as a whole'.

In these manoeuvres the Unionist Free Traders played no important role. Devonshire, however, was especially well versed in the private events of the Balfour-Chamberlain confrontation. Lord Wolverton told him the results of the first major post-election impasse early in February when Balfour went to Highbury:

> On Friday A. J. B. dined with Joe, Mrs Joe, and Austen. They dined at 8 and never left the dining room til 12:45. Matters became rather heated at the finish, no compromise seemed possible, and poor Mrs Joe dissolved in tears. . . .[27]

The duke also received urgent requests from Goschen, Hugh Cecil, and Lansdowne to throw his support to Balfour and thus help him to resist Chamberlain's demands. But the duke was so angry with Balfour that he would do nothing for him. To Lansdowne's disappointment, the duke refused to agree to the Unionist Free Trade peers dining with the rest of the Unionist peers at the customary semi-official banquet before the opening of parliament. Devonshire did not think that the

> result of the election has in any way modified my opinions that the distinction between free traders and all shades of Tariff Reform should be as strongly marked as possible, and I am afraid therefore we must dine apart. I do not understand Goschen's opinion . . . St Aldwyn [Hicks Beach] I leave to you.[28]

Soon after this frosty reply, the duke received a long letter from Goschen who lamented that he had been mistaken in writing to *The Times* on 20 January, calling on all Unionist factions to work together, for Chamberlain continued 'as truculent as possible'. As for Balfour, Goschen feared that he would 'be of no more use to us in the future than he has been in the past'. He was so angry at the 'atrocious telegram' Balfour had sent to Durham against Elliot that he would not even reply to Lansdowne's invitation.

Many Unionist Free Traders were not so much angry with Balfour as perplexed about their future role in parliament. For example, Lord St Levan asked the duke what

> is to be our position in the next Parliament, and belonging neither to the Government nor to the Opposition (if it represents Tariff Reform), are we to be relegated to the Cross Benches? All are as willing as ever to work for the Old Cause, but I, and those who work with me, should be very grateful for a little information as to what our future position is to be.[29]

If Unionist Free Traders refused (or were not asked) to give help to Balfour, they all desperately hoped he would hold his position even if a formal split in the party ensued. Such a split would no doubt handicap the party for a few years. However, Unionist Free Traders were certain that Tariff Reform would continue to be a failure at the polls. When the party became disillusioned with protection, then unity could be achieved around the free trade nucleus.

This was the background of attitudes and hopes held by Unionist Free Traders as the Lansdowne House party meeting, a concession to Chamberlain's demands, was set for 15 February. Free Traders, observing Balfour's steadfastness in holding off Chamberlain in the early days of February, became quite optimistic about the outcome of the meeting. Hugh Cecil expressed this guarded optimism to the duke on 11 February:

> A. J. B. is here [Hatfield] but he has not talked much about politics. His physical tiredness is very great and it has therefore seemed impossible to harass him very much. What he said is anti-Joe and I do not think he will move in Joe's direction at all. But I doubt whether he will depart from the region of mist where he has lived so long. . . . Nevertheless . . . it seems to me for the present we ought to try and co-operate with him if we can. . . . He and we both wish to prevent Joe capturing the party and committing it to a definite scheme of Tariff Reform and if we do not co-operate with him what else are we to do![30]

The hopes of the Unionist Free Traders, however, were swiftly dispelled on 14 February, the day before the meeting, when an exchange of letters between Balfour and Chamberlain was published. There is no doubt that this 'Valentine' correspondence represented a victory for Chamberlain. Balfour retained the leadership, but agreed to two major concessions which marked his most decisive step in Chamberlain's direction. He at last agreed to advocate as party policy both a general tariff and colonial preference. Thereafter, Balfour's Valentine letter was regarded as almost Holy Writ by the Tariff Reformers. Armed with the letter, they proceeded to use it as an ideological weapon to banish Unionist Free Traders into the political wilderness.

Unionist Free Trade dismay at the Valentine correspondence was well expressed by Hugh Cecil who complained to the duke that

> none of us could tell that he [Balfour] was suddenly to identify himself with J. C.—even to the point of treating opposition to the taxation of corn as grounds for exclusion from parliament. For, of course, J. C. will oppose every Free Trade Unionist and since A. J. B. is resolved not to help them, exclusion is the certain result.[31]

Lambton was so disillusioned he did not even bother to attend the party meeting. Elliot wrote in his journal of the 'miserable, contemptible part Balfour has played'. Goschen was furious that Balfour had 'sprung' the letters on the party.

Balfour himself was very depressed at the Lansdowne House meeting, for Newton's recollection was of an exuberant audience of party members almost wholly in favour of Tariff Reform with a 'stumbling Balfour appearing in the role of a captive'.

After short speeches by Balfour and Chamberlain, the duke solemnly stated that his group would continue to act independently. Hugh Cecil then delivered an insulting speech, directed at Balfour, asking whether free traders were to be excluded completely from the party. Their chagrin was intensified when it was decided, inevitably, that Chamberlain should lead in the House until Balfour got a seat.

In the aftermath of the election the Unionist Free Traders represented a pathetic group. During 1903 and early 1904 they had held the balance of power in the Unionist party and even for a while in parliament as a whole. In 1906 they were disregarded in all Unionist post-election decisions. Reduced to a handful of MPs, they were of only marginal significance in the new parliament. Nor were they hardened into an effective unity by their adversity. Immediately after the Valentine letters, the old paralysing disagreements broke out among them. Also, Devonshire was very indecisive and could not make up his mind on what action to take. He wrote pathetically to Elliot asking him not to accept the Liberal nomination to run against Balfour in the City. Although he thought 'Balfour's behaviour justified any sort of protest', the duke could not support Elliot because at the party meeting he had inadvertently put his hand up in favour of the resolution expressing confidence in Balfour's leadership.[32]

The Unionist Free Traders made a last determined effort in the election of 1906 to reverse or at least to stem their drift towards extinction. They had only sixteen MPs and of these really only nine or ten active members. Although individuals acted decisively at times, the Unionist Free Traders, as a whole, never made any worthwhile concerted effort after 1906. So in effect the years from 1906–10 represent a painful and impotent epilogue.

Chapter 10 THE ECLIPSE OF THE UNIONIST FREE TRADERS

I

AFTER THE 1906 election the Unionist Free Traders were a pathetically small group. In parliament George Bowles, Robert Cecil, George Younger, and Sir Edward Clarke were the only newcomers elected in 1906. Then as some old Whig grandees and Tory leaders died or ceased to be active, the movement lost more of its standing. Ritchie died in January 1906, Goschen in February 1907, and, after a year's illness, Devonshire died in March 1908. In his last two years the duke was only a nominal leader. His attitude is described by James:

> After the General Election of 1906, the Duke of Devonshire became much more Conservative than he had previously been . . . [and] toward the end of his life he would not have given the first place in rank of importance to Free Trade. . . . I know he regarded the assumption of responsibility when he . . . urged the electors of Lewisham to vote for the Liberal candidate as a regrettable mistake. . . .[1]

Although James was seventy-eight in 1906, he alone of the Unionist Free Trade peers remained active against Tariff Reform. George Hamilton was completely involved in the Poor Law Commission, Balfour of Burleigh lived in partial retirement, and St Aldwyn had withdrawn from Unionist Free Trade affairs. Among the younger men, the two most able, Hugh Cecil and Elliot, were without seats after 1906 and there seemed little likelihood of either being adopted as a Unionist candidate in the near future. Hugh Cecil's predicament was graphically outlined by his brother Robert:

> Bonar Law himself told me, speaking on behalf of the Central

Office of the Tariff Reform League, that they would rather lose 20 seats than allow my brother to be returned to Parliament.[2]

After 1906 the Unionist Free Traders were even more dominated by Conservatives than they had been earlier. The few Whig Unionists who were still alive by 1907–8 were mostly out of parliament. Indeed only four of the Unionist Free Traders in the House of Commons were Liberal Unionists.

Although he was the obvious candidate, the fact that Chamberlain led the party in the Commons during Balfour's short absence, until the latter was elected for a City seat on 11 March 1906, underlined the predominance of the Tariff Reformers. After February 1906 the refusal of Unionist Free Traders to accept Balfour's Valentine letter meant that the Tariff Reformers would have greater freedom to attack them. Since part of Balfour's capitulation had consisted in his consent to a democratisation of the party machinery, the reorganisation would give more power to the constituency associations, most of which were dominated by Tariff Reformers. In May 1906, Robert Cecil complained to his cousin that 'the committee for the reorganisation of the Central Office is composed almost wholly of Tariff Reformers. . . . It is really essential to us to know how far the policy of . . . excommunication is to be allowed to go.'[3] Of even greater concern was the problem that Liberal social reform became for most Unionist Free Traders an even worse threat than Tariff Reform. The introduction of old age pensions early in 1908 and the Lloyd George Budget of 1909 made any co-operation with the Liberals impossible for most Unionist Free Traders.

Fatally, for the Unionist Free Traders, the Tariff Reformers gained complete control of the party as the Liberals moved toward the Left. To maintain his position, Balfour late in 1907 moved towards 'a definite doctrinal rapprochement with the whole hoggers'.[4] His acceptance of their programme allowed the Chamberlainites to embark upon a final purge of free traders within the party. Because of their growing antipathy to the Liberals, the Unionist Free Traders could not mount an effective counter-attack. Balfour of Burleigh expressed their dilemma:

> To put it briefly we are between the Devil and the Deep Sea. Shall we go to the Devil of Protection with our friends, or the Deep Sea of Socialism with our political adversaries.[5]

For a few months after the election, however, the Unionist Free Traders were not reduced to the stark alternatives posed by Balfour of Burleigh. The Liberals did not begin to embark on Radical social legislation until late in the spring of 1906. Moreover, after the Valentine letters, and especially after Chamberlain's stroke in July, Tariff Reform suffered a temporary slump in the party.

Immediately after the Valentine letters, the Unionist Free Traders were in a very aggressive mood. This tough approach was laid down at the special meeting of the Unionist Free Trade Club held on 6 March just before the debate on Sir James Kitson's motion condemning protection based on food taxes and a general tariff. At the meeting Devonshire reiterated his decision that, while remaining a Unionist, he must repudiate the Valentine letters. After his speech a resolution was passed condemning the Balfour-Chamberlain correspondence. Then, according to Elliot's Journal, James repudiated Balfour 'on behalf of the Club . . . as our leader'.

The Times noted how James's 'repudiation' was received with cheers, and concluded that the Unionist Free Traders must 'now be regarded as a party'. This was not correct, however, for the declaration of independence from Balfour, and particularly James's speech, almost caused the two Cecils and their supporters to resign. Hugh wrote Devonshire that he would 'write a letter making it clear that . . . there is no general repudiation of . . . [Balfour]. And this I suppose may apply to the Club'.[6] Elliot, Strachey, and their friends were furious that the Cecil view prevailed. Strachey was particularly annoyed, for he had proposed the formation of a Unionist Free Trade party cooperating with Rosebery. The duke, however, would not countenance a separate party, and Strachey had to inform his brother that 'the Duke . . . says that if my resolution were carried, he should have to resign the chairmanship of the Club and of course I cannot risk that'.[7]

The first public post-election test for the Unionist Free Traders arose on 12 March over the vote on Kitson's motion. In the debate the Unionist Free Traders were inconspicuous. Only Clarke spoke, asserting on 12 March that 'people would rather vote for Home Rule for Ireland than have a tax on corn or meat'. After this speech, Clarke was driven from parliament by Tariff Reform pressure. Sir Joseph Lawrence and other London Tariff Reformers warned him that political memories are long. 'When you next want the votes of Tariff Reformers . . . look to those whom you looked on 12 March 1906 for your cheers'. In May Clarke, exhausted and near nervous collapse, resigned his seat. He felt that he had been shamefully treated by Balfour, who would neither recognise him nor shake his hand after his speech against Tariff Reform. (In the by-election Sir Frederick Banbury, one of the most doctrinaire right-wing Tariff Reformers, won the constituency.) In the division on Kitson's motion, eight Unionist Free Traders voted with the government and the others, along with some Balfourites, abstained. *The Times* chided the thirty-seven unpaired abstentions for disloyalty and took care to list each one.

Having demonstrated their continuing attachment to free trade, the Unionist Free Traders began to co-operate with Balfour against Liberal measures. They were encouraged for though Tariff Reformers urged Balfour to lay out a comprehensive fiscal programme, at this time he refused to yield. Balfour wished to concentrate on resisting Liberal legislation while at the same time conciliating the new Labour forces. Thus he and Lansdowne allowed the Trade Disputes Bill to pass the Lords while ensuring that many other Liberal measures, in particular the Education Bill, did not pass the upper chamber.

Most Unionist Free Traders approved of Balfour's attack on Liberal legislation and only regretted that the Trades Disputes Bill had not also been stopped. In the debates over the Bill, the *Spectator* claimed with satisfaction that Cecil and Lambton in the Commons and Goschen in the Lords had made the best speeches 'against placing the Trade Unions in a position of privilege'. Strachey was also pleased that Lambton led the attack against 'the unnecessary proposal' to feed children in elementary schools. Most Unionist Free Traders were as hostile as Strachey to social reform. Robert Cecil recalled how he, Bowles, Lambton, and W. F. D. Smith acted as a little band to engage in 'guerilla warfare' against social legislation.[8] So tireless were they in their criticism of Liberal measures that a number of Unionist papers protested strongly when Tariff Reformers launched a public purge against them in January 1909. In defending Cecil, *The Times* in January 1909 declared that 'he has made a more conspicuous mark in the House of Commons than any of the rising men amongst his colleagues'.

II

While Tariff Reform was in the doldrums, the surviving Unionist Free Traders played an important role in parliament. Balfour refused to comply with the demands of the Tariff Reformers to ostracise them: 'If such a policy succeed in making the party unanimous', he said to Austen Chamberlain, 'it would be at the price of keeping it small'. In addition, Joseph Chamberlain was depressed that the proposed reorganisation of the party appeared to him to be a sham. Sandars and Acland-Hood were striving to postpone any modernisation 'of our long-standing scheme of Central management and Control'.[9] When some reorganisation was completed by July 1906, moreover, the Central Advisory Committee, which was established to keep the party leader in touch with Unionist followers in the country, left the initiation of policy with Balfour. His representatives could always out-vote the Chamberlainite members. Acland-Hood also rejected the Tariff Reform demand that the Chief Whip be elected, stating publicly that he 'could not imagine anything more disastrous to the party welfare'. The Chief Whip could rebuff this demand because many Unionists were tired of Chamberlain's dogged insistence on emphasising fiscal change.

Another reason for the slump of Tariff Reform was the healthy state of the economy. The prosperity of the years 1905–7 was based on the great output of new ships and the expansion of foreign as opposed to colonial trade. While the economy boomed, Tariff Reform had little appeal, a fact recognised by the fiscal reformers and one which placed them in the uncomfortable position of appearing to wish for bad times.

An even greater misfortune for the Tariff Reformers occurred when Chamberlain was incapacitated by a stroke on 11 July 1906. As he had no heir-apparent and for fear that his movement might disintegrate, the nature and extent of Chamberlain's illness was not disclosed for some time. In the autumn it was made public that, owing to severe gout and 'a fall which injured his foot and damaged his eyesight', he had to cancel all his engagements. This sudden departure of Joseph Chamberlain from the political scene led to confused speculation. Balfour discreetly tried to find out just how serious Chamberlain's 'indisposition' was. Sandars reported early in 1907 that a doctor he consulted had, after looking at a photograph of the invalid Chamberlain, felt absolutely certain the problem was severe paralysis of one side. Such a condition, Sandars went on to elaborate, 'means recovery must be *very, very* doubtful'.[10]

Chamberlain's incapacity removed the most prominent Unionist advocate of social reform. He had not opposed the Trade Disputes Bill and in his last speech, to the Liberal Unionists at Birmingham, he declared that they had two great tasks: to advocate social reform and to uphold imperial interests. To press ahead with the first would now be easier since 'the bitterest opponents had been the old and now defunct whigs who opposed fiscal as they opposed social reform.'

By the end of the year, however, interest in Tariff Reform and widespread dissatisfaction with Balfour revived. For Unionists who realised the need for social reform but were apprehensive of financing such measures by increases in direct taxation, Tariff Reform, which would raise revenue by indirect taxation, seemed the only alternative to Liberal finance. Indeed, Sandars informed Balfour that he had heard that 'several Radical manufacturers have subscribed [to the Tariff Reform League] being afraid of predatory socialism and being keen on the possible advantages of a tariff'. He claimed that the Chamberlainites had gained a new lease of life. Finally, he cautioned Balfour that 'with the exception of the *Daily Telegraph* we have not a single organ of the London press which will support the orthodox party leader against this development'.[11]

As Tariff Reform once again grew more powerful within the party, the Confederacy began to play an active role. The best account of this extraordinary phenomenon in English politics—a secret society with all the trappings of oaths, threats, and codes—is given by Page Croft, one of the originators of the organisation.[12] Page Croft describes how he, Sir Thomas Comyn Platt, and a few others met late in 1905 to discuss means to keep

Tariff Reform from being dropped by the official leaders. From this genesis the organisation soon expanded to over fifty members, thirty of whom became MPs. It was directed by an influential council of twelve, who were elected annually. All members were sworn to secrecy.

The main object of this vanguard of Tariff Reform was to purge the party of all free traders. As Page Croft outlined their intentions, 'young men drawn from the aristocracy and country gentlemen' were to devote themselves to fighting any seat held by a free fooder. By 1909 Croft's boast, that they had put such fear into all Conservative Associations that no Unionist Free Trade candidates could be adopted, was correct. So pervasive were their activities that in writing to Robert Cecil, Charles Mallet of the Free Trade Union added 'P.S. I hope your postman is not a Confederate, I've no other envelopes.' There is no evidence that Joseph and Austen Chamberlain took any part in their activities, but the Confederates could hardly have existed without at least their sympathy. No activity undertaken in the name of Tariff Reform sowed as much bitterness among free traders, Balfourians, and even some moderate Tariff Reformers, as did the policies of the Confederates.

By the beginning of 1907 it was clear that Tariff Reform was once again powerful enough to threaten Balfour's position. On 22 January 1907, Sandars described the increased power of the Tariff Reformers, emphasising that Balfour could no longer remain silent. Everything depended on his speech at the National Union meeting on 15 February: if he did not make a clear statement on Tariff Reform, his followers would melt away.[13] Balfour replied that he would tell the party the 'truth in love' at Hull on 1 February without waiting until 15 February, 'when however I could repeat the lesson if it were necessary'. At Hull Balfour conciliated the Chamberlainites by stressing the importance of Tariff Reform for imperial consolidation, social reform, and the protection of British manufacturers.

Many Tariff Reformers felt that Balfour had yielded to their pressure. Indeed, Balfour reluctantly agreed to support a fiscal amendment to the Address at the opening of the 1907 session. Despite this concession, an intractable Tariff Reformer in the debate referred to Balfour as 'the heaviest drag on the wheel of

Tariff Reform' and urged him to 'come down from the Olympian heights of philosophy and golf'. By April even Balfour had to agree that Tariff Reform was capturing all the local associations. Mindful of such omens, Balfour on 14 November made a very important speech at the National Union meetings in Birmingham. His major points were that until the recent Colonial Conference, he had had serious doubts as to whether preference could be carried through, but it was 'irrational still to entertain these fears' and so he was ready to consider the implementation of preference. He laid down four propositions on fiscal reform which he hoped would be accepted by all members of the party: namely he was in favour of broadening the basis of taxation; safeguarding the productive industries from unfair competition; strengthening the position in foreign markets, and establishing preferential commercial arrangements with the colonies.

The Chamberlainites by the end of 1907 had thus recovered the initiative in the party. Rejecting much of his former ambiguity on fiscal policy, Balfour increasingly identified party fortunes with Tariff Reform, particularly as his great rival was no longer a threat. In addition, Acland-Hood, 'in 1906 considered an arch enemy of the whole hoggers', had by July 1907 claimed that no candidate unwilling to accept a duty on corn could expect any help from the Central Office.[14] Thus, after nearly four years, the Tariff Reformers finally began to dominate the policy of the Central Office. Since fiscal reformers already controlled the National Union and most Unionist constituency organisations, what hope was there for the Unionist Free Traders? Moreover, by 1908, it seemed that an early Unionist return to office was assured. During 1907 Liberal majorities began to fall at by-elections and the government lost one seat to the Unionists and two to Labour. The next year witnessed a long series of Liberal defeats as the Tariff Reformers won eight seats. By January 1909 the Central Office was calculating on a majority of twenty at the next general election.

III

Resurgent Tariff Reform left the Unionist Free Traders in a desperate position. The former free Traders, McArthur and Peel, elected at by-elections in October 1907 and November 1908 were only selected as candidates because they publicly announced their conversion to Tariff Reform. Hayes Fisher and Yerburgh, anxious to stand again for parliament, wrote an open letter to *The Times* on 6 May 1907 in which they stated that their main political hope was to see the Empire strengthened through the implementation of Chamberlain's proposals. Despite these capitulations, however, most important free fooders still remained implacable enemies of the Tariff Reformers. Hugh Cecil insisted to Balfour that 'Pray rid your mind of the idea that any co-operation is possible between me or any U. F. T. and the Tariff Reformers so long as the fiscal question is with us. I am fully resolved to destroy Tariff Reform and believe in my ability to do it'.[15]

Although extremists like Cecil and the Confederates saw no middle ground on which to compromise, many moderate Unionists, anxious for party unity and mindful of the ability of the free fooders, wished to bring them back into the fold. The most important communications about a possible arrangement took place between Cromer and Lansdowne. By the end of 1907 Cromer was the dying duke's heir-apparent as head of the Unionist Free Traders. He had declined, for reasons of health and policy, to become foreign secretary in Campbell-Bannerman's ministry. When he arrived in England from Egypt in 1907, his *laissez-faire* conscience was offended by many Liberal measures and, despising Tariff Reform as much as social reform, he took up a position on the cross benches. Finding that the only group holding political views congenial to his own were the Unionist Free Traders, Cromer made a series of speeches in which he 'advised Unionists to put Tariff Reform on the shelf and the Liberals to get rid of Old Age Pensions'. Cromer then became president of the Unionist Free Trade Club on 2 June 1908. A man of powerful but inflexible intellect, Cromer was as doctrinaire a free trader as Strachey. He had enjoyed great prestige as a proconsul and was greeted by some as the ideal leader for the Unionist Free Traders. However, Cromer lacked experience in English domestic politics. Consequently, he overestimated his (and Unionist Free Trade) influence and proved to be quite out of touch with the electorate.

According to Cromer, Lansdowne expressed a wish to see him and encouraged him to put the views of the Unionist Free Traders on paper. Although he had secured the consent of Devonshire and the executive committee of the Unionist Free Trade Club to carry out negotiations with Lansdowne, Cromer stressed that the views expressed were entirely his own, and set out a number of prerequisites. Any arrangement should be made public in an exchange of letters between Balfour and the Duke of Devonshire. He also stated categorically that no arrangement with the Unionist Free Traders was possible unless the Confederates were denounced by the official leaders. (This demand destroyed whatever slender chances there were for a reconciliation, since Balfour refused to give such an assurance which he believed 'would do more harm than good' by re-opening party divisions.) Cromer further stipulated then that Tariff Reform candidates should neither be run against the incumbent Unionist Free Traders nor run in constituencies where Unionist Free Traders constituted a majority of the electorate. In return, the Unionist Free Traders would abide by the same conditions in constituencies where the majority opinion was clearly for fiscal reform.

Cromer insisted that free fooders should not be required to vote for 'an extreme Tariff Reformer' if no free trader was standing. Indeed, he stipulated that for Unionist Free Traders to support candidates 'in favour of "Mr Balfour's programme" ', such candidates must agree to oppose both protection and any proposal to tax food or raw materials. In making these demands Cromer maintained that his conditions in no way contravened Balfour's Birmingham propositions. He warned that unless an arrangement was arrived at, Unionist Free Traders would consider themselves at complete liberty to accept whatever course of action they might think best in support of their 'special views'.

These unrealistic proposals ignored the extent to which Chamberlainism dominated the party. In a long reply, Lansdowne answered Cromer's demands one by one.[16] He pointed out that since the reform of the Unionist organisation, constituencies had full freedom to select their own candidates, and that if they wanted Tariff Reformers there was nothing that could be done by a decree from the Central Office. In addition, Lansdowne stated politely that Cromer must have misinterpreted the Birmingham speech, and he closed with these words:

> I am afraid you will regard these criticisms as less helpful and sympathetic than you would wish, but nothing would, I assure you, give me greater pleasure than a concordat which would enable men like yourself and others whom I reckon amongst my oldest political friends, to work cordially with us . . . [but] it is virtually impossible to restrict the activities of the most restless supporters.

All Lansdowne could offer was the hope that 'goodwill' would help to bring about unity.

The only formal major attempt at a reconciliation between the Unionist Free Traders and the rest of the party was doomed to failure from the outset. As Sandars commented to Lansdowne, 'it is rather difficult to know how to answer Cromer's letter because his childlike ignorance of party or party politics confuses nearly every assertion and argument he employs'.[17]

Although an agreement could not be negotiated—and neither side was ever confident of success—attempts were made at individual settlements. In these limited negotiations Walter Long and Robert Cecil took the leading roles. Long was a moderate Tariff Reformer who despised the Confederates. Representing the views of many High Church and landowning Tories and disliking intensely what he called the Austen Chamberlain-Bonar Law 'clique', Long was anxious to bring free traders like the Cecils into harmony with the rest of the party. Late in 1907 he wrote to Balfour saying he wished that 'sometime you would send me a memo of your wishes and ideas as to the Free Trade Unionists, I mean as to their future place in the party'.[18] Then, early in 1908, Long wrote to Robert Cecil offering his services as a mediator between the free traders and the Tariff Reformers, stating he would make every personal sacrifice to stop the 'dry rot' destroying the Unionist Party.

The need for an accommodation became urgent as the Tariff Reformers began to exert more pressure in January 1908. On 15 January the Confederates forced the free fooder Henry Bentinck to accept the Birmingham policy without reservations in order to be selected as the candidate for Nottingham South.

By 19 January Robert Cecil was raging at Balfour that the Confederates had induced the chairman of George Bowles' association to disown him: 'You will no doubt have heard of the fresh attack by the Confederates *aided by the Central Office* on the Unionist Free Traders and especially on Bowles'.[19] According to Cecil, the Confederacy's campaign against the Unionist Free Traders was developing so fast that all of them were in acute danger. This development appears to have dampened Long's ardour, for he said that all MPs would have to accept the Birmingham programme. Since Long was backing down from his earlier vows of support, Cecil tried threats:

> Have you any news for me. I am in a difficulty. . . . Advances are being made to us from the other side. They have come from several different quarters . . . some of us think they should be entertained. . . . If Winterton and Co. . . . [are allowed to eject us] we ought to seek [protection] outside the party.[20]

Long was sufficiently taken aback to say that he would consult Balfour but apparently nothing more was done.

Indeed, the only compromise ever agreed upon between Unionist Free Traders and Tariff Reformers was a private accommodation—known as the Marylebone pledge—between Robert Cecil and his constituency. This bargain meant that if a Unionist ministry brought forward a budget which Cecil could not accept, he would resign his seat and offer himself for re-election. But the 'pledge'—which Cecil wanted applied to other free traders—was only an interim measure, and as the Tariff Reformers became stronger during 1909 even this compromise was brushed aside.

The new strength of Tariff Reform was reflected in by-elections as early as January 1908 and it grew throughout the year. On 17 January Mid-Devon, a Liberal seat since 1885, fell to a Tariff Reformer. Of particular importance was the victory on 7 February of Edward Goulding—popularly known as 'Joe's man Friday'. These impressive victories had their effect on the Unionist party. On 4 March Goulding moved an amendment stating that the consumer would benefit from preference. Balfour's acceptance of the amendment marked the first time that the party officially supported an amendment advocating food taxes. This development was greeted with dismay by Robert Cecil:

> I have received our Whip this morning . . . which I can only interpret as in support of Goulding's amendment moved and seconded by Confederates. That is in favour of Protection undisguised. . . . You have modified your view that you would not lead a Protectionist party. . . .[21]

Cecil concluded that he did not now see how he could stay in the Unionist party.

Now that Tariff Reform had become so powerful, Balfour knew he could do little for his cousins and felt that they might well be lost to the Unionists. In an unhappy and resigned manner he wrote a twenty-four page letter to Selborne about his predicament. He considered 'Linky' the ablest Unionist outside the House, but said that his name had not been put forward as a candidate even in Lancashire where the free food section had the strongest hold. He further asserted that family relations had become so strained over fiscal reform that he more than once had considered resigning the leadership. In the light of Robert Cecil's latest missive, he thought his cousins would try to link up with Rosebery in a new party.[22] (The idea of a centre party was a chimerical aspiration in the years 1906–10, but it exerted a fascination at times for people such as Robert and Hugh Cecil, as well as Strachey.)

During March and April the Tariff Reformers were concentrating on the contest in North-West Manchester between Churchill and the Unionist candidate, William Joynson Hicks. The Tariff Reformers had threatened Joynson Hicks so that a week before the election he repudiated all connections with the Unionist Free Trade Club and the Manchester Free Trade League. If the Unionist Free Traders could not make their presence felt in Manchester, there was not much hope for them elsewhere.

From January to April there was constant dissension among the Unionist Free Traders over the question of supporting Churchill. Cromer, the Cecils, George Hamilton, and now Strachey were against support. Elliot, Lambton, and some others—a minority of the Club and mainly Liberal Unionists—were for collaboration with the Liberals. These opposing points of view were strenuously debated at a meeting of the Executive

Committee of the Unionist Free Trade Club on 5 February 1908. Cromer and his Tory associates won and the philosophy of 'masterly inactivity' was therefore continued.[23] As this by-election had such a demoralising effect on the Unionist Free Traders it must be examined in detail.

Since its creation in 1885 North-West Manchester had been a Conservative seat until Churchill won it in 1906 by over 1,200 votes. The Unionist Free Traders were strong in the constituency, as in the city as a whole. Early in 1908, when it was obvious that Campbell-Bannerman was near retirement and that Churchill would be promoted to cabinet rank, free traders and Tariff Reformers prepared for what they considered a crucial test of strength. Asquith became Prime Minister on 8 April 1908, Churchill was appointed President of the Board of Trade on 13 April, and the poll was fixed for 24 April.

Elliot continued to speak on Churchill's behalf at meetings in Manchester; Strachey, on the other hand, became so obsessed with the 'socialistic' measures of the Liberals that he avowed: 'I spoke for Winston at the last election but I certainly could not do so now'. When it appeared likely that Joynson Hicks would pledge himself not to vote for any change in the fiscal system during the present parliament, most Unionist Free Traders were prepared to support him. Robert Cecil even intended to go to Manchester and speak on behalf of Joynson Hicks.

The Tariff Reformers, however, flushed with their by-election successes, threatened to run a Confederate against Joynson Hicks unless he gave satisfactory assurances, a threat which prompted E. Tootal Broadhurst, a prominent cotton manufacturer and President of the Manchester Free Trade League, to remark that 'apparently now the official leaders of the party have joined the Confederacy'. When Joynson Hicks gave in, his capitulation caused a furore among the Unionist Free Traders, even causing them to consider putting up a candidate of their own at the Manchester by-election. Robert Cecil was so incensed that he cancelled his engagement to speak on behalf of Joynson Hicks. In the end all the fulminations of the Unionist Free Traders came to nothing. Elliot summed up their inconsequential role:

> As a Club we have never taken part in any election. . . . The divergence of views may be seen from the fact that at the recent

> Manchester election I wrote a letter backing Churchill whilst Lord Avebery wrote a letter to Dundee opposing him! . . . The plain truth of the matter is that we—the Club—do not constitute a *political party* at all in any practical sense.[24]

In what Clarke describes as the government's 'blackest hour', Churchill lost the election by a narrow margin.[25] Unionist papers were exultant that the citadel of free trade had fallen. Randolph Churchill claims that the 'transcendent reason' for his father's defeat was the desertion of the Unionist Free Traders.

It continued to be a bleak year for the Unionist Free Traders. Robert Cecil was under pressure from rather bizarre Tariff Reformers. For example, a certain A. Cadbury Jones, who signed himself Secretary General of the 'Societas Rosicruciana in Anglia', warned that it was very unwise of Cecil to appear on the Unionist Free Trade Club circulars and that 'such an act of open defiance to our wishes will cost you the seat'.[26] More seriously, Goulding took the lead in excluding him from the Constitutional Club. In reply to Cecil's letter about Goulding's action, the chief whip bluntly dismissed Cecil's complaints:

> The leader of the Party stakes his adherence to a certain policy in which he is keenly supported by the great majority of the Party. You and your friends do not agree with that policy. What you ask is that the leader is to denounce those who accept his policy. . . . Surely this is a 'reductio ad absurdum!'[27]

The Unionist Free Traders were further demoralised by the introduction in 1908 of legislation which they considered socialistic. In particular they were alarmed by the Old Age Pensions Act. Unionist Free Trade apprehension about the trend of Liberal legislation came out in a general review of their position in December 1908. Their reappraisal was held amid the rumours that Lloyd George intended to present a Radical budget in the 1909 session which would, according to Cromer, 'constitute a turning point in our fiscal policy'. Liberal intentions had been signalled by Asquith in a speech to the National Liberal Club on 10 December 1908 when he asserted that 'the Budget of next year will stand in the very centre of our work'. Politicians recognised from this speech that 'Liberal finance was to provide the answer to Tariff Reformers in the

Country, it was to revitalise their party in the constituencies, and it was to be the method by which the veto of the House of Lords could be by-passed at last'.[28]

Unionist Free Trade perplexities were discussed in long memoranda circulated among the leaders of the free trade faction and contained in the Cromer Papers. The main themes were that Unionist Free Traders should stand together, at least until the next election. However, since the next budget would convert many waverers in the country to Tariff Reform, the fate of the government would be sealed. Cromer thus advised the Unionist Free Traders to side with moderate Tariff Reformers when an election came. Most leading Unionist Free Trade leaders were now ready, reluctantly, to agree with Cromer's analysis, with only Balfour of Burleigh, James, and Elliot (who was in India) dissenting. Balfour of Burleigh wanted to do everything possible to help those who 'fight Unionist Free Trade battles in the House of Commons. They hold the key of the position we all want to maintain and the Confederates know it'. James disagreed violently that Unionist Free Traders should vote for moderate Tariff Reformers, reminding Cromer that:

> There are different degrees of Unionism within the Club. There is the Conservative—who has nothing of the Liberal with him save Free Trade. But there is also the Liberal Unionist of 1886, who has much of Liberalism left in him apart from Free Trade. They will vote differently.

Thus, on the eve of the 1909 session, the Unionist Free Traders, apart from a small minority, were ready to come to terms with official Unionism. But in January 1909 their movement back into the party was halted, and they made one last attempt to stop the Tariff Reformers from eradicating them completely.

Chapter 11 THE FINAL PURGE

I

THE CAMPAIGN started with an anonymous article in the January 1909 edition of the *National Review* signed 'Confederate'. This was the opening of a systematic and well-publicised assault on the Unionist Free Traders. The Tariff Reformers felt certain that they would win the next election but only by a narrow majority over the Liberals and their allies. Thus Tariff Reformers feared that if fifteen to twenty Unionist Free Traders were elected they could effectively sabotage a protectionist budget. Then, the Confederates maintained, a dissolution would be forced. At the election, the Unionists, weakened by internal divisions, would be defeated and a fiscal revolution postponed once again while the Liberals came back to power.

The Tariff Reformers tried to remove once and for all any heretics in their midst so that they could face the introduction of a controversial budget, and possibly the electors, as a disciplined and united body. The anonymous 'Confederate' boasted that they 'already had a guaranteed election fund to run Tariff Reform candidates against all known Free Food Unionists', and that 'the Confederacy comprises many men whose pockets are as deep as their political convictions, and just as full'. As a final melodramatic touch the writer stated that 'the last proselyte has been made; henceforth those who are not with us, are against us'.

This article was followed on 18 January by the *Morning Post*'s declaration against all free fooders. The editor, H. A. Gwynne, produced a 'carefully prepared list of members believed to be unfavourable to the Birmingham programme either partially or in its entirety'. He claimed that Percival Hughes, the Conservative agent, had sanctioned the list.

This attack produced immediate reactions among Unionist Free Traders. Cromer informed Elliot, who was visiting his brother, Lord Minto, in India, that 'we must evidently fight. I cannot tell you how much I regret your absence'. Edward Brunker, secretary of the Unionist Free Trade Club, told Elliot of steps being taken. At Robert Cecil's request, it was decided to try to seek assurances from Asquith of Liberal help in the constituencies. It was also resolved at an emergency meeting of the Unionist Free Trade Club to start a campaign fund. Finally, invitations were sent to all blacklisted Unionists to attend a private policy meeting on 17 February.

Unionist Free Traders were encouraged to retaliate by the cool and often hostile reaction of much of the Unionist press to the Confederate declarations. On 22 January *The Times* devoted a leading editorial to the theme of the Unionist party and its dissidents, concluding that 'for our own part we must confess to profound distrust of the driving out policy'. Both the *Daily Telegraph* and the *Standard*, as well as many Unionist provincial papers, endorsed the view of *The Times*. Lord Northcliffe even went so far as to write privately to Robert Cecil offering his help and stating that 'keen as I am on Tariff Reform I strongly object to the Confederacy. . . .'[1] Even Lord Ridley disapproved and on 1 February wrote to *The Times* repudiating any link of the Tariff Reform League with the Confederates. The Liberal press was scathing in its denunciation of Confederate tactics and the *Westminster Gazette* devoted a series of articles in January and February to the problem of the Confederates and the free fooders. But despite this sympathy for the free fooders, Balfour never did anything to help them or to denounce the Confederates. He was silent because he was finally convinced that the only way to maintain his party and save his own position was by going all out for fiscal reform. Austen Chamberlain noted with approval that Balfour had approved the *Morning Post* article. Balfour's calculated decision to throw in his lot with the Tariff Reformers is best expressed by Sandars:

> The *National Review* I have read. . . . I think it madness to cherish by compromise or any arrangement the presence on the Unionist benches of men who wish or may even break away from us. From the *Tariff Reform standpoint* it is better to lose our Unionist friends and possibly their constituencies . . . than to have them returned![2]

Unaware of Balfour's decision to abandon them completely, the Unionist Free Traders went ahead with their plans to counteract the Confederates. However, their campaign failed entirely. They failed to get any assurances of support from the Liberals; they were unable to build up a substantial campaign fund; and they failed to prevent the capitulation of many of the blacklisted MPs to Tariff Reform demands.

The Unionist Free Traders started optimistically enough. On behalf of the Club, Robert Cecil wrote to Asquith on 21 January 1909 to inquire what would be the Liberal attitude to Unionist Free Trade MPs if they were attacked by Tariff Reformers. Cecil said that the attitudes of many free traders, whether to fight or to retire, would depend considerably on Asquith's answer. The prime minister replied negatively that he regretted but the matter would have to be determined by local conditions and that each case would have to be assessed on its merits.[3] This reply showed that official Liberalism was not interested in helping the Unionist Free Traders—a number of whom had after all been among the most effective critics of government policies. Though individual Liberals desired to work with the Unionist Free Traders, a majority in the party echoed the *Daily News* of 25 January:

> It is best to avoid all ambiguity and circumlocution and to say at once that the Liberal party does not want the Free Fooders. . . . Already the party is overloaded with the relics of the Whigs and the Imperialists.

Any Unionist Free Trade plans to defend incumbent MPs were contingent upon heavy financial assistance. Robert Cecil advocated making an appeal for financial assistance from all who could afford to contribute. Cromer and Strachey both gave £50 immediately. Harold Cox wrote to say that he had a definite promise of £5,000 from a friend and had hopes of two more offers of the same magnitude besides some promises of smaller sums. Salisbury himself was prepared to put up £500, and W. F. D. Smith was ready to help. But many other rich men like Henry King refused outright. On 23 February Brunker, the Secretary of the Club, reported to Cecil that the campaign fund was '£1,300, nearly £400 in cash'.[4] Obviously Cox's backers had not come through with the sums promised. The total subscribed was insufficient if an intensive and protracted campaign was to be carried on against the Confederates. There is no evidence the fund was ever increased.

By February it still appeared as if the Unionist Free Traders would take a strong stand. Brunker's confidential letter to Elliot on 5 February 1909 indicates the scale of their aspirations.[5] The Unionist Free Traders were committing all their speakers. Cromer, Balfour of Burleigh, George Hamilton, and the Cecils were all reported ready to campaign. Brunker concluded on an optimistic note:

> We do not believe there will be a general election for a considerable time. We therefore appear to have some time to prepare a blow which might astonish some people. . . . We want organisers and agents, we want Unionists . . . a lot depends on that, but money we must get and a lot. . . . One thing is certain: the Cecils appear convinced the time has come for them to declare their independence from the official party and that very fact ought to bring the conviction to many.

Robert Cecil publicly denounced the Confederates as 'foolish and unimportant young men' who had all the paraphernalia of a medieval secret society. On 26 January a 'Confederate' replied publicly that 'the Confederacy will not be questioned nor will deign to defend itself against the effete absurdities of Cobdenism in disguise'. Cecil had important allies in the party who detested these Confederate attempts to turn him out. For example, Sir Edward Carson went down to Marylebone on 30 January to speak on Cecil's behalf, and asserted that it would be a calamity for the Unionist party if he was not in the next parliament. Turbulent interjections accompanied Carson's speech and the meeting dissolved into a near riot with shouts of 'Tariff Reform' and chants of 'we'll hang Lord Robert Cecil from a sour apple tree'.

The Tariff Reformers were prepared to make a special case for Cecil. Indeed, Cecil later claimed that 'various Tariff missionaries', including Chaplin, Bonar Law, and even Joseph Chamberlain himself, attempted to convert him.[6] But since Cecil maintained that he was bound by pledges to work with Abel Smith and George Bowles, he could only accept the same treatment as his two colleagues. In their cases the Tariff Reformers were not inclined to be lenient. Thus when Cecil told Goulding he would only accept an arrangement that was extended to Bowles and Smith, the Tariff Reformers attacked all three.

According to the *Westminster Gazette* two other Unionist Free Traders, Lambton and Brotherton, categorically refused to submit to the Confederates. Cross of Glasgow proclaimed that he would run as an Independent rather than grapple with the Confederates. In two other cases Unionist Free Traders retired. Thornton, for reasons he could not put on paper could not stay in Clapham. But, he said, he could better serve the cause of the Union and free traders by becoming 'unshackled politically'. And Hornby, though old age and blindness obliged him to retire, stoutly denied that his withdrawal from active politics had anything to do with Tariff Reform pressure.

The Tariff Reform campaign, however, was remarkably successful in coercing most free fooders at least into accepting Balfour's four Birmingham propositions. On 20 January the *Morning Post* announced with satisfaction that both Younger and King fully subscribed to the Birmingham speech. On 21 January Colonel Williams announced his capitulation and added that, as he now had the confidence of the party, he would stand again. By 15 February the *Morning Post* reported that only Mildmay and Rutherford were doubtful and only eight of the free fooders—Bowles, Brotherton, Robert Cecil, Cross, Lambton, Sloan, Abel Smith, and Wolff—were still intransigent.

A clear indication of the general and rapid success of the Tariff Reform campaign can be seen in the voting on the amendment to the Address on 20 February. For the first time in any parliamentary resolution, this set out the proposition that Ireland stood to gain by a thorough policy of fiscal reform. (It was a clear attempt to attract the Irish Nationalists, most of whom were protectionists in outlook.) On this amendment only ten Unionists abstained, while ten others who had capitulated to Tariff Reform voted for the amendment.[7]

Before the division the Unionist Free Traders had already started to retreat from the militant attitudes they had espoused in late January and early February. Their will to fight obviously slackened as the Liberals gave them no help, as fund raising produced disappointing results, and as most of their fellows bowed to Confederate demands. The special meeting of the Club on 17 February was a very subdued gathering. A special fund was started to help harassed Unionist Free Traders. But the fund was only to be used where definite attacks were made on incumbent members, and nothing more was said either of reprisals or of attacking Confederates.

By March all political issues began to be overshadowed by speculation about the budget Lloyd George was to introduce at the end of April. Unionist Free Traders found their struggles dwarfed and much of their energy taken up by worries concerning the budget. In answer to those who advocated a more vigorous course, Cromer replied cautiously that 'so much depends on the forthcoming budget that a very general feeling exists that we had better hold our hand until it is issued'.

II

When Lloyd George presented the budget on 27 April the ensuing controversy extinguished the remaining hopes of Unionist Free Traders that they could maintain a separate identity and organisation. He introduced the budget in a four and a half hour speech concluding with the assertion that 'this is a war Budget . . . for raising money to wage implacable warfare against poverty and squalidness'. Its chief features were: a sharp increase in death duties; the innovation of a super tax on incomes of £5,000 or more; and the introduction of new land taxes of which the most significant was a 20 per cent tax on the unearned increment in value when land changed hands.

The budget strengthened the hand of the extreme Tariff Reformers by allowing them to present their programme as the only alternative to Liberal 'confiscatory' finance. Gollin develops this idea by showing that Garvin 'again and again during these weeks [the summer of 1909] . . . emphasised that Tariff Reform was the sole alternative to socialistic finance, naval decay, and the consequent disruption of the Empire.' Balfour was forced to accept the arguments of the extreme Tariff Reformers for rejection of the budget. Although he kept his decision private, he had opted for rejection by the beginning of August, and resolved to recognise Tariff Reform as the basis for his party's opposition to the Finance Bill. At the Bingley Hall in Birmingham on 24 September Balfour 'committed himself "irrevocably" to the Tariff Reformers' policy of rejection'.[8]

In the turmoil of these developments many Unionist Free Traders were encouraged to sink their differences with their party and unite in denouncing the budget. Strachey in particular dropped his opposition and began to attack the Liberals fiercely in the *Spectator*. Strachey's new course illustrates the anguished predicament of the Unionist Free Traders. For most of them free trade was synonymous with limited government and integrity in public life. Thus they attached immense importance to the possibilities of political corruption if protection were to be implemented. Their advocacy of free trade was also a moral crusade against *étatisme*: against the increase in government powers and interference which would, they believed, assuredly result from tariffs. With the coming of the budget, both dangers—corruption and big government—were for Unionist Free Traders more certain to arise from Liberal policy than from Tariff Reform measures. More than anything else, the budget took the heart out of their opposition to Chamberlainism and broke their will to continue fighting. As Brunker wrote to Robert Cecil, 'we are paralysed by the Budget'. St Aldwyn lamented to Robert Cecil that

> this Budget seems to me to have given the final shove to the movement of the Unionist party to Tariff Reform. A man may be a Free Trader by reason and conviction . . . *but if he has anything to lose* . . . he will certainly prefer an indefinite T. R. policy to the fiscal policy which is initiated by the present Budget.[9]

Although the Unionist Free Traders were against Lloyd George's measure, almost all of them were opposed to rejection by the Lords. In the Upper House, St Aldwyn, James, Balfour of Burleigh, and, above all, Cromer, argued strongly against rejection. However, as Roy Jenkins points out, 'the free trade element in the party was . . . suspect and the advice which came from it was given far less attention than it deserved'.[10]

The reasons for the Unionist Free Trade opposition to rejection ranged from the belief that such action would be electorally disastrous to the more sophisticated view that it would contravene an essential constitutional convention. Although he detested the budget, Cromer pleaded with Lansdowne that rejection would be 'beyond all doubt disastrous to the fortunes of the Unionist party'. James was more concerned with constitutional principles than expediency. When Cromer swallowed his dislike of rejection and urged free fooders to rally to the Unionist party, James wrote to Elliot:

> I entirely differ from Cromer's utterances. If we are not free traders we are nothing. The prospect before us is most alarming but all my old Liberal ideas have been recalled, and first and foremost now I go against this country being ruled by 500 peers of fixed Conservative views.[11]

Balfour of Burleigh was convinced that, unpleasant as he found the budget, the Lords should not throw it out, for he saw no evidence in the country that the 'average man in the street wants it thrown out'. Elliot was of the same opinion: 'It would startle the public *much* to see a measure which has occupied the House of Commons all the summer disposed of after a few hours' one-sided debate in the House of Lords'. St Aldwyn pleaded with Balfour, claiming that the budget was 'certainly not a revolution, and can be altered or repealed by the next House of Commons. Rejection seems to me the worst gamble I have ever known in politics for it would play right into the hands of the Liberals'. In their moderation the Unionist Free Traders were far more prescient than the Tariff Reformers as to the means of winning elections.

While the budget was being debated the Unionist Free Traders were foundering. On 22 June, at the annual meeting of the Club, Cromer devoted most of his speech to what he considered the iniquities of Liberal finance. This made many of the strong free traders in the Club extremely angry. Indeed, Cromer's words, and those of Hugh Cecil, almost broke up the Club. Cecil claimed that apart from a small group of extremists, Unionist Free Traders had 'no quarrel but only certain differences of opinion' with the Tariff Reformers.[12] No incident illustrates more clearly the collapse of the Unionist Free Traders than Cecil's capitulation. Since 1903 he had been the most influential and violent opponent of Tariff Reform among the younger Unionist Free Traders. By June 1909 he was prepared to swallow his hostility to Chamberlainism if there was a chance of defeating the Liberals to preserve the Lords.

Throughout the summer Unionists, antagonised by the budget, drifted away from the Free Trade Union and the Unionist Free Trade Club. Avebury wrote to Elliot, explaining his resignation from the Free Trade Union:

> It seems to me that the two great dangers of the day are Socialism and Protection: the first would rob us of our freedom and the second of our commerce.
>
> I value Commerce very much, but Freedom even more.
>
> Moreover, Socialism is the danger of the moment, the fight over Protection may or may not come.

The control of local associations by the Tariff Reformers also accelerated the flight of many Unionist Free Traders from the Club. A rank-and-file member, Bernard Vernon, informed Elliot that he wished his name removed from the list of members of the Club. He explained that he would

> probably be standing for Parliament at the next General Election, and I cannot afford to fly in the face of the opinion of the majority of my future supporters.
>
> In fact without acceptance of the principle of 'Tariff Reform' no Conservative could secure a nomination in any constituency. . . .
>
> If the Unionist party wants Tariff Reform they must have it. . . . In any case I am not a big enough person to stand in the breach.[13]

Unionists far more powerful than Vernon had been systematically excluded from political affairs merely because they belonged to the Unionist Free Trade Club. For example, Brunker related to Robert Cecil how Lord Monkbretton was invited to stand as a London County Council candidate. Everything went smoothly until he was asked at a meeting if he was a member of the Club; Monkbretton admitted he was, and never heard anything more about his candidature.

III

With their membership collapsing the Unionist Free Traders seemed destined to disappear entirely as an organisation. Two factors, however, postponed their disintegration until just after the election of January 1910. First, they desired to protect the position of the few embattled Unionist Free Trade MPs, and secondly, many Unionist Free Traders thought an election might well produce an inconclusive result for both the Tariff Reformers and the Liberals. A fluid political situation might then exist which would allow them to act independently.

In fact the position of the few Unionist free Trade MPs was made a little easier for a while late in 1909. Many influential men in the Unionist party were still anxious for Robert Cecil, Bowles, and Abel Smith to have a place in the Unionist ranks in the next parliament. Consequently, with Selborne as mediator, one last attempt at compromise was undertaken for the three men. With the knowledge of Robert Cecil, Selborne negotiated with Austen Chamberlain. By 6 September Cecil wrote with relief to Cromer that there was every prospect of the difficulties in East Marylebone, Norwood, and East Herts being settled.

As Cecil informed Cromer, the compromise was on the terms suggested by Selborne. The three—Cecil, Bowles, and Smith—would undertake never to permit their opposition to Tariff Reform to endanger a Unionist government. If it became necessary for them to resign their seats, they would allow the Unionist whips to decide the time at which the resignations should take effect. In Cecil's opinion these proposals seemed 'such an advance over anything previously offered that we just had to accept them'.[14]

This tentative compact was greeted with great satisfaction by the *Spectator*, which claimed that the Tariff Reformers 'seem to realise the need to concentrate all anti-socialist forces'. Indeed, Austen told Mary Chamberlain that he was heartily glad Cecil had accepted the terms, since 'Bob has done so well in the House that it was very disagreeable to fight him outside it'. He added that Abel Smith and Bowles had received the same terms though the latter did not equally deserve them. Lambton, on the other hand, the Tariff Reformers wanted to oppose but could not touch. 'Corbett and Cross', Austen said, 'will be fought, and that is the whole of the cave'.[15] Even Joseph Chamberlain appeared to favour the compromise, for he wrote an open letter on 20 September to the Marylebone association which, though ambiguous, could be interpreted as favouring Cecil's candidacy.

Cromer was pleased with the compromise, but he was apprehensive because 'the arrangement has never been publicly approved by the leaders. The extremists represented by the *Morning Post* deny its existence, and continue their fanatical opposition to Robert Cecil and the Unionist Free Traders.'[16] These anxieties about the 'compact' were fully realised, for Balfour could not restrain the extremists, having committed the Unionist party to fighting the forthcoming election on the issue of Tariff Reform. Unchecked, the *Morning Post* extremists won their battle against the Unionist Free Traders.

Urged on by the Confederates, the local Tariff Reformers bolstered by Bonar Law persevered in Marylebone, ignored the arrangement negotiated by Selborne, and ran the strong Tariff Reformer Richard Jebb against Cecil. The same situation developed in Norwood and East Herts where Tariff Reformers were selected. Cecil found this final clash intolerable and when Hornby of Blackburn, who was retiring, said he would give them his full support, Cecil and Bowles set out forlornly for Blackburn to stand as Unionist Free Traders. Thus only four candidates —Bowles, Robert Cecil, Lambton, and Brotherton—contested seats, while Hugh Cecil was unopposed. His influence was sufficient for him to be selected to contest Oxford University along with Sir William Anson. For a while the distinguished archaeologist and Tariff Reformer, Sir Arthur Evans, threatened to oppose him but at Lansdowne's request, and with Lord Milner acting as a 'go-between', Evans eventually withdrew.

The Unionist Free Trade Club was so paralysed by internal divisions that it could not formulate a clear policy for the election. At the general meeting of the Club on 7 December it was decided that members should be left at liberty to vote as they pleased, but they were urged to make it clear to any candidates whom they supported that they were opposed both to Tariff Reform and to Home Rule. Only the meagre hope that a centre party might be a possibility after the election held the Club together. But as the election drew nearer the right wing of the free fooders drew closer to the official Unionists. After Hugh Cecil's Manchester speech of 15 November advocating support of the Tariff Reformers even the cautious Balfour of Burleigh was moved to protest. He wrote to Cromer that, although he would 'do much for Lord Hugh', he would not follow him 'in taking up the Tariff Reform cudgels'. With the election imminent, however, Cromer became so alarmed that on 17 December at Sheffield he strongly urged all Unionist Free Traders to vote for their party in the interests of 'national defence, the Union, the Church, and the preservation of a second Chamber'. And—in more strident terms than he had ever used before—he once more attacked the Liberal drift towards socialism. This speech made the dissolution of the Club after the election almost certain.

The election of January 1910 was the final disaster for the Unionist Free Traders. Their decline was marked by the large number of apostate free fooders who ran as full Tariff Reformers. Bentinck in Nottingham, Hayes Fisher in Fulham, Peel at Harrow, Stirling-Maxwell in Glasgow, Yerburgh in Chester, and McArthur at Liverpool were all former free fooders who had discarded their free trade beliefs. Less active former free fooders—Morrison, Mount, Bagot, and Malcolm—also ran with Tariff Reform endorsement. Of those who had been blacklisted in 1909 and had capitulated, Mildmay, Younger, Magnus, Williams, King, Wolff, Sloan, and the young Hicks Beach ran, and all but Sloan and Rutherford were elected.

Thornton, Hornby, W. F. D. Smith, Abel Smith, Long, and Kennaway had retired. Other former Unionist Free Traders showed up in different guises. Cross ran as an independent in Glasgow Central and was defeated. Corbett won his division in Glasgow as an Independent Liberal. Gorst and Edgar Vincent, men looked upon as the staunchest of Tories in the period 1903–6, ran as Liberals and were defeated. The irrepressible Gibson 'Tommy' Bowles ended up winning King's Lynn as an Independent. In London, where the Unionist Free Traders had been very strong in the 1906 election, not one candidate ran, prompting the *Morning Post* on 17 January to boast that 'another feature of the fight in London is the complete effacement of the

Unionist Free Traders'. Of the incumbent Unionist Free Traders who stood again, Robert Cecil and George Bowles lost the campaign in Blackburn without any outside assistance save for 'F. E. Smith, who made a brilliant speech on our behalf'.[17] In South-West Durham Lambton was defeated by a Labour candidate. Only in Oxford University, where Hugh Cecil was unopposed, did a Unionist Free Trader succeed, and Cecil only succeeded because he had ceased to be an active free trader. Thus, by the end of January the *Morning Post* could justifiably exult that

> silently throughout the election the work of purging the Unionist party has proceeded. That work has been accomplished in the constituencies by the elimination of Unionist Free Trade candidates. There have been hard struggles on both sides . . . [and] the final stand of the Unionist Free Traders was made at East Marylebone.

The Unionist Free Traders had once numbered sixty-five members in the House of Commons. After the 1906 election there were still close to thirty left. But after January 1910 only the much-changed Hugh Cecil was in parliament. Their demise was lamented in terse but moving words by Lambton:

> The new House of Commons has only one Unionist Free Trader now, and only one member of independent views, Hugh Cecil, and he sits for a University.[18]

Yet Cecil was a very passive free trader by 1910, and by 1911 all his interests and energies were concentrated on a fanatical attachment to the House of Lords and a violent opposition to the Parliament Bill. As Amery comments, the Parliament Bill changed political alignments, even reuniting Cecils and Chamberlains!

Since it was obvious immediately after the election that there would be no juggling of party alignments, and consequently no opportunity for the Unionist Free Traders to fish in troubled waters, it was senseless to go on. In bitterness and rancour the Unionist Free Trade Club was dissolved. Cromer wrote to Elliot on 21 January 1910 that he was certain that the Club must now be dissolved and that, in any case, he would not remain with it as it 'hampered' him and 'interfered' with his influence.

Moreover, he also resigned as President of the Manchester Free Trade League claiming that he 'could not co-operate with a body containing members such as Ramsay MacDonald'.[19] From the other wing, James also asserted that the Club must be broken up, for he could not stay with Cromer as president since 'he was always opposing free trade'.

On 12 March the last meeting of the Executive Committee of the Club was held and after much acrimony it was decided to hold a general neeting to dissolve the Club. Cromer, Strachey, and George Hamilton then sent out a circular asking all members to join a Constitutional Free Trade Association to defend free trade, oppose socialism, and defend the Union. The Association would give support to and vote for the Unionist party. In retaliation at the call for a new organisation, James, Elliot, and seventeen others of the ninety-five members of the Club met to draw up their own circular letter opposing the views of the Cromer clique and urging all members of the Unionist Free Trade Club to join the Free Trade Union. These differences were suspended at the special meeting to dissolve the Club on 22 March. Cromer proposed and Elliot seconded, in what the latter described as a 'lugubrious business', the resolution for dissolution, and the last Unionist organisation opposed to Tariff Reform vanished.

IV

Paradoxically, it was only after the Unionist Free Traders were extinguished as a corporate body that Tariff Reform suffered a temporary, prewar, decline within the party. The realisation on the part of Balfour, the great mass of moderate Tariff Reformers, and a few whole-hoggers like Garvin, that they could not win an election on fiscal reform led first to the referendum pledge of November 1910 and then to the dropping of food taxes from the party programme early in 1913. The referendum was a tactical device proclaimed by Balfour on the eve of the December 1910 election. After consultation only with Lansdowne, he announced, to the dismay of the Chamberlains, that 'he had not the slightest objection to submitting the principles of tariff reform to a referendum'. On these matters Unionist Free Traders such as Hugh Cecil, Cromer, and particularly Strachey fought hard to diminish the influence of the Tariff Reformers but their pressure was not decisive.[20] And in 1913 it was the revolt of the moderate Tariff Reformers combined with the decisive action of Lord Derby, who dominated Unionist politics in free trade Lancashire, which convinced Bonar Law, Balfour's successor, that he had to give way and cut out food taxes.[21]

Despite the eclipse of the original Unionist Free Traders, free trade sentiment remained in the Unionist party right up to 1932 (and indeed beyond). Had the Unionist Free Traders acted as ruthlessly and vigorously for their cause as Chamberlain did for his, they might not have been reduced to the solitary and equivocal Hugh Cecil between 1903 and 1910. The fact that, from the outset, Balfour went a good way toward accepting the policies of the Tariff Reformers, who were much the dominant faction, eroded the strength of the Unionist Free Traders. The ambivalent attitudes of their leaders, Hicks Beach, Devonshire, and Cromer, and the divisions between the Liberal Unionist and the Conservative free traders—the latter more prepared to accept the policies of Balfour and more reluctant to leave their party—partially explain the indecisiveness of the Unionist Free Traders.

The dependence of the group on the leadership of the old Whigs and a few older Tories tied it to men whose most vigorous days had passed and whose influence was on the wane. By 1903 all the old Whigs—Northbrook, Devonshire, Goschen, and James—were over seventy years of age and the leading Tory free trader—Hicks Beach—had retired from active politics in 1902. Consequently, the struggle of the Unionist Free Traders often had the appearance of a desperate rearguard action waged by Tory groups such as the Cecils, who fought to prevent Chamberlain and his heirs from re-vamping the Conservative party, and by Whigs who fought against extinction.

As so many Unionist Free Traders held strongly traditional views of politics—for example, holding to the primacy of aristocratic 'influence' and to the slogan of 'men not measures'—they were hostile to political change and inflexibly committed to the *status quo*. Certainly they never were able to adopt the techniques of mass organisation and fund raising so successfully practised by the Tariff Reformers. Indeed, they were so self-righteous that they lavished contempt on the methods of the Tariff Reformers. From rank and file men like Hornby and King, controlling their constituencies as little fiefs, to the grandees with wider influence, many of the Unionist Free Traders represented declining political forces whose demise was only hastened by the challenge of Tariff Reform. Consequently, many of the vital free trade elements such as the Churchills, Becketts, Elliots, and Robert Cecils of the movement, were hamstrung by the negative attitudes and cautious policies of the majority of the Unionist Free Traders. In some ways, the brilliant younger free fooders were men of Peelite metal without the all too necessary Peel and lived at a time when party lines were far more rigidly defined than in the late 1840s and 1850s. By the spring of 1904 there was clearly little chance of avoiding political eclipse except by joining the Liberals.

That there was a profound current of protectionism in the party and to some extent in the country there is no doubt, as the survival, and indeed the success, of Tariff Reform after Chamberlain's incapacitation and subsequent death demonstrates. But the victory of the Chamberlainites was by no means inevitable. Whether a Unionist party that remained wedded to free trade could have posed a viable alternative to Liberalism is an open question. However, as far as electoral success was concerned, Tariff Reform contributed decisively to the Unionist débâcle of 1906 and failed to bring victory in the two 1910 elections, as well as that of 1923, which Stanley Baldwin fought mainly on that issue. Nevertheless, it is clear that some Tariff Reformers, particularly Joseph Chamberlain—and his son Neville during the late 1920s—advocated the most constructive ideas within the Unionist party—social reform, a recognition of the need for new sources of revenue, and a policy of closer imperial relations.

While most of the Unionist Free Traders had few imaginative or constructive policies apart from maintenance of the present economic system, they were at least, save for a few like the Cecils, more moderate on many questions than the majority of the Tariff Reformers. Most Unionist Free Traders were against the abuse of the Lords' veto after 1906, opposed the rejection of the budget, and advocated conciliation in the 1911 crisis over the Parliament Bill. Few Unionist Free Traders had the inclination towards violence which characterised the extreme Tariff Reformers in the Confederacy movement and subsequently during the Irish crisis of 1912–14. The course of English politics would no doubt have been smoother and less polarised before 1914 if the Unionist Free Traders had kept the influence in the party which many of them exerted before Chamberlain's new course in 1903.

No politician respected courage more than Chamberlain—and he often claimed it was the quality least often found among politicians. Yet he, and many others, their perspectives obscured by the heat of the battle, refused to recognise the individual courage of many of the Unionist Free Traders. Devotion to free trade often destroyed their careers and, at a minimum, exposed Unionist Free Traders to hostility from the party machine and obloquy in the constituencies. The easiest and most understandable course to take, rather than face such frustration, was to shelter under Balfour's policies, at least until he capitulated to Tariff Reform. Those who refused to compromise, but attempted to remain within their party, played the most difficult role of all. After he had crossed the floor, Churchill categorically rebutted Liberal sneers of Unionist Free Trade timidity. After his motion of 8 March 1905 condemning preference based on food taxes, he replied firmly to Margot Asquith's letter which had expressed surprise that twelve free fooders had 'summoned up courage' to vote with the Liberals: 'You are wrong about the Free Fooders. No other similar body of men would have displayed such consistency amid such conflicting strains'.[21] The tragedy for the Unionist Free Traders is not only that as a group they failed to defeat Tariff Reform in their party, but that their ruin led to the loss of many individual politicians of distinction.

References

Chapter 1 THE BACKGROUND (pages 11–30)

1 Hicks Beach, Lady Victoria. *Life of Sir Michael Hicks Beach* (1932), 2, 159.
2 Blunt, W. S., *My Diaries* (1920), 489.
3 Hurst, Michael. *Joseph Chamberlain and West Midland Politics, 1886–1895* (1962) and 'Joseph Chamberlain, the Conservatives and the Succession to John Bright, 1886–1889', *The Historical Journal*, 7, 1964. Passim.
4 Garvin, J. L. *Life of Joseph Chamberlain* (1934), 1, 435.
5 Webb, Beatrice. *Our Partnership*, ed B. Drake and M. Cole (1948), 125.
6 Fraser, Peter. *Joseph Chamberlain* (1966), 311.
7 Amery, Julian. *Life of Joseph Chamberlain* (1950), 4, 453. Chamberlain admired Balfour and valued the support he had given him all through the dark days of the South African War.
8 Churchill, Winston. *Great Contemporaries* (1937), 196.
9 Winterton, Lord. *Prewar* (1932), 17.
10 Garvin, 3, 532.
11 Maxwell, Sir Herbert. *Evening Memories* (1932), 245–6.
12 Amery. *Chamberlain*, 4, 394–400.
13 Holland, Bernard. *Life of the Duke of Devonshire* (1911), 2, 292.
14 Sir Edward Hamilton Diaries, Add MSS 48679, f 133: 22 July 1902.
15 Balfour, Lady Frances. *A Memoir of Lord Balfour of Burleigh* (1924), 121.
16 Hewins, W. A. S. *The Apologia of an Imperialist* (1929), 1, 63. See also Joseph Chamberlain Papers, JC18/18/22: The Origins of the Tariff Reform Movement, A. Chamberlain to Mrs Dugdale, 4 March 1931, 16.
17 Balfour Papers, Add MSS 49761, f 56: Sandars to Balfour, 9 October 1902.
18 Hamilton, Lord George. *Parliamentary Reminiscences and Reflections* (1917), 2, 315.
19 Devonshire Papers, 340.2943: Balfour to Devonshire, 27 August 1903, marked *Private*.
20 Balfour to the King, 19 November 1902, quoted in Amery, *Chamberlain*, 4, 523.

21 Campbell-Bannerman Papers, Add MSS 41217, f 245: Campbell-Bannerman to Herbert Gladstone, 20 January 1903.
22 Garvin, 2, 551.
23 Young, Kenneth. *Arthur James Balfour* (1963), 212.
24 Balfour Papers, 49761, f 3: Sandars to Balfour, 8 March 1902, and f 26: Sandars to Balfour, 4 September 1902.
25 Mary Chamberlain Papers, AC/4/3/1140: Mary Chamberlain to Mrs Endicott, 22 April 1903.

Chapter 2 THE RISE OF THE UNIONIST FREE TRADERS (pages 31–48)

1 Devonshire Papers, 340.2943: Balfour to Devonshire, 27 August 1903, marked *Private*.
2 Amery, Leopold. *My Political Life* (1953), 1, 236.
3 Gollin, Alfred. *Balfour's Burden* (1965), 39.
4 Ritchie Papers: Memorandum on the Preference Crisis and Resignation, undated but obviously written late in September or early in October 1903.
5 Devonshire Papers, 340.2943: Balfour to Devonshire, 27 August 1903, marked *Private*. Amery quotes these words of Balfour but claims that there is nothing in the Chamberlain papers about the alleged arrangement, 5, 227.
6 Ritchie Papers: Mowatt to Ritchie, Saturday, nd but obviously 23 May 1903, marked *Confidential*.
7 Balfour Papers, 49759, ff 5–6: Cecil to Balfour, 24 May 1903.
8 Balfour Papers, 49722, f 39: Churchill to Balfour, 25 May 1903.
9 Campbell-Bannerman Papers, 41220, f 108: Harcourt to Campbell-Bannerman, 29 May 1903, marked *Secret*.
10 Ritchie Papers: Devonshire to Ritchie, 29 May 1903.
11 Devonshire Papers, 340.2910: Ritchie to Devonshire, 30 May 1903.
12 Cabinet Papers, 37/66/1, 'The Cabinet Crisis of 1903', 11 May 1905: Devonshire to Balfour, 31 May 1903, marked *Strictly Confidential*. 'Now' must represent a slip of the pen for 'not' since no policy had been adopted at the time of this letter.
13 Gollin, *Balfour's Burden*, 66.
14 Devonshire Papers, 340.2912: Lansdowne to Devonshire, 1 June 1903.
15 Devonshire Papers, 340.2914: Selborne to Devonshire, 4 June 1903, marked *Private*.
16 Ritchie Papers: Wyndham to Ritchie, 2 June 1903, marked *Confidential*.
17 Devonshire Papers, 340.2915: Balfour to Devonshire, 4 June 1903.
18 Strachey Papers: Churchill to Strachey, 21 May 1903.
19 Rosebery Papers: Churchill to Rosebery, 29 May 1903, marked *Private*.

20 Cromer Papers, FO 633/18: Hugh Cecil to Cromer, 10 February 1908.
21 Gardiner, A. G. *The Life of Sir William Harcourt* (1923), 2, 554.
22 Spender, J. A. *Life of Sir Henry Campbell-Bannerman* (1923), 2, 97. Campbell-Bannerman to the Chairman of his constituency association.
23 Campbell-Bannerman Papers, 41220, f 108: Harcourt to Campbell-Bannerman, 29 May 1903, marked *Secret.*
24 Hicks Beach, 2, 192: 10 June 1903.
25 Morley's remark is quoted in Spender, *Campbell-Bannerman*, 2, 110.
26 Balfour Papers, 49708, f 126: Balfour to Selborne, 26 June 1903.
27 Strachey Papers: Goschen to Strachey, 18 June 1903, marked *Private.*
28 Askwith, Lord. *Lord James of Hereford* (1930), 275.
29 Salvidge, Stanley. *Salvidge of Liverpool* (1934), 47.
30 Hicks Beach, 2, 194.
31 Campbell-Bannerman Papers, 41220, f 133: Harcourt to Campbell-Bannerman, 7 July 1903.
32 Campbell-Bannerman Papers, 41217, f 286: Hugh Cecil to Herbert Gladstone, 6 July 1903, marked *Most Private and Confidential*, copy.
33 Devonshire Papers, 340.2935: Devonshire to Hugh Cecil, 18 July 1903, copy.
34 Balfour Papers, 49759, f 56: Balfour to Hugh Cecil, 16 July 1903.

Chapter 3 THE CONFLICT IN THE CABINET (pages 49–63)

1 Balfour to Lady Elcho, 9 August 1903, quoted in Dugdale, Blanche. *Arthur James Balfour* (1937), 1, 351.
2 Hamilton, 2, 321.
3 Cabinet Papers, 76/82/1, 'The Cabinet Crisis of 1903', final draft entered on 11 May 1905 and listed under no name but obviously compiled by Sandars.
4 Cabinet Papers, 36/65/47, drawn up by Balfour on 1 August and printed for use of the cabinet on 5 August, marked *Confidential.* See also Judd, D. *Balfour and the British Empire* (1968), 115.
5 Unpublished 'Political Journal' of Arthur Elliot, 5 August 1903, 15, 112–13.
6 Devonshire Papers, 340.2936A: Memorandum, 12 August 1903.
7 Cabinet Papers, 41/28/18, Balfour to the King, 14 August 1903.
8 Devonshire Papers, 340,2938: Balfour to Devonshire, 13 August 1903.
9 Ritchie Papers: Balfour of Burleigh to Devonshire, 16 August 1903, copy.
10 Rosebery Papers: Churchill to Rosebery, 13 August 1903, marked *Private.*

11 Ritchie Papers: Devonshire to Ritchie, 16 August 1903.
12 Balfour Papers, 49761, f 87: Sandars to Balfour, 18 August 1903, marked *Confidential.*
13 Devonshire to Balfour, 23 August 1903, quoted in Holland, 2, 325–6.
14 Balfour to Devonshire, 17 August 1903, quoted in Holland, 2, 330–1.
15 Holland, 2, 334.
16 Cabinet Papers, 76/82/11, 'The Cabinet Crisis of 1903': Devonshire to Balfour, 9 September 1903.
17 Amery, *Chamberlain,* 5, 383–4.
18 Gollin, *Balfour's Burden,* 118.
19 There is no clear evidence to support Young's (215) assertion of a free trade cabal although Balfour was convinced that they had intrigued against him. Speaking in parliament on 7 March 1904 of the attitudes of the three ministers who resigned in September, he stated that 'every kind of suggested coalition combination' reached his ears. Churchill's statement that the free trade ministers were working to depose Balfour, contained in his essay on Balfour in *Great Contemporaries,* 198, has no doubt powerfully nourished the theory.
20 Devonshire Papers: James to Devonshire, 8 September 1903.
21 Balfour Papers, 49761, f 24: Sandars to Balfour, 26 December 1903.
22 Dugdale, 1, 358.
23 Amery, *Chamberlain,* 5, 402.
24 Ritchie Papers: Draft of an Address to His Constituents, early October 1903.
25 Elliot Papers: Ritchie to Elliot, 16 September 1903.
26 Devonshire Papers, 340.2992A: Memorandum of Events on Resigning, 6 October 1903.
27 Devonshire Papers: Devonshire to the Duchess of Devonshire, undated but obviously 17 September 1903, unsorted correspondence.
28 According to Lord Derby, Ritchie was urged on by the Duchess of Devonshire. (Churchill, Randolph. *Lord Derby* (1959), 81.) Sandars claimed that the pressure of James was decisive (Amery, *Chamberlain,* 5, 435).
29 Ritchie Papers: Ritchie to Devonshire, 28 September 1903 and Devonshire to Ritchie, 29 September 1903.
30 Elliot Papers: Ritchie to Elliot, 2 October 1903.
31 Hicks Beach Papers, PCC/25: Beach to Harcourt, 19 September 1903.
32 Churchill to Rosebery, 9 October 1903, Churchill, Randolph. *Winston S. Churchill,* companion vol 2, part 1 (1969), 227.
33 Spencer Papers: Campbell-Bannerman to Spencer, 23 September 1903.
34 Strachey Papers: Haldane to Strachey, 18 September 1903.
35 Devonshire Papers: Hamilton to Devonshire, 3 October 1903.

Chapter 4 THE TARIFF REFORM CAMPAIGN OPENS (pages 64–75)

1 Beatrice Webb, 292–3, described in June 1904 the effects of the campaign on Chamberlain. 'He is obsessed with the fiscal question—has lost his judgement over it—refuses to think or talk of anything else. He looks desperately unhealthy . . . bad colour, and general aspect of "falling in". But I should imagine there is plenty of force in the man yet. . . .' Mary Chamberlain felt it was a 'fatal' mistake that Chamberlain took only two months' holiday and not four (Amery, *Chamberlain*, 6, 557).

2 Clegg, H. A., Fox, Alan, and Thompson, A. F. *A History of British Trade Unions: Since 1889* (Oxford, 1964), 1, 367–8.

3 MacDonald, Ramsay. *The Zollverein and British Industry* (1903), 16–19.

4 Mitchell, Wesley. *Business Cycles* (New York, 1928), 432.

5 Clapham, Sir John. *An Economic History of Modern Britain* (1938), 3, 41.

6 *Annual Register*, 31 December 1903, 242. On 29 September Consols stood at 86 7/8, the lowest price since 1866. On 31 December they were only at 88.

7 Devonshire Papers, 340.3016: Williams to James, 22 October 1903. James bitterly complained to the duke about Williams' letter. 'I enclose you a *very* offensive letter from Powell Williams. He had never assumed this tone with me before. . . .' (Devonshire Papers, uncollated correspondence: James to Devonshire, 23 October 1903).

8 Herbert Gladstone Papers, Add MSS 46106, f 127, Notes of Committee Meeting at Free Trade Union and Memorandum on the Position and Work of the Free Trade Union, 13 January 1904.

9 Fitzroy, Alemric. *Memoirs*, 1, 170, entry for 3 December 1903.

10 Devonshire Papers, 340.3008: Goschen to Devonshire, 9 October 1903, marked *Private*.

11 Askwith, 284–5.

12 Amery (*Chamberlain*, 6, 502) states ruefully that Hicks Beach's support may have encouraged Balfour to keep his policy distinct from Chamberlain's.

13 Campbell-Bannerman Papers, 41217, f 74: Campbell-Bannerman to Gladstone, 14 January 1904, marked *Private*.

14 See R. Churchill, *Churchill*, companion vol 2, part 1 for crucial Cecil–Churchill correspondence, 243–4 and 255.

15 Spencer Papers: Adkins to Spencer, 1 December 1903.

16 Elliot Journal, 24 November 1903, 15, 153.

17 Selborne Papers: Devonshire to Selborne, 22 December 1903.

18 D'Abernon Papers, Add MSS 48937: Albert Zelly to Vincent, 21 January 1904.

19 Discussing the duke's power, a perceptive anonymous writer in the *Fortnightly Review*, January 1904, commented:

'I do not believe the Duke of Devonshire would influence a hundred working class votes in the whole of Great Britain excluding those that derive employment from him. But his influence with the landowning class is immense. It is greater than that of any public man in England, that is why landowners have hesitated to throw in their lot with J.C.'

20 Rosebery Papers, 78: Devonshire to Rosebery, 17 December 1903.

21 Rosebery Papers, Liberal League correspondence: Allard to Rosebery, 18 December 1903.

22 Quoted in the *National Review*, January 1906.

23 Griffith-Boscawen, Arthur. *Fourteen Years in Parliament* (1907), 283–4.

24 Halévy, Elie. *History of the English People in the Nineteenth Century* (1929), 5, 357. See also Amery, *Chamberlain*, 6, 544–5. Chamberlain apparently never pressed Balfour about an election, for Amery sadly comments that the two men appear neither to have met nor written to each other after September. Amery feels that the 'last real opportunity' to carry Tariff Reform was, thereby, lost.

25 Mary Chamberlain Papers, AC 7/3/1188: 11 December 1903.

26 Hicks Beach, 2, 200.

27 Balfour Papers, 39701, f 209: Sandars to Balfour, 23 December 1903.

Chapter 5 THE UNIONIST FREE TRADERS AT THEIR ZENITH (pages 76–93)

1 McCready, H. W. 'The Revolt of the Unionist Free Traders', *Parliamentary Affairs*, 16 (1963), 189.

2 Rosebery Papers: Perks to Rosebery, 21 December 1903. A little later on an incident in London lent strong credence to belief in the financial strength of Chamberlain's camp. Writing to J. L. Garvin about the establishment of the Tariff Commission, Sir Henry Brittain (in 'One or Two Recollections of Mr Joseph Chamberlain') commented on a dinner held at the Hyde Park Hotel on 14 January 1904: 'Having carefully developed the plans and cut and dried the necessary arrangements [we] took the hat round after dinner and collected nearly £27,000, which gave the Commission a very satisfactory start.' Chamberlain Papers, JC 19/7/5.

3 Herbert Gladstone Papers, 46106, ff 119–22: Notes on Party Affairs, December 1903.

4 Campbell-Bannerman Papers, 41225, f 220: Spencer to Campbell-Bannerman, 7 December 1903.

5 Sacks, Benjamin. *The Religious Issue in the State Schools of England and Wales 1902–1914* (Albuquerque, 1961), 62.

6 Haldane Papers: Haldane to Rosebery, 11 November 1903.

7 Asquith Papers: Gladstone to Asquith, 29 October 1903, marked *Secret*.

8 Elliot Papers: Munro Ferguson to Elliot, 3 December 1903 and Masterman to John Baily, sent to Elliot, 3 December 1903.
9 Devonshire Papers, 340.3011: Hugh Cecil to Devonshire, 2 December 1903.
10 Holland, 2, 373.
11 Devonshire Papers, 340.3038: Devonshire to Rosebery, 12 December 1903, copy, and Devonshire Papers, 340.3039: Rosebery to Devonshire, 15 December 1903.
12 Asquith Papers, 46, ff 112–13: Gladstone to Campbell-Bannerman, 20 December 1903, copy, and Campbell-Bannerman Papers, 41212, f 55: Campbell-Bannerman to Gladstone, 22 December 1903, marked *Private.*
13 Asquith Papers, 20, ff 124–7: Memorandum of a Conversation by Lord James of Hereford, 21 December 1903. Churchill informed Hugh Cecil, vacationing in Khartoum, of these negotiations, commenting that 'Lewisham has produced a salutary effect upon the Liberal officials' (Hatfield, Quickswood Papers, 63/17: Churchill to Cecil, 27 December 1903, marked *Private*).
14 Spencer Papers: Devonshire to Spencer, 2 January 1904, marked *Private.*
15 Asquith Papers: James to Asquith, 5 January 1904.
16 Spencer Papers: Devonshire to Spencer, 11 January 1903.
17 Austen Chamberlain Papers, AC 18/3/23: Gerald Balfour to Austen Chamberlain, 26 December 1903.
18 Spencer Papers: Campbell-Bannerman to Spencer, 14 January 1904.
19 Spencer Papers: Asquith to Spencer, 12 January 1904.
20 Fitzroy, 1, 180, entry for 19 January 1904.
21 Holland, 2, 371.
22 Campbell-Bannerman Papers, 41223, f 267: Campbell-Bannerman to Bryce, 15 January 1904. Campbell-Bannerman stressed that 'with such a fight before us we must make the fullest use of these U. F. T. stalwarts. Could Clifford and Co. see that this is as much their game as ours?'
23 Bryce Papers: Clifford to Bryce, 2 February 1904.
24 Rosebery Papers: Haldane to Perks, 25 December 1903.
25 Spencer Papers: Devonshire to Spencer, 31 January 1904.
26 Quickswood Papers, 63/19–24: Churchill to Cecil, 1 January 1904, marked *Private*; Spencer Papers: Asquith to Spencer, 12 January 1904: and Spencer Papers: Campbell–Bannerman to Spencer, 15 January 1904.
27 Quoted in Chilston, Viscount. *Chief Whip: The Political Life and Times of Aretas Akers-Douglas* (1961), 326.
28 Dugdale, 1, 411.
29 Griffith-Boscawen, 289.
30 Elliot Papers: 'Votes of Free Food League Members', August 1904. See also Appendix I, Part B.
31 Chilston, 327.

32 Balfour Papers, 49672, ff 79–83: Sandars to Balfour, 20 February 1904, marked *Confidential*, and Balfour Papers, 49672, f 84: Balfour to Sandars, 22 February 1904.
33 Webb, 283, entry for 1 March 1904.
34 Devonshire Papers, 340.3075: Churchill to Devonshire, 16 February 1904.
35 Cromer Papers, FO 633/18: Elliot to Cromer, 17 May 1908.

Chapter 6 THE CHARACTERISTICS OF THE UNIONIST FREE TRADERS (pages 94–114)

1 For all numerical calculations concerning the Unionist Free Traders see Appendix 1.
2 Lists abound of those who were allegedly Unionist Free Traders. See in particular, Herbert Gladstone Papers, 46106, ff 119–22 and 147–50, 1903 and 1904; Quickswood Papers, 1/143 and 1/444, late 1903. The lists agree substantially, although some discrepancies exist. Elliot is the most reliable because of the detailed information he compiled on the Free Food League and its successor (which he founded), the Unionist Free Trade Club.
3 Clarke, P. F. *Lancashire and the New Liberalism* (Cambridge, 1971), 280.
4 Elliot, 'Journal', 23 October 1903, 15.
5 Halevy, 5, 339. The main complaints in the iron and steel industries centred on the attempts of American and German manufacturers to get rid of their surplus by dumping in England. But if dumping hurt the British smelting industry, 'it assisted all those branches of manufacture for which pig iron and steel were not the finished article, but raw material'. Some 1,200,000 workers were employed in the branches of manufacture and construction which made use of the cheap 'raw materials'.
6 Wright, Jean. 'The Tariff Reform Movement 1903–14', unpublished Oxford B Litt thesis, 1959, 514.
7 Erickson, Charlotte. *British Industrialists: Steel and Hosiery, 1850–1950* (Cambridge, 1959), 150.
8 MacDonald, 61.
9 A. L. Bowley wrote that 'if we exported nothing, the service of our ships [our "invisible exports"] would pay for imports to the amount of £90,000,000. . . .' *England's Foreign Trade in the Nineteenth Century* (1903), 120.
10 Semmel, Bernard. *Imperialism and Social Reform* (1960), 151.
11 Schumpeter, Joseph. *Imperialism and Social Classes* (New York, 1951), 81, and Semmel, 145.
12 Clapham, 3, 55.
13 Thomas, J. A. *The House of Commons 1832–1901: A Study of its Economic and Functional Character* (Cardiff, 1939), 6.

14 Unless otherwise stated, information on directorships is taken from the *Directory of Directors* or *Dod's*.

15 The sample of seventy-five Tariff Reformers is drawn from the list of Chamberlainites given in *The Times* on 30 January 1906. Of the 109 listed, sixty-four had sat in parliament in 1903. Another eleven professed Tariff Reformers, who were defeated in 1906, are included: Henry Chaplin, Arthur Griffith-Boscawen, Sir Frederick Banbury, Alfred Haslam, Sir Henry Seton-Karr, Leverton Harris, Bonar Law, Sir Joseph Lawrence, Sir Herbert Maxwell, Sir John Randles, and Sir Henry Meysey-Thompson.

16 Page Croft, Henry. *My Life of Strife* (1949), 43.

17 Griffith-Boscawen, 275.

18 Asquith, Margot. *The Autobiography of Margot Asquith* (1962), 264.

19 Quoted in Strachey, Amy. *St Loe Strachey and His Paper* (1931), 151.

20 Cecil of Chelwood, Viscount. *All the Way* (1949), 113.

21 Balfour Papers, 49759, ff 93–4: Balfour to Hugh Cecil, 2 March 1905.

22 Robertson Scott, J. W. *The Story of the Pall Mall Gazette* (1950), 323.

23 Cecil, Lord Hugh. 'The Unionist Party and its Fiscal Sore', *The Nineteenth Century*, 75, 585.

24 Nicolson, Nigel. *People and Parliament* (1958), 141. It was Cecil's last letter, for a week later, on 19 December 1956, he died.

25 National Liberal Club election folios, 1906, 1, 185–6 and 1, 181.

26 Balfour Papers, 49737, f 40: Robert Cecil to Balfour, 25 January 1906.

27 Elliot's comment to his brother Lord Minto, that he 'had been too long in the place [the House of Commons] to look upon Harry Chaplin leading the van of progress', shows how contemptuous many free fooders were of Chamberlain's claim that Tariff Reform was progressive (Elliot Papers: 2 December 1904).

28 *National Review*, July 1903 and Amery, L. *My Political Life*, 1, 251.

29 Churchill, *Great Contemporaries*, 45.

30 The Unionist Free Traders were more realistic—and prescient—than the Tariff Reformers about the probable effects of attempting to implement Chamberlain's scheme. The Imperial Economic Conference in Ottawa in 1932, with all the 'fighting, haggling and snubbing' to which British ministers were subjected, was 'not the love-feast for which Conservative imperialists and protectionists had hoped' (Mowat, C. L. *Britain Between the Wars* (1956), 417–18).

31 Elliot. *Life of Lord Goschen* (1911), 2, 245 and Hicks Beach, 2, 197–8.

32 MacCallum Scott, R. *Winston Churchill* (1906), 232–3; Amery, L. *My Political Life*, 1, 254; *4 Hansard*, 129: 823 (9 February 1904); and Cecil, Lord Hugh. *Conservatism* (1912), 194.

33 Wright, 205.
34 Quoted in Amy Strachey, 153.
35 Strachey Papers: Strachey to Margot Asquith, 15 December 1908, marked *Confidential.*
36 Zetland, Marquis of. *Lord Cromer* (1932), 323, and D'Abernon, Lord. *Portraits and Appreciations* (1931), 325.
37 Cornford, James. 'The Transformation of Conservatism in the Late Nineteenth Century', *Victorian Studies*, 7 (1963), 58.
38 Clegg, Fox, and Thompson, 299 and 226–7.

Chapter 7 THE UNEASY ALLIANCE OF BALFOUR AND CHAMBERLAIN (pages 115–133)

1 See Chamberlain's letter in Wallace, W. S. *The Memoirs of the Rt Hon Sir George Foster* (Toronto, 1933), 126, for 26 January 1904: 'If I could settle matters my own way, I would put the opposition in for twelve months.'
2 Young, 313.
3 See Amery, *Chamberlain*, 6, 559, who claims that Balfour still feared a Devonshire ministry arising and so ordered the amendment. But by March the possibility of a new coalition was so improbable that this cannot have been Balfour's main motive.
4 Austen Chamberlain Papers, AC/7/3/37: A. Chamberlain to J. Chamberlain, 16 May 1905, marked *Private.*
5 Mary Chamberlain Papers, AC/4/3/1223: Mary Chamberlain to Mrs Endicott, 25 May 1904.
6 Balfour Papers, 49761, f 118: Sandars to Balfour, 14 September, marked *Confidential.*
7 Austen Chamberlain Papers, AC/17/3/79: A. Chamberlain to Balfour, marked *Confidential.*
8 Balfour Papers, 49762, f 116: Sandars to Balfour, 14 September 1904, marked *Confidential.*
9 Balfour Papers, 49771, f 151: Acland-Hood to Balfour, 22 September 1904.
10 Balfour Papers, 49757, f 301: Salisbury to Balfour, 6 September 1904.
11 Balfour Papers, 49762, ff 151–3: Sanders to Balfour, 6 October 1904, marked *Confidential.*
12 Petrie, Sir Charles. *The Life and Letters of the Rt Hon Sir Austen Chamberlain* (1939), 1, 156, and Amery, *Chamberlain*, 6, 634.
13 Balfour Papers, 49762, f 164: Sandars to Balfour, 16 October 1904, marked *Confidential*, and Hicks Beach Papers, PCC/89: Hicks Beach to Devonshire, 10 October 1904.
14 Dugdale, 1, 410.
15 Balfour Papers, 49708, ff 29–31: Selborne to Balfour, 20 December 1904.

16 Balfour Papers, 49774, f 59: J. Chamberlain to Balfour, 12 February 1905.
17 Balfour Papers, 49794, ff 61–5: Balfour to J. Chamberlain, 18 February 1905.
18 Elliot Papers: Memorandum by Robert Cecil on Tariff Reform Attacks on Unionist Free Traders, 18 February 1905.
19 Amery, *Chamberlain*, 6, 568.
20 Balfour Papers, 49735, ff 176–8: A. Chamberlain to Balfour, marked *Private*.
21 Balfour Papers, 49763, f 108: Sandars to Balfour, 18 March 1905, marked *Confidential*.
22 Austen Chamberlain Papers, AC/17/38: A. Chamberlain to J. Chamberlain, 21 March 1905, and Mary Chamberlain Papers, AC/7/3/1276: J. Chamberlain to Mrs Endicott, 14 March 1905.
23 Balfour Papers, 49738, ff 124–7: Lansdowne to Balfour, 18 May 1905.
24 Balfour Papers, 49759, f 105: Balfour to Hugh Cecil, 27 May 1905.
25 Quoted in Young, 222.
26 Balfour Papers, 49759, f 101: Hugh Cecil to Balfour, 5 June 1905, and f 113: Balfour to Hugh Cecil, 11 July 1905, marked *Private*.
27 Elliot, 'Journal', 8 October 1905, 17, 43.
28 Balfour Papers, 49774, f 86: Balfour to J. Chamberlain, 2 November 1905, and Balfour Papers, 49771, ff 131–2: Acland-Hood to Balfour, 22 December 1905.

Chapter 8 THE UNDERMINING OF THE UNIONIST FREE TRADERS (pages 134–150)

1 Balfour Papers, 49762, f 126: Sandars to Balfour, 22 February 1904.
2 Seely, J. E. B. *Adventure* (1930), 108.
3 Carter, Violet Bonham. *Winston Churchill* (1965), 87.
4 Elliot Papers: Robert Cecil to Elliot, 25 March 1905.
5 Hamilton Diaries, 48682, f 19: 16 February 1905.
6 Elliot Papers: Devonshire to Elliot, 23 January 1905.
7 Elliot, 'Journal', 19 March 1905, 16, 150.
8 Devonshire Papers, 340.3136: Goschen to Devonshire, 27 April 1905.
9 Elliot, 'Journal', 7 July 1905, 17, 3.
10 Balfour Papers, 29771, ff 142–4: Acland-Hood, Notes on Lord Robert Cecil's Memorandum, 'early' 1906.
11 Balfour Papers, 49771, f 122: Acland-Hood to Sandars, 6 December 1904.
12 Balfour Papers, f 53: Balfour to Hugh Cecil, 6 December 1904.
13 H. Gladstone Papers, 46616, ff 126 and 133: James to Gladstone, particularly the letters 12 March and 4 December 1904; 46106, f 126: Notes on Party Affairs, 23 February 1904; and 46616, f 145: James to Gladstone, 9 February 1905.

14 Elliot Papers: Strachey to Haldane, 27 February 1905, and Haldane to Strachey, 1 March 1905.
15 Elliot, 'Journal', 4 April 1905, 16, 157.
16 Elliot Papers: Devonshire to Elliot, 23 December 1904.
17 Fraser, Peter. 'The Liberal Unionist Alliance: Chamberlain, Hartington, and the Conservatives, 1886–1904', *English Historical Review*, 77 (1962), 78.
18 Lucy, Sir Henry. *The Balfourian Parliament* (1906), 326–7: 29 June 1904.
19 For a list of some of the members and many of the peers see Elliot, *Goschen*, 2, 285.
20 Elliot, 'Journal', 1 March 1905, 16, 142.
21 Robert Cecil Papers: Henry King to Robert Cecil, 8 February 1909.
22 Cromer Papers, FO 633/19: Cromer to Hugh Cecil, 12 February 1908, marked *Private*.
23 Balfour Papers, 49762, f 187: Sandars to Balfour, 3 December 1904, marked *Private*, and f 180: Sandars to Balfour, 30 November 1904.
24 Elliot, 'Journal', 26 January 1905, 16, 126.
25 Elliot Papers: Cecil to Elliot, 10 February 1905 and Devonshire to Elliot, 25 January 1905.

Chapter 9 THE ELECTION OF 1906 (pages 151–170)

1 Page Croft, 70. Internal evidence indicates that X was Charles Seely, Unionist Free Trade MP from Lincoln.
2 Balfour Papers, 49759, f 70: Hugh Cecil to Balfour, 6 December 1905.
3 Balfour to Devonshire, 8 December 1905, quoted in Holland, 2, 392.
4 Askwith, 291.
5 Devonshire Papers, uncollated correspondence: James to Devonshire, 3 December 1905.
6 Russell, A. K. 'The Election of 1906', unpublished Oxford D Phil thesis, 1963, 212.
7 Quickswood Papers, 4/189–81: 'Proposed Draft Report of the Executive Committee of the Unionist Free Trade Club to the Second Annual General Meeting', 'Spring of 1906'.
8 On 23 November 1905, Bryce had predicted to Herbert Gladstone that while most Unionist 'organisations' supported Chamberlain, 'many moderate Tories [would] . . . drop out quietly as the [Liberal] moderates did after the Newcastle programme of 1891' (H. Gladstone Papers, 41211, f 309). After the election the *Pall Mall Gazette* deplored the high abstention rate among Unionist voters. For example, in Fulham, where Hayes Fisher had lost what was con-

sidered a very safe seat, the Unionist poll was 25 per cent lower than the number of registered Unionist electors (17 January 1906).

9 Balfour Papers, 49759, f 67: Hugh Cecil to Balfour, 20 October 1905.

10 Balfour Papers, 49857, f 36: Balfour to Robert Cecil, 8 January 1906, marked *Private.*

11 Balfour Papers, 49857, f 125: Alex Baird to Balfour, 6 January 1906 and f 144: Baird to Balfour, 12 January 1906.

12 Mackail, J. W., and Wyndham, G. *Life and Letters of George Wyndham*, nd, 2, 535.

13 Russell, 212 and 214.

14 Ibid.

15 Austen Chamberlain Papers, AC/17: Chamberlain to Long, 25 November 1905, marked *Private.*

16 Balfour Papers, 49737, f 33: Robert Cecil to Balfour, 7 January 1906.

17 Page Croft, 44–5.

18 Russell, 543.

19 Spender, *Campbell-Bannerman*, 2, 216–17.

20 Channing, Francis Allston. *Memories of Midland Politics* (1918), 328–9.

21 Robert Cecil Papers: Lord Durham to Cecil, 1 February 1906, marked *Private.*

22 Newton, Lord. *Retrospection* (1941), 146–7.

23 Balfour Papers, 49721, ff 127–30: Müller to Balfour, 5 February 1906, marked *Secret* and *Confidential.*

24 See Blewett, N. 'Free Fooders, Balfourites, Whole Hoggers. Factionalism within the Unionist Party 1906–1910', *Historical Journal*, 11, (1968), 18.

25 Devonshire Papers, 340.3192: Wolverton to Devonshire, 5 February 1906.

26 Newton, Lord. *Lord Lansdowne* (1929), 347.

27 Devonshire Papers, 340.3191: St Levan to Devonshire, 3 February 1906.

28 Devonshire Papers, 340.3200: Hugh Cecil to Devonshire, 11 February 1906.

29 Devonshire Papers, 340.3206: Hugh Cecil to Devonshire, 16 February 1906.

30 Elliot Papers: Devonshire to Elliot, 17 February 1906.

Chapter 10 THE ECLIPSE OF THE UNIONIST FREE TRADERS (pages 171–186)

1 Cromer Papers, FO 633/18, James to Cromer, 13 January 1908, marked *Confidential.*

2 Robert Cecil Papers: Cecil to Philip Magnus, 18 December 1907.

3 Balfour Papers, 49757, f 51: Robert Cecil to Balfour, 24 May 1906, marked *Private.*
4 Blewett, 18.
5 Cromer Papers, FO 633/19: Memorandum by Balfour of Burleigh, 9 January 1909.
6 Devonshire Papers, 340.3209: Hugh Cecil to Devonshire, 7 March 1906.
7 Strachey Papers: St Loe Strachey to Harry Strachey, 2 March 1906.
8 Chelwood. *All the Way*, 104.
9 Balfour Papers, 29763, f 107: Sandars to Balfour, 14 May 1906, marked *Private.*
10 Balfour Papers, 49764, f 33: Sandars to Short, 4 March 1907.
11 Balfour Papers, 49764, ff 11–16: Sandars to Balfour, 22 January 1907.
12 Page Croft, 43–4.
13 Balfour Papers, 49765, ff 11–12: Sandars to Balfour, 22 January 1907.
14 Blewett, 26.
15 Balfour Papers, 49759, f 211: Hugh Cecil to Balfour, 27 July 1907.
16 Cromer Papers, FO 633/18: Lansdowne to Cromer, 30 January 1908, marked *Private.*
17 Balfour Papers, 49728, f 306: Sandars to Lansdowne, 'early 1908'.
18 Balfour Papers, 49776, f 222: Long to Balfour, 5 December 1907, and Robert Cecil Papers: Long to Robert Cecil, 4 January 1908.
19 Balfour Papers, 49737, f 88: Robert Cecil to Balfour, 19 January 1908.
20 Rober Cecil Papers: Robert Cecil to Long, 24 February 1908, marked *Private.*
21 Balfour Papers, 49737, f 88: Cecil to Balfour, 4 March 1908.
22 Balfour Papers, 49708, ff 106–30: 6 March 1908.
23 Cromer himself uses this phrase to describe the Unionist Free Traders' attitude in a letter to Elliot, in the Elliot Papers: Cromer to Elliot, 7 March 1908.
24 Cromer Papers, FO 633/18: Elliot to Cromer, 17 May 1908, marked *Private.*
25 Clarke. *Lancashire*, 376–7.
26 Robert Cecil Papers: Cadbury Jones to Robert Cecil, 11 July 1908.
27 Robert Cecil Papers: Acland-Hood to Robert Cecil, 17 November 1908.
28 Gollin, A. M. *J. L. Garvin and the Observer* (1960), 94–5.

Chapter 11 THE FINAL PURGE (pages 187–203)

1 Robert Cecil Papers: Northcliffe to Robert Cecil, 26 March 1909, marked *Private.*

2 Balfour Papers, 49766, ff 205–6: Sandars to Short, 5 January 1909.
3 Asquith Papers: Asquith to Robert Cecil, 23 January 1909, ff 7–8, marked *Confidential.*
4 Robert Cecil Papers: Brunker to Cecil, 23 February 1909.
5 Elliot Papers: Brunker to Elliot, 5 February 1909.
6 Cecil, Viscount. *A Great Experiment* (New York, 1941), 31.
7 The free fooders who abstained were Hornby and Thornton, who were going to retire, and Bowles, Brotherton, Cecil, Cross, Lambton, Sloan, Abel Smith, and—surprisingly in the light of his earlier capitulation—Williams. Mildmay, Butcher, King, Younger, Long, Kennaway, Magnus, Wolff, Rutherford, and W. F. D. Smith voted with the Chamberlainites.
8 Gollin. *Garvin*, 101 and 122.
9 Robert Cecil Papers: Brunker to Robert Cecil, 6 September 1909 and St Aldwyn to Robert Cecil, 28 May 1909, marked *Private.*
10 Jenkins, Roy. *Mr Balfour's Poodle* (1954), 62–3.
11 Elliot Papers: James to Elliot, 12 December 1909.
12 Elliot, 'Journal', 27 June 1909, 19, 101.
13 Elliot Papers: Avebury to Elliot, 28 October 1909, and Vernon to Elliot, 31 July 1909.
14 Cromer Papers, FO 633/18: Robert Cecil to Cromer, 6 September 1909.
15 Chamberlain A. *Politics from Inside* (1936), 181: 4 September 1909.
16 Cromer Papers, FO 633/18: Cromer to Lansdowne, 8 October 1909, marked *Private.*
17 Cecil. *All the Way*, 114.
18 Cromer Papers, FO 633/19: Lambton to Cromer, 29 January 1910.
19 Elliot Papers: Cromer to Elliot, 21 February 1910; Zetland, 325; and Elliot, 'Journal', 21 February 1910, 17, 170.
20 Churchill, R. *Derby*, 146–83.
21 Margot Asquith, 234.

Select Bibliography

A. Private Papers

Althorp, Northamptonshire	Earl Spencer Papers
Beaverbrook Library, London	St Loe Strachey Papers
Birmingham University Library, Birmingham	Austen Chamberlain Papers
	Joseph Chamberlain Papers
	Mary Chamberlain Papers
Bodleian Library, Oxford	Earl of Oxford and Asquith Papers
	Viscount Bryce Papers
	Earl of Selborne Papers
British Museum	Lord D'Abernon Papers
	Lord Avebury Papers
	Earl of Balfour Papers
	Sir Henry Campbell-Bannerman Papers
	Viscount Cecil of Chelwood Papers
	Sir Edward Hamilton Papers
	Viscount Gladstone Papers
	Lord Ritchie of Dundee Papers
	James Alfred Spender Papers
Chatsworth, Derbyshire	Duke of Devonshire Papers
Gloucester Record Office, Gloucester	Lord St Aldwyn Papers
Hatfield House, Hatfield	Lord Quickswood Papers
National Library of Scotland, Edinburgh	Arthur Elliot Papers
	Viscount Haldane of Cloan Papers
	Earl of Rosebery Papers

New College, Oxford — Viscount Milner Papers
Public Records Office, London — Earl of Cromer Papers

B. Serial Publications

(1) Government Documents. *Cabinet Papers*; *Parliamentary Debates*; *House of Commons Sessional Papers.*

(2) Newspapers, Year Books, Directories, and Pamphlets. *Annual Register*; *Daily Chronicle*; *Daily News*; *Daily Telegraph*; *Directory of Directors*; Dod's *Parliamentary Companion*; *Edinburgh Review*; *Fortnightly Review*; *Manchester Guardian*; *Morning Post*; National Liberal Club, *Election Folios for 1906*, 2 vols; *National Review*; *The Observer*; *Pall Mall Gazette*; *Spectator*; *Standard*; *St James Gazette*; *The Times*; *Unionist Free Food League Pamphlets* and *Unionist Free Trade Club Pamphlets* (contained in the Elliot Papers); *Westminster Gazette.*

C. Books and Articles

The number of books and articles consulted is very large. The list below is confined to books and articles mentioned in the text or cited in notes. Unless otherwise stated the place of publication is London.

Amery, Leopold. *My Political Life*, vol 1 (Hutchinson, 1953)
Askwith, Lord. *Lord James of Hereford* (Ernest Benn, 1930)
Asquith, Margot. *The Autobiography of Margot Asquith* (Eyre & Spottiswoode, 1962)
Balfour, Arthur James. *Some Economic Notes on Insular Trade* (Longmans, Green 1903)
Balfour, Lady Francis. *A Memoir of Lord Balfour of Burleigh* (Macmillan, 1924)
Blewett, Neal. 'Free Fooders, Balfourites, Whole Hoggers. Factionalism with the Unionist Party 1906–10', *Historical Journal*, 11 (1968)
Blunt, Wilfred S. *My Diaries* (Martin Secker, 1932)
Bonham-Carter, Violet. *Winston Spencer Churchill* (New York, Harcourt, Brace, 1965)
Bralley, H. 'St Loe Strachey and the Politics of Dilemma: A Study of Political Journalism During the Edwardian Era'. Unpublished South Carolina PhD Dissertation, 1971

'Calchas' [J. L. Garvin]. 'The Eve of the Campaign', *Fortnightly Review*, 74 (September, 1903)
Cecil, Lord Hugh. 'The Unionist Party and its Fiscal Sore', *Nineteenth Century*, 65 (April 1909)
—— *Conservatism* (Thornton, Butterworth, 1912)
Cecil, Viscount. *A Great Experiment* (New York, Oxford University Press, 1941)
—— *All the Way* (Hodder & Stoughton, 1949)
Chamberlain, Austen. *Politics from Inside, 1906–1914* (Cassell, 1936)
Channing, Francis A. *Memories of Midland Politics* (John Murray, 1918)
Chilston, Viscount. *Chief Whip.* (Routledge & Kegan Paul, 1961)
Churchill, Randolph. *Lord Derby* (Heinemann, 1959)
—— *Winston S. Churchill*, vol 2 (Heinemann, 1967)
—— Companion vol 2, part 1 (1969)
Churchill, Winston. *Amid these Storms* (New York, Charles Scribner, 1932)
—— *Great Contemporaries* (New York, G. P. Putnam, 1937)
Clapham, Sir John. *An Economic History of Great Britain*, vol 3 (Cambridge University Press, 1938)
Clarke, P. F. *Lancashire and the New Liberalism* (Cambridge University Press, 1971)
Clegg, H. A., Fox, Alan, & Thompson, A. F. *A History of British Trade Unions since 1889*, vol 1 (Oxford, Clarendon Press, 1964)
Croft, Henry P. *My Life of Strife* (Hutchinson, 1949)
Cornford, James. 'The Transformation of Conservatism in the Late Nineteenth Century', *Victorian Studies* (1963)
Denison, Sir George. *The Struggle for Imperial Unity* (Toronto, Macmillan, 1921)
Dugdale, B. *Arthur James Balfour*, 2 vols (New York, G. P. Putnam, 1937)
Elliot, A. R. D. *Life of Lord Goschen*, 2 vols (Longmans, Green, 1911)
Ensor, R. C. K. *England 1870–1914* (Oxford, Clarendon Press, 1936)
Erickson, Charlotte. *British Industrialists: Steel and Hosiery 1850–1950* (Cambridge University Press, 1959)

Esher, Lord. *Journals and Letters*, vols 2 and 3 (Ivor Nicholson, 1934)

Fitzroy, Sir Alemric. *Memoirs*, 2 vols (Hutchinson, 1923)

Fraser, Peter. 'The Liberal Unionist Alliance: Chamberlain, Hartington, and the Conservatives 1886–1904', *English Historical Review*, 77 (1962)

—— 'Unionism and Tariff Reform: The Crisis of 1906', *Historical Journal*, 5 (1963)

—— *Joseph Chamberlain* (Cassell, 1966)

Gardiner, A. G. *Life of Sir William Harcourt*, 2 vols (Constable, 1923)

Garvin, J. L., & Amery, J. *Life of Joseph Chamberlain*, 6 vols (Macmillan; Garvin vols 1, 2 and 3: 1932, 1933 and 1934; and Amery vols 4, 1950, and 5 and 6, 1969)

Gollin, A. M. *The Observer and J. L. Garvin 1908–1914* (Oxford University Press, 1960)

—— *Balfour's Burden* (Anthony Blond, 1965)

Griffith-Boscawen, A. S. T. *Fourteen Years in Parliament* (John Murray, 1907)

Halévy, E. *History of the English People in the Nineteenth Century*, vols 5 and 6 (Ernest Benn, 1961)

Hamilton, Lord George. *Parliamentary Reminiscences and Reflections*, 2 vols (John Murray, 1916, 1922)

Headlam, M. F. 'Arthur Elliot' in the *Dictionary of National Biography 1922–1931* (Oxford, 1937)

Hewins, W. A. S. *Apologia of an Imperialist*, 2 vols (Constable, 1929)

Hicks Beach, Lady Victoria. *Life of Sir Michael Hicks Beach*, 2 vols (Macmillan, 1932)

Holland, Bernard. *Life of Spencer Compton, Eighth Duke of Devonshire* (Longmans, Green, 1911)

Hurst, Michael. *Joseph Chamberlain and West Midland Politics, 1886–1895* (Oxford: printed for the Dugdale Society, 1962)

—— 'Joseph Chamberlain, the Conservatives and the Succession to John Bright, 1886–1889', *The Historical Journal*, 7, (1964)

Jenkins, Roy. *Mr Balfour's Poodle* (Heinemann, 1954)

Judd, Denis. *Balfour and the British Empire* (Macmillan, 1968)

Lucy, Sir Henry. *The Balfourian Parliament* (Hodder & Stoughton, 1906)
McCready, H. W. 'The Revolt of the Unionist Free Traders', *Parliamentary Affairs*, 16 (1963)
MacDonald, J. Ramsay. *The Zollverein and British Industry* (Grant Richards, 1903)
Mackail, J. W., & Wyndham, G. *Life and Letters of George Wyndham*, 2 vols (Hutchinson, nd)
Maxwell, Sir Herbert. *Evening Memories* (A. Maclehose, 1932)
Mowat, C. L. *Britain Between the Wars, 1918–1940* (Methuen, 1950)
Newton, Lord. *Lord Lansdowne* (Macmillan, 1929)
Nicolson, Nigel. *People and Parliament* (Wiedenfeld and Nicolson, 1958)
Petrie, Sir Charles. *Life and Letters of Sir Austen Chamberlain*, 2 vols (Cassell, 1939)
Rempel, R. A. 'The Abortive Negotiations for a Free Trade Alliance to Defeat Tariff Reform: October 1903–February 1904', *Proceedings of the South Carolina Historical Association* (1966)
Russell, A. K. 'The Election of 1906', unpublished Oxford DPhil thesis (1963)
Sacks, B. *The Religious Issue on the State Schools in England and Wales 1902–1914* (Albuquerque, University of New Mexico Press, 1960)
Salvidge, S. *Salvidge of Liverpool* (Hodder & Stoughton, 1934)
Schumpeter, Joseph. *Imperialism and Social Classes* (Cambridge, Mass, Harvard University Press, 1951)
Seely, J. E. B. *Adventure* (Heinemann, 1930)
Semmel, Bernard. *Imperialism and Social Reform* (Allen & Unwin, 1960)
Spender, J. A. *Life of Sir Henry Campbell-Bannerman*, 2 vols (Hodder & Stoughton, 1923)
Strachey, Amy. *St Loe Strachey: His Life and His Paper* (V. Gollancz, 1931)
Thomas, J. A. *The House of Commons 1832–1901: A Study of its Economic and Functional Character* (Cardiff, University of Wales Press, 1939)

Wallace, W. S. *Memoirs of Sir George Foster* (Toronto, Dent, 1933)

Ward, Wilfred. 'A Political Fabius Maximus', *Nineteenth Century*, 58 (1905)

Webb, B. *Our Partnership* (Longmans, 1948)

Winterton, Lord. *Prewar* (Macmillan, 1932)

Wright, Jean. 'The Tariff Reform Movement, 1903–1914', unpublished Oxford BLitt thesis, 1959

Appendices

I

Unionist Free Trade MPs in the Balfourian Parliament

(1) List of Unionist Free Food League MPs in the Elliot Papers: 'early' December 1903. (MPs who met on 1 July 1903 to oppose Chamberlain are indicated by an asterisk.)

*Baird, J. A., Glasgow Central
*Hicks Beach, Bristol West
*Beckett, E., Whitby
*Bentinck, H., Nottingham S
*Bond, E., Nottingham E
Bowles, Colonel, Enfield
*Bowles, Gibson, King's Lynn
*Campbell, J. A., Glas and Aber Us
*Cavendish, R. (LU), N Lonsdale
*Cecil, H., Greenwich
*Churchill, W., Oldham
Coghill, D., Stoke on Trent
*Cohen, B., Islington E
*Corbett, A. D. (LU), Glas Tradeston
Cross, A. (LU), Glas Camlachie
*Denny, Colonel, Kilmarnock
*Dickson Poynder, J., Chippenham
*Dickinson, R., Wells
Elliot, A. (LU), Durham
*Fisher, H., Fulham
*Galloway, Wm, SW Manchester
*Gorst, J., Cambridge U
*Goschen, G., East Grinstead
Gray, E., West Ham N
Greville, R., Bradford E
*Guest, I. (LU), Plymouth
*Guthrie, M. (LU), Bow and Bromley
Ormesby Gore, S. F., Oswestry
*Hain, E. (LU), St Ives
Hamilton, G., Ealing
*Hatch, E., Gorton
*Hoare, S., Norwich
*Hobhouse, H. (LU), Somerset E
*Johnstone, H., Horsham
King, H., Hull Central
Kemp, G. (LU), Heywood
*Knowles, L., Salford W.
*Lambton, F. (LU), Durham SE
*McArthur, C., Liverpool Exchange
*Malcolm, I., Stowmarket
Stirling-Maxwell, J., Glasgow Coll
Mitchell, E. (LU), Fermanagh W
*Morrison, J., Wilton
*Mount, W., Newbury
*Peel, W. R. (LU), S Manchester
*Pemberton, J., Sunderland
*Renshaw, C., Renfrew W.
Ritchie, C., Croydon
*Russell, T. W. (LU), Tyrone S
*Seely, C. H. (LU), Lincoln
*Seely, J., Isle of Wight
*Simeon, B. (LU), Southampton
*Smith, A., E Herts
Smith, H. C. (LU), Tyneside
*Smith, W. F. D., Strand
*Shaw Stewart, H., Renfrew E
*Taylor, A., Liverpool E Toxteth
*Thornton, P., Clapham
*Tritton, C., Norwood
*Vincent, E., Exeter
Whitely, H., Ashton-under-Lyne
*Williams, Colonel, Dorset W
Wills, F. (LU), Bristol N
*Wood, J. (LU), Down E

*Yerburgh, R., Chester

65 MPs

*Bagot, J., Kendal
*Sloan, T. (LU), Belfast S
*Lucas, R., Portsmouth
*Morrell, G., Woodstock
(Attended 1 July 1903 meeting but had resigned from League by December 1903)

4 MPs

(2) Never joined the Free Food League but voted against the Government in one or more fiscal divisions.

Brotherton, E., Wakefield
Hutton, J., Richmond, Yorkshire
Mildmay, F. (LU), Totnes
Rollit, A., Islington S
Rothschild, L. (LU), Aylesbury
Younger, Wm, Stamford

6 MPs

(3) Neither joined the Free Food League nor voted against Balfour but were re-elected in 1906 as free traders.

Hornby, Wm, Blackburn
Powell, Sir F., Wigan
Rutherford, J., Darwen
Sassoon, E. (LU), Hythe
Kennaway, Sir J., Honiton
Wolff, G., Belfast E

6 MPs

(4) Miscellaneous.

Wilson, J. (LU), Falkirk (crossed to Liberals over Tariff Reform, February 1904)
Greene, H., Shrewsbury (retired early in 1905 in disgust at Tariff Reform)

2 MPs

Total: 83

II

Unionist Free Food League: Votes of Members in the House of Commons. (Elliot Papers: Drawn up late in August 1904.)

Name	*Fiscal motions*			
	Morley's	*Pirie's*	*Black's*	*Campbell-Bannerman's*
Baird	No	Abs	Abs	Abs
Beach	No	No	No	Abs
Beckett	Aye	Abs	Aye	Abs
Bentinck	Abs	Abs	Abs	No

Name	*Fiscal motions*			
	Morley's	*Pirie's*	*Black's*	*Campbell-Bannerman's*
Bond	No	Abs	Abs	Abs
Bowles, G.	Aye	Aye	Aye	Abs
Campbell	No	Abs	No	No
Cavendish	Aye	Aye	Aye	Abs
Cecil	Aye	Aye	Aye	Abs
Churchill	Aye	Aye	Aye	Aye
Corbett	Aye	Abs	Aye	Abs
Cross	No	No	No	Abs
Denny	Abs	Aye	Abs	Abs
Elliot	Aye	Aye	Aye	Abs
Fisher	No	Abs	No	No
Gorst	Aye	Aye	Aye	Abs
Goschen	Aye	Aye	Aye	Abs
Greville	Aye	Abs	No	Abs
Guest	Aye	Aye	Aye	Aye
Guthrie	Abs	Abs	Abs	Abs
Hain	Aye	Aye	Aye	Abs
Hamilton	Aye	Aye	Aye	Abs
Hatch	Aye	Aye	Aye	Aye
Hobhouse	Abs	Aye	Aye	Abs
Kemp	Aye	Aye	Aye	Aye
Knowles	No	No	No	No
Lambton	Aye	Aye	Aye	Abs
McArthur	Abs	Aye	Abs	Abs
Mitchell	Abs	Abs	Abs	Abs
Morrison	No	No	No	No
Peel	No	Abs	Abs	No
Pemberton	Aye	Aye	Aye	Abs
Poynder	Aye	Aye	Aye	Aye
Renshaw	Abs	Abs	Abs	Abs
Ritchie	Aye	Ayc	Abs	Abs
Seely, J.	Aye	Aye	Aye	Aye
Seely, C. H.	Aye	Abs	Abs	Abs
Shaw Stewart	Abs	Abs	No	Abs
Simeon	Aye	Aye	Aye	Abs
Smith, W. F. D.	No	Abs	Abs	Abs
Smith, A.	Aye	Abs	No	No
Smith, H. C.	Aye	Abs	Abs	Abs
Stirling-Maxwell	Abs	Aye	Abs	Abs
Taylor	Aye	Aye	Aye	Abs
Thornton	No	No	No	No
Tritton	No	No	No	No
Vincent	Abs	Aye	No	Abs
Whitely	No	No	No	No
Wills	Abs	Abs	Abs	Abs
Wood	Aye	Abs	Abs	Abs
Yerburgh	Abs	Aye	No	Abs
				51 MPs

III

Unionist Free Traders who became Liberals over the fiscal question

Before 1906 Election		*After 1906 Election*	
February 1904	Russell, T. W. (LU)	February 1906	Taylor, A.
February 1904	Wilson, J. (LU)	August 1908	Corbett, A. C. (LU)
March 1904	Seely, J.	May 1909	Cross, A. (LU)
April 1904	Guest, I. (LU)	December 1909	Gorst, Sir J.
May 1904	Churchill, W.	December 1909	Vincent, Sir E.
May 1904	Dickson Poynder, J.		
August 1904	Kemp, Colonel G. (LU)		
August 1904	Hain, E. (LU)		
March 1905	Hatch, E.		
March 1905	Mitchell, E. (LU)		
March 1905	Wood, J. (LU)		
January 1906	Cavendish, R. (LU)		

17 MPs

IV

Unionist Free Traders who had retired, gone to the Lords, or died by 1906

Hicks Beach
Beckett, E. (Lords)
Bowles, Colonel
Campbell, J. A.
Coghill, D.
Denny, Colonel
Ormesby-Gore, S. F. (Lords)
Greene, H.
Greville, R.
Guthrie, M. (LU)
Hamilton, G.
Hoare, S.
Hobhouse, H. (LU)
Hutton, J.
Malcolm, I.
Renshaw, C.
Ritchie, C.
Simeon, B. (LU)
Smith, H. (LU)
Tritton, C.
Wills, F. (LU)
Younger, Wm

Johnstone, H. (deceased)

23 MPs

V

(1) Unionist Free Traders in the Balfourian Parliament who contested the 1906 election.

Key: * 'hard core' candidates
† candidates faced with a Tariff Reform opponent
‡ candidates faced by a Tariff Reform opponent who withdrew
§ candidates who changed constituencies for the election

Bagot, J., Kendal
Baird, J. A., Glasgow Central
Stirling-Maxwell, J., Glas. College
Mildmay, F., Totnes

‡Bentinck, H., Nottingham S
Bond, E., Nottingham E
†*Bowles, Gibson, King's Lynn
Brotherton, E., Wakefield
†*Cecil, Hugh, Greenwich
Cohen, B., E Islington
†*Corbett, C. (LU), Glas Tradeston
*Cross, A. (LU), Glas Camlachie
Dickinson, R., Wells
†*Elliot, A. (LU), Durham
‡Fisher, H., Fulham
Galloway, Wm, SW Manchester
†*Gorst, J., Cambridge U
§*Goschen, G., Bolton
Gray, E., West Ham N
*Hornby, H., Blackburn
Kennaway, J., Honiton
King, H., Hull Central
*Knowles, L., Salford
*Lambton, F. (LU), Durham SE
§*Lucas, R., Bury Lancs
McArthur, C., Liverpool Exchange
Morrell, E., Woodstock
Morrison, J., Wilton
Mount, E., Newbury
§Peel, Wm (LU), Harrow
†*Pemberton, J., Sunderland
Powell, F., Wigan
†*Rollit, A., S Islington
Rothschild, L., Aylesbury
Rutherford, J., Darwen
Sassoon, E. (LU), Hythe
†*Seely, C. H. (LU), Lincoln
†*Sloan, T. (LU), Belfast
‡Smith, A., E Herts
Smith, W. F. D., Strand
Shaw Stewart, H., E Renfrew
*Taylor, A., Liverpool E Toxteth
‡Thornton, P., Clapham
‡Vincent, E., Exeter
Whitely, H., Ashton-under-Lyne
Williams, Colonel, Dorset W
Wolff, G., Belfast
Yerburgh, R., Chester

48 MPs

(2) Unionist Free Traders not in the Balfourian Parliament who contested the 1906 election.

Bowles, Geo, Norwood
*Burdett, H., N Paddington
‡Cecil, R., E Marylebone
Clarke, E., City
*Drage, G., Blackburn
†*Smith, W. C., Glasgow and Aberdeen
†*Strachey, St L. (LU), Edinburgh and St Andrews
Younger, G., Ayr Burghs

8 MPs

VI

List of MPs who belonged to the Unionist Free Trade Club. Those in the Club after 1906 as MPs are indicated by an asterisk

*Bowles, Geo
Bowles, Gibson
Cavendish, R.
Cecil, H.
*Cecil, R.
*Corbett, C.
*Cross, A.
Denny, Colonel
Dickson-Poynder, J.
Elliot, A.
Goschen, G.
Gorst, J.
Guthrie, M.
Hain, E.

Hamilton, G.
Hatch, E.
Hobhouse, H.
*Lambton, F.
Morrison, J. A.
Ritchie, C.
Seely, C. H.
Shaw Stewart, H.
*Smith, A.
Smith, H.
*Smith, W. F. D.
*Stirling-Maxwell, J.
Taylor, A.
Wills, F.
Yerburgh, R.

29 MPs

VII

*Unionist Free Traders in the House of Commons, 1906–10. Those 'proscribed' by the 'Morning Post' are indicated by *; those under 'suspicion' by the paper are shown by †.*

*Brotherton, E.
Butcher, H.
*Bowles, Geo
*Cecil, R.
Clarke, E.
*Corbett, C.
*Cross, A.
†Hicks Beach, M.
*Hornby, H.
*Kennaway, J.
*King, H.
*Lambton, F.
*Long, Colonel
†Magnus, P.
†Mildmay, F.
Powell, F.
Rothschild, L.
†Rutherford, J.
Sassoon, E.
*Sloan, T.
*Smith, A.
*Smith, W. F. D.
*Thornton, P.
Tuke, B.
*Williams, R.
*Wolff, G.
*Younger, G.

27 MPs

Index

Acland-Hood, Sir Alexander, 12, 75, 107, 123–33, 137, 142–3, 155, 165, 175, 178
Adkins, Sir Ryland, 71
Akers-Douglas, Aretas, 12, 75, 86, 88, 118, 158
Aliens Act (1905), 115, 131
Amery, Julian, 19, 24, 55, 74, 142, 199
Amery, Leopold, 26, 32, 65, 105, 109–11
Annual Register, 32, 67, 71, 81, 96, 113, 144
Army Reform, 27–8, 117
Ashley, Percy, 39
Ashley, W. J., 65
Asquith, Herbert Henry, 40, 65, 77–81, 84, 125, 136, 145, 184, 188–9
Asquith, Margot, 105, 112, 203
Avebury, Lord, 43, 113, 195

Baldwin, Alfred, 102
Baldwin, Stanley, 202
Balfour, Arthur James: attitudes to free traders, 93, 107, 143; cabinet crisis (1903), 49–63; character, 15–16, 23, 28–9, 47; fiscal programmes (Birmingham), 178, 180–2, (Edinburgh), 123–4, 129–30, 140, 158, (Sheffield), 60–1, 70, 75, 88–9, 115, 118, 139–40, 149, 158; political philosophy, 74, 116–17; Tariff Reform, 31–43, 116–33, 178, 188–9, 192–3, 197, 200–1
Balfour, Gerald, 33, 39, 51, 55, 81, 86, 88, 118, 143
Balfourites, 12, 74, 86, 94, 104, 158, 161, 174, 177, *see also* Balfour, A. J.
Beach, Sir Michael Hicks, 12, 18–21, 36, 41–7, 53, 60–2, 66–71, 75, 81, 88, 91, 93, 100, 104, 107, 110–14, 119, 124, 136, 140–1, 152, 165, 171, 193, 201; character, 39–40, 139
Beach, Lady Victoria Hicks, 12, 75
Beckett, Ernest, 27, 78, 99–100, 107, 136
Blue Paper, 49–52
Blunt, Wilfred, 30
Bonar Law, Andrew, 21, 86, 88, 102, 171–2, 181, 190, 197
Borden, Robert, 18
Bowles, George, 159, 171, 174, 190–1, 196–9
Bowles, Gibson Thomas, 104, 108, 155–7, 163, 166, 198
Bridgeman, W. C., 121–2
British Empire, 13–14, 17, 32–3, 65, 110–11, 117, 176, 202
Broadhurst, E. Tootal, 160, 184
Brodrick, St. John, 27, 86
Brunker, Edward, 188–90, 193
Bryce, James, 83
Burke, Edmund, 108
Burleigh, Lord Balfour of, 12, 21, 51–2, 56–8, 71, 112, 114, 148, 166, 171–3, 186, 193–4
Burns, John, 72, 144

Cabinet, 86, 121, 128; (1902), 19–27; truce, 37–9; crisis (1903), 49–63; Liberal cabinet, 136, 151, 184
Campbell-Bannerman, Sir Henry, 25, 40–1, 46–7, 62–3, 70, 72, 76–84, 92–3, 117, 133, 151, 179, 184
Canada, 17–19, 25; Canadian Liberal party, 18
Carson, Sir Edward, 190
Cavendish, Richard, 90, 100, 107, 138
Cavendish, Victor, 51, 95, 107
Cecil, Lord Hugh, 12–13, 21, 27–8, 36, 40, 45–7, 62, 70–1, 79, 83–93, 96, 104, 107–12, 125–7, 138–43, 147–57, 160, 165–73, 179, 183, 194–5, 199, 201–2
Cecil, Lord Robert, 12, 95, 105, 107, 127, 136, 141, 145, 148, 155, 159, 171–7, 181–6, 188–202
Cecil, Robert, fourth Marquis of Salisbury, 107, 123, 155, 189
Cecil, Robert, third Marquis of Salisbury, 14, 19, 55, 71, 107
Chamberlain, Austen, 21, 26, 57–9, 81, 116, 119, 122–4, 127–8, 147, 158, 167, 175, 177, 181, 188, 196–7, 199
Chamberlainites, 45, 72, 85, 94, 120, 124–5, 145, 154, 164–7, 172, 178, *see also* Tariff Reform
Chamberlain, Joseph: cabinet crisis (1903), 49–63; campaign, 64–8, 73–5, 84–5; early career, 14–15; imperialism, 14, 17, 110–11, 202; inquiry, 42–3; methods, 12, 33–4, 108–9, 112, 116, 147; preference, 23–7; relations with Balfour, 23, 117, 119, 122–3, 166–70; social reform, 19, 44, 114, 176, 202; speeches (Birmingham), 30–2, (Glasgow), 64–5, 115, 125; stroke, 173–6
Chamberlain, Mary, 29–30, 38, 74, 84, 167, 196
Chamberlain, Neville, 202
Chaplin, Henry, 41, 106, 110, 120, 133, 190
Chinese Labour, 117, 120, 122, 134–5
Churchill, Lord Randolph, 23, 26, 135
Churchill, Randolph, 185
Churchill, Winston, 12, 21, 27–8, 36, 39, 45, 52, 62, 65, 70–1, 79–81, 84, 88–92, 104–5, 111, 127, 135–6, 139, 143, 151, 165, 183–5, 202–3
City, 43, 98–9, 104
Clapham, Sir John, 67, 99
Clarke, Sir Edward, 106–8, 160, 171–4
Clarke, Peter, 106, 185
Clifford, Dr John, 72, 82–3
colonial conference, 157; (1897), 17; (1902), 17; (1907), 178
colonies, 13–14, 17, 20, 32, 111, 158, 178
Committee for Imperial Defence, 115, 121
Confederates, 104, 176–90, 203
Conservative party, 22, 70, 91, 95, 110, 147, 151; Central Office, 123, 127, 143, 172, 175, 178, 180–1; National Union, 60, 123–5, 130–3, 177–8
Constitutional Club, 166, 185
Constitutional Free Trade Association, 200
Corn Registration Duty, 18, 66
Courtney, Leonard, 106
Cromer, Lord, 40, 92, 100, 112–14, 148, 179–90, 194–201; character, 179
Cunningham, William, 65

Daily Chronicle, 105, 156
Daily News, 32, 35, 45, 73, 85, 189
Daily Telegraph, 72–3, 82, 85, 88, 139, 176, 188
Denison, Colonel George, 13
Derby, Lord, 201
Devonshire, Duchess of, 60

Devonshire, Duke of, 15, 37, 47, 69–73, 79–93, 110, 124, 137–8, 146–53, 171–3, 201; cabinet crisis (1903), 49–63; character, 37, 54; election (1906), 164–70; Liberal Unionists, 12, 22, 44, 67–8, 120, 137–8; preference, 38
Dickson-Poynder, Sir J., 78, 82, 92, 136, 138
Dugdale, Blanche, 86, 116
Durham, Lord, 107, 165

Economic Notes on Insular Free Trade, 49, 51, 54, 56
Edinburgh Review, 44, 149
Education Act (1902), 22–3, 27, 69, 77, 79, 83, 144
Edward VII, 25, 34
Elcho, Lady, 49, 130
Elections: by-elections, Argyllshire, 55, Aston, 13, Dulwich, 68, 71–4, Lewisham, 68, 71–4, Ludlow, 68, 74, 76, Mid-Herts, 85, 121, N.E. Lanark, 121–2, N.W. Manchester, 183–5, Oswestry, 121–2; general (1832), 105, (1892), 14, (1895), 14, (1900), 14, (1906), 114, 151–71, 202, (Jan 1910), 196–9, 202, (Dec 1910), 200, 202, (1923), 202
Elliot, Arthur, 12, 41, 51, 58, 62, 71, 78–9, 91–6, 104, 106, 112–14, 132, 135, 138–56, 163, 166, 169–73, 183–6, 194–5, 199–202
Endicott, Mrs, 30, 128
Ensor, R. C. K., 40
Entente Cordiale, 91, 115, 117, 121, 131
Esher, Lord, 38, 85, 121
Evans, Sir Arthur, 197

fair traders, 64, 106
Farrer, Sir Thomas, 14
fiscal question, *see* Tariff Reform
Fisher, Admiral, 115
Fisher, W. Hayes, 139, 160, 179, 198
Fitzroy, Sir Almeric, 68, 83, 99, 106, 121, 127–9
food taxes, *see* preference
Fortnightly Review, 111
Fraser, Peter, 117
Free Churchmen, *see* Nonconformists
free fooders, *see* Unionist Free Food League
free trade: principles, 11, 73, 193; *see also* Unionist Free Traders, Unionist Free Food League
Free Trade Union, 46, 68, 177, 195, 200

Gardiner, A. G., 45
Garvin, J. L., 44, 65, 109, 111, 192, 200
Germany, 17, 30, 97–9
Gladstone, Herbert, 25, 46, 78, 80, 83, 90, 135, 144
Gladstone, W. E., 13, 64–5, 71
Gollin, A. M., 32, 53, 56, 61, 192
Gorst, Sir John, 41, 104, 107, 109, 114, 135, 162, 198
Goschen, George, 90, 100, 107, 143, 155, 160, 166
Goschen, Lord, 12, 23, 26, 40, 43–5, 60, 62, 69, 71, 77, 90–1, 99, 104, 112–14, 140, 145, 149–50, 166–9, 171, 174, 201
Gould, Carrauthers, 125
Goulding, Edward, 182–3, 185, 191
Griffith-Boscawen, A. S. T., 74, 104, 117–18
Guest, Ivor, 28, 92, 135
Gwynne, H. A., 187

Haldane, Richard, 63, 68, 78, 84, 144–5
Halévy, Elie, 74, 98
Hamilton, Lord George, 12, 22, 50–1, 56–60, 63, 70–1, 80, 83, 88, 91, 109, 134, 140, 148, 171, 183
Hamilton, Sir Edward, 20–1, 24, 35, 48, 138

Harcourt, Sir William, 40–1, 46–7, 62
Harmsworth Alfred, 44, 149, 188
Harmsworth, Harold, 76
Hartington, *see* Devonshire
Hatch, Ernest, 144, 153
Hereford, Lord James of, 12, 40, 44, 56, 60, 68, 71, 80–3, 90–3, 113, 135, 140, 144–8, 152–3, 171, 173, 186, 193–4, 200–1
Hewins, W. A. S., 21, 65
Hills, Jack, 141–3, 156, 163
Home Rule, 13, 38, 54, 77, 105, 109, 144–5, 151, 153, 173–4
Hornby, Sir Henry, 101, 105–6, 109, 161, 191, 197, 202
House of Lords, 112, 186, 193–4, 202
Hughes, Percival, 187
Hughligans, 27–8, 39, 42, 79, 91, 108, 136

inquiry, *see* preference
Ireland, 131, 173, 191, 203
Irish Nationalists, 151, 191

Jameson, Dr, 107
Jenkins, Roy, 193
Joynson-Hicks, William, 183–4

King, Sir Henry, 100, 105, 148, 157, 162–3, 189, 198, 202

Labour, 66, 93, 113–14, 151, 178; *see also* working class
Labour Representative Committee, *see* Labour
Lambton, Frederick, 102, 106–7, 128, 144, 165, 169, 174, 183, 191, 197, 199
Lancashire, 97, 102–3, 106, 159–61, 183, 201
Lansdowne, Lord, 12, 37–8, 91, 120–1, 129, 137, 167, 179–81, 197, 200
Laurier, Sir Wilfred, 18, 27
Lawrence, Sir Joseph, 174
Lewisham letter, 71–3, 79, 137, 142, 171
Liberal Imperialists, 62–3, 72–3, 76–9, 89, 151
Liberal party, 40–1, 47, 62–3, 66, 69–73, 76–93, 122, 127–8, 133–6, 141, 144–5, 151, 163, 185–7, 202–3
Liberal Union Club, *see* Liberal Unionists
Liberal Unionist Association, *see* Liberal Unionists
Liberal Unionists, 15, 22–3, 43, 65, 67, 81, 91–2, 95, 110, 119–20, 133, 137, 147, 151, 172, 176, 183; *see also* Devonshire
Licensing Act (1904), 115, 121
Llewellyn Smith, Sir H., 39
Lloyd George, David, 33–4, 70, 72, 81, 136, 145; Budget (1909), 172, 185, 192–4, 202–3
Londonderry, Lord, 132–3
Long, Walter, 181–2
Lowther, James, 106, 110
Lucy, Sir Henry, 147
Lyttelton, Alfred, 86, 88, 127

MacDonald, Ramsay, 15, 67, 97, 200
Mackinder, Halford, 65
Manchester Free Trade League, 160, 183–4, 200
Manchester Guardian, 113, 156, 159–62
Marylebone pledge, 182, 196–7
Masterman, C. F. G., 73–4, 79
Maxse, Leo, 43, 65, 73, 110, 156
Maxwell, Sir Herbert, 106, 118–19, 120, 129
Middleton, Captain, 28–9
Mildmay, Francis, 87, 144, 157, 191, 198
Milner, Lord, 197
Minto, Lord, 106, 188
Mitchell, Wesley, 67
Morley, John, 42–3, 86–7, 125, 144, 151

Morning Post, 150, 156, 165–6, 187–8, 191, 197–9
Mowatt, Sir Francis, 21, 24, 35
Müller, Iwan, 82, 165

National Liberal Club, 185
National Liberal Federation, *see* Liberal party
National Review, 21, 72, 156, 187
Newton, Lord, 165, 169
Nineteenth Century, 131–2
Nonconformists, 22, 27, 77–8, 80, 83–5, 93
Northcliffe, *see* Harmsworth

Observer, 150
old age pensions, 19, 44, 66, 112–14, 172, 179; (Act of 1908), 185
Onslow, Lord, 58

Page Croft, Henry, 104, 141–2, 163, 176–7
Pall Mall Gazette, 161
Parliament Bill, 199, 202–3
Pearson, Arthur, 44, 149
Peelites, 43, 202
Peel, Sir Robert, 109, 116, 202
Peel, William, 161, 188
Perks, Sir Robert, 76, 84
Platt, Sir Thomas C., 176
Powell, Sir Francis, 106, 136, 161
preference, 16–19, 34–5, 64, 129, 159, 178; food taxes, 46, 55, 67, 126, 139, 143, 158, 173, 200, 203; inquiry, 37–43, 83
protection, *see* Tariff Reform

Queen's Hall rally, 71

Radicals, *see* Liberal party
Radical Liberal Unionists, *see* Liberal Unionists
retaliatory tariffs, 42–3, 89, 115, 157–8, 161
Ridley, Lord, 158, 188
Ritchie, C. T., 14, 20–7, 30–41, 50–3, 56–62, 68, 71, 81, 99, 134, 148, 171; character, 25–7, 61
Rosebery, Lord, 39, 52, 62, 73, 77–82, 183
Rosicrucian Society, 185
Royal Commission on the Poor Law, 171
Russell, A., 164
Russo-Japanese War, 86, 115, 125, 131

St Aldwyn, *see* Hicks Beach
Salisbury, *see* Cecil
Salvidge, Archibald, 44
Sandars, Jack, 22, 48, 53, 57, 75, 88–9, 116, 122–4, 127–9, 132, 134, 149, 175–7, 181, 188
Schumpeter, Joseph, 98
Schuster, Felix, 99
Seely, Charles, 145, 152, 163
Seely, J. E. B., 27, 41, 92, 135–6
Selborne, Lord, 37–8, 43, 115, 120, 125, 137, 147, 183, 196
Semmel, Bernard, 98, 103–4
Smith, Abel, 141–2, 147, 157, 190–1, 196–8
Smith, F. E., 105
Smith, W. F. D., 160, 174, 189
Social Darwinism, 111
socialism, 67, 111, 172, 184, 195, 198, 200
South Africa, 25, 111
South African War, 14–15, 17, 106–7
Spectator, 39, 112, 138, 149, 153, 165, 174, 193, 196
Spencer, Lord, 62, 77–8, 81–5
Spender, J. A., 25, 164
Standard, 44, 85, 149, 188
Strachey, John, 105
Strachey, St Loe, 12, 39, 43–4, 63, 91, 106, 112–14, 138, 144–5, 147, 150, 153, 173–4, 183–4, 189, 193

Taff Vale judgement, 28, 66, 91, 114
Tariff Reform: Commission, 99, 103–4; economic interests, 97–104; finances, 68, 76; League, 44–6, 65, 71, 79, 103–4, 123–6, 141–2, 148, 158–9, 172; origins, 17–23; political characteristics, 11, 104–14, 193–202; Valentine letters, 169–70; referendum, 200; social reform, 44, 66, 176, 202
Taylor Austin, 144, 160, 165
The Times, 73, 96, 107, 121–2, 135, 137, 141, 150, 153, 162, 167, 174–5, 179, 188
Thornton, Sir Percy, 105, 109, 144, 157–60, 191
Tories, 12, 45, 91, 106, 110, 181, 198, 201
Trade Disputes Act (1906), 174, 176
Trades Union Congress, 66

Unemployed Workmen Bill, 131
Unionist Coalition, 11, 14–21, 28–30, 43, 64, 72, 75, 120, 163–6, 202–3
Unionist Free Food League, 39, 45–6, 71–2, 77–8, 81, 86–8, 92, 117–19, 123, 137, 140, 146–58, 203; numbers, 69, 95–7, 138
Unionist Free Trade Club, 92, 94–7, 136, 145–53, 179–86; numbers, 148; finances, 148; divisions, 173; termination, 194–200
Unionist Free Traders: and Balfour, 90–3, 130–1, 134–40, 152–3; cabinet crisis (1903), 49–59; and Confederates, 179–92, 197–9; economic interests, 99–104; emergence, 39–41, 45; groupings, 12–13, 70, 201–2; and imperial views, 110–11; and inquiry, 43–4, 47; and Liberals, 76–93, 144–5, 183–4, 188–9; numbers, 94–7, (1906 election), 154–63, (after 1906 election), 166, 170–2, 199; political characteristics, 104–14; and social reform, 89, 112–14, 160, 174
United States, 17, 24, 30, 97–103

Valentine letters (1906), 169–70, 172–3
Vincent, Edgar, 41, 72, 100, 106, 124, 135, 198
Vincent, Howard, 102–3, 106

Ward, Wilfred, 131–2
Webb, Beatrice, 14, 89, 104, 109
Wells, Captain, 29, 125, 132
Westminster Gazette, 25, 110, 125, 127, 188, 191
Wharton amendment, 118–19, 132, 134
Whigs, 12, 15, 19, 22, 26, 39, 45, 68–70, 77, 92, 120, 171–2, 176, 189, 201
Williams Powell, 65, 68
Winterton, Lord, 16, 109, 182
working class, 33, 54, 66–7, 131, 159
Wyndham, George, 37–8, 86, 110, 158

Younger, George, 162, 171, 198

Zollverein, 17